JUST PEACEMAKING

The New Paradigm for the Ethics of Peace and War

NEW EDITION

EDITED BY GLEN STASSEN

The Pilgrim Press
Cleveland

The Pilgrim Press, 700 Prospect Avenue, Cleveland, Ohio 44115-1100
thepilgrimpress.com
© 2008 Glen Stassen

Library of Congress Cataloging-in-Publication Data

    Just peacemaking : the new paradigm for the ethics of peace and war / edited
by Glen Stassen.
      p. cm.
    Includes bibliographical references.
    ISBN 978-0-8298-1793-5 (alk. paper)
    1. Peace—Religious aspects—Christianity.   2. Christianity and justice.
I. Stassen, Glen Harold, 1936–

BT736.4.J88 2008
261.8'73—dc22   2008041308

CONTENTS

COLLABORATORS

STEVEN BRION-MEISELS is board co-chair of Peace Action, Washington, D.C., and deputy director of Peace Games, Cambridge, Massachusetts.

NICHOLAS READ BROWN is a Ph.D. candidate in Christian ethics, Fuller Theological Seminary, Pasadena, California.

DAVID BRONKEMA is director of International Development and associate professor of International Development, Eastern University, Philadelphia, Pennsylvania.

PAMELA BRUBAKER is professor of religion, California Lutheran University, Thousand Oaks, California.

JAMES B. BURKE is assistant professor of theology and director, Center for Ministry and Spirituality, Lewis University, Romeoville, Illinois.

JOHN CARTWRIGHT is professor of Christian ethics, emeritus, Boston University, Boston, Massachusetts.

MEENAKSHI CHHABRA is assistant professor in the Graduate Program of Interdisciplinary Studies at Lesley University, Cambridge, Massachusetts.

DAVID CORTRIGHT is president of Fourth Freedom Forum and research fellow at the Kroc Institute for International Peace Studies at the University of Notre Dame, Notre Dame, Indiana.

MICHAEL E. DYSON is University Professor, Georgetown University, Washington, D.C.

DUANE K. FRIESEN is professor of Bible and Religion, emeritus, Bethel College, North Newton, Kansas.

ALAN GEYER is former Canon Ethicist, the Washington National Cathedral, Washington, D.C.

BARBARA GREEN is director of the Churches Center for Theology and Public Policy, Washington, D.C.

GARY GUNDERSON is senior vice president and director of the Center of Excellence in Faith and Health, Methodist LeBonheur Healthcare, Memphis, Tennessee.

JUDITH M. GUNDRY is research fellow and associate professor (adjunct) of New Testament, Yale University Divinity School, New Haven, Connecticut.

DAVID HOLLENBACH, S.J., holds the University Chair in Human Rights and International Justice at Boston College, Chestnut Hill, Massachusetts.

COLLABORATORS

THEODORE KOONTZ is professor of ethics and peace studies, Associated Mennonite Biblical Seminary, Elkhart, Indiana.

JOHN LANGAN, S.J., is rector, Jesuit Community, Georgetown University, and Joseph Cardinal Bernardin Professor of Catholic Social Thought, Kennedy Institute of Ethics, Georgetown University, Washington, D.C.

EDWARD LEROY LONG JR. is professor emeritus of Christian ethics, Drew University, Madison, New Jersey.

DAVID LUMSDAINE is research tutor, Oxford Centre for Mission Studies, Oxford, England.

PATRICIA MCCULLOUGH is past co-chair of the Nuclear Weapons Freeze Campaign and clinical psychologist in private practice specializing in children and adolescents, Cleveland, Ohio.

PETER PARIS is Elmer G. Homrighausen Professor of Social Ethics, emeritus, Princeton Theological Seminary, Princeton, New Jersey.

RODGER A. PAYNE is professor of political science, and director of the Grawemeyer Award for Ideas Improving World Order, University of Louisville, Louisville, Kentucky.

BRUCE RUSSETT is Dean Acheson Professor of International Politics, Yale University, New Haven, Connecticut, and editor, *Journal of Conflict Resolution.*

DONALD W. SHRIVER is former professor of Christian ethics and president, Union Theological Seminary, New York.

PAUL W. SCHROEDER is professor of history and political science, emeritus, University of Illinois, Urbana, Illinois.

MICHAEL JOSEPH SMITH is the Thomas C. Sorensen Professor and director of the Program in Political and Social Thought, University of Virginia, Charlottesville, Virginia.

GLEN STASSEN is Lewis B. Smedes Professor of Christian Ethics, Fuller Theological Seminary, Pasadena, California.

DAVID STEELE is senior reconciliation facilitator, Baghdad office, Center for Post-Conflict Peace and Stability Operations, United States Institute of Peace.

RONALD STONE is professor of Christian ethics, emeritus, Pittsburgh Theological Seminary, Pittsburgh, Pennsylvania.

SUSAN THISTLETHWAITE is professor of theology, Chicago Theological Seminary, Chicago, Illinois, and Senior Fellow, the Center for American Progress, Washington, D.C.

Introduction

JUST PEACEMAKING AS THE NEW ETHIC FOR PEACE AND WAR

Pamela Brubaker
James B. Burke
Duane K. Friesen
John Langan, S.J.
Glen Stassen

We now have three paradigms for the ethics of peace and war: pacifism, just war theory, and just peacemaking theory. The development of the just peacemaking paradigm is a response to clear need, and increasingly so in our time. An ethic of peace and war that still operates with only pacifism and just war theory is outdated.

For example, terrorism requires more than an ethic that says terrorism is unjust; it requires an ethic that points to practices that prevent it. Just war theory is designed to deal with the justice or injustice of war, and it says clearly that terrorism is unjust. Terrorism's purpose "is to destroy the morale of a nation or a class, to undercut its solidarity; its method is the random murder of innocent people. Randomness is the crucial feature of terrorist activity. If one wishes fear to spread and intensify over time, it is not desirable to kill specific people identified in some particular way with a regime, a party, or a policy. Death must come by chance." Definitions of terrorism should not be twisted to serve the ideological interests of one side. Terrorism intentionally violates the *sine qua non* rule of just war that one can attack only military targets and never intentionally attack noncombatants.[1] It is always wrong.

Having a clear ethic that clarifies the reasons why terrorism is especially unjust is necessary. But it is not sufficient. The more urgent question is: What are effective ways to prevent it? And are we obligated to support those preventive practices? For these questions, just war theory *alone* gives us tunnel vision. Its function is to condemn terrorism, justify appropriate military action against terrorists, and rule out inappropriate military action. But effective action against terrorism requires much more than relying on military action alone. If our ethics focuses only on when military action is right or wrong, it focuses our discussion on military action and away from preventive actions.[2] We need *initiatives* to correct the injustices that cause terrorism; *structures of justice* that dry up the sources of recruitment of terrorists; we need *international networks of cooperation* against terrorism. Precisely such initiatives, structures of justice, and international cooperation are what just peacemaking theory points us to.

For another example, pacifism witnesses against violent action and for nonviolent action. That rightly leads many pacifists to seek answers to the question: "What effective nonviolent ways can we use to prevent terrorism?" But if pacifism lacks clear guidance about which practices do work to prevent terrorism, then pacifism can degenerate into withdrawal. In fact, Mennonite and Quaker pacifism have engaged in specific practices of just peacemaking. John Keegan praises the courageous service of pacifists in World War I,[3] and Ken Burns' documentary on World War II (*The War*) captures the same pacifist heroism in that war's medic corps. Hence pacifism, too, needs the effective initiatives, structures of justice, and international cooperation that just peacemaking theory points to.

TURKISH AND RUSSIAN ANTITERRORISM COMPARED

A comparison of Russia's and Turkey's method of combating terrorism is instructive. Turkey has wrestled with decades of terrorism by ethnic-minority, Muslim Kurds in southeastern Turkey seeking independence, just as Russia has wrestled with terrorism by ethnic-minority, Muslim Chechens in southern Russian seeking independence. Russia chose a scorched-earth approach, attacking repeatedly with large military force. The result was enormous devastation, many deaths, and an increase in terrorism. Fareed Zakaria wrote in December 2003 that in the four previous months,

> seven Chechen suicide bombers, all but one of them women, have detonated explosives that have taken 165 lives, including

their own. . . . In the early 1990s, there were no Chechen suicide bombers, despite a growing, violent movement against
Russian rule. . . . Reporters who covered the Chechen war in
the early 1990s mostly agree that there were very few "international Islamists—Saudis, Afghans, Yemenis—present. They
grew in numbers . . . as a direct result of the "brutal, botched
and unnecessary" Russian military intervention of 1994–96.[4]

Turkey had an analogous problem with the Kurdish rebellion and
terrorism led by the PKK (*Partiya Karkeren Kurdistan*). Since its beginning in 1984, the war with the PKK had killed more than 30,000
persons. After failing to defeat the terrorists by attacking them with
widespread force, in the mid-1990s the Turkish army developed a
much more disciplined approach to avoid attacking civilians, and the
government introduced health and education for the Kurdish area.[5]
One just peacemaking practice is *sustainable economic development*, and
the key to that is community development—development of the civic
society of local communities. Kurdish areas had been economically
worse off and neglected by the central government. But the government changed course to pay attention to sustainable economic development, and "initiated huge investments in the southeast, exemplified
by the $32 billion Southeastern Anatolia Project, to improve the long-
languishing region's economic prospects. Indeed, between 1983 and
1992 the southeast received twice as much investment per capita as
any other region in Turkey. . . ."[6] Recognition was given to Kurdish
language and community customs. The government invested extensively in improving education, including for girls and women. Instead
of trying to break down Kurdish tribal structures, as previously attempted, they gave them recognition and sought to enlist them in the
struggle for economic development, community development, and
political representation. "Considerable economic development has
taken place."[7] This is not "rewarding terrorists"—a charge that has
frozen some governments into the inability to do justice where justice
is right. This is separating the people from the terrorists—showing
the people they can get justice more effectively by working nonviolently than violently.

Another just peacemaking practice has been to *advance human
rights, democracy, and religious liberty*. Kurds have actually gained more
representation in the Turkish parliament than their proportion of the

3

population. This has been in part a response to pressure from the European Union (EU) and Turkey's drive to be accepted as a member of the EU. Kurds have seen the move toward joining the EU as promising them improved democratization as well as economic development.[8] "Civil associations in Turkey are growing in strength and exerting increasingly effective pressure on the government. . . ."[9]

The pressure, and the allure, of the EU suggests the importance of *working with emerging cooperative forces in the international system*—another practice of just peacemaking. And the international community was also important in arresting Ocalan, the leader of the terrorist organization. He had been living in Syria, safe from Turkey's military, but Syria expelled him as part of its effort to improve relations with Turkey and to respond to international pressure against terrorism. Ocalan sought refuge in Italy and other countries, but instead Italy arrested him.

Turkey then negotiated with him and achieved his cooperation in ending the terrorism in exchange for forgoing the death penalty. Here is the just peacemaking practice of *cooperative conflict resolution.* "In 1996 the journalist Franz Schurmann called the PKK 'the biggest guerrilla insurgency in the world.'" But by May, 2000, the PKK had basically quit.[10]

It is painful and tragic, and also ironically symbolic, that on November 20, 2003, we saw two more days of terrorism in Turkey. But they were not Kurdish terrorism against the Turks. They were al-Qaeda terrorism against Israel and the British-American "coalition of the willing." On the day when President Bush and Prime Minister Tony Blair of the United Kingdom (UK) were meeting in London, terrorists attacked the British HSBC bank and the British consulate in Instanbul. Twenty-six people were killed, including British Consul Roger Short. Five days previously, two Jewish synagogues in Istanbul had been bombed, killing twenty-three people and wounding more than three hundred. There had been several small attacks on U.K. and U.S. diplomatic premises April 3, April 8, May 31, and June 11.[11]

It is a tragic symbol. It symbolizes that the anger in Turkey has been shifted from Kurdish anger against the government to al-Qaeda anger against Israel and the alliance between the United States and Britain. It might suggest what works and what does not work in combating terrorism. The Iraq War, which dramatically violated just peacemaking practices, stimulated Kurdish drives for independence once again, and the PKK is once more active, in Iraq, though dramatically less so than prior to Turkey's efforts for just peacemaking practices.

RECRUITMENT OF TERRORISTS

Preventing terrorism requires a focus on preventing causes that lead to recruitment of terrorists. It is the U.S.-supported autocracies, such as Saudi Arabia and Egypt, that produce terrorists against the United States. Israel appears to Palestinians as an autocracy because Palesinians from Gaza and the West Bank are isolated from each other by the Israeli military occupation and by Israel's control of the transportation and economic infrastructure, thus causing desperate poverty, and many bitterly frustrated Palestinians turn to terrorism. The conclusion must be that the United States should be nudging these governments in the direction of *human rights and democracy*, a key just peacemaking practice. President Bush declared this his intention. However, Bush's inattention to the Palestinian/Israeli conflict the first six years of his presidency, his unbalanced support of Israel and loss of U.S. credibility in being an honest broker, and the Iraq war undermined his stated intentions. In 2003 al-Qaeda was not in Iraq. The irony is that the military occupation of Iraq has turned out to be one of the most effective recruiting tools for terrorists in Iraq, undermining human rights and democracy. The U.S. State Department reports that the number of terrorist incidents and deaths has increased exponentially. In 2003, the first year of the Iraq war, 208 international terrorist attacks caused 625 deaths. In 2004, 3,168 attacks caused 1,907 deaths. In 2005, the number skyrocketed to 11,111 attacks and 14,602 deaths. And in 2006, the number of attacks increased to about 14,500. In 2007, there were "nearly the same number of terrorist attacks worldwide in 2007 as the year before—about 14,500. But many more people were killed, especially as the number of suicide bombers rose, says the 312-page report, which is required by Congress and compiled using statistics from the National Counterterrorism Center."[12] Unilateral policies caused anger to increase, terrorist recruitment to increase, terrorist attacks to increase, security to decrease, and international respect for the United States to decrease.

Almost every Arab country is less free than it was forty years ago. "In such societies, severe repression drives all politics underground, placing the moderate opposition at a disadvantage, and encouraging political extremism." Double-digit unemployment causes the edu-

5

cated but unemployed youth to grow increasingly angry and frustrated. It's not the poorest states, but the autocratic states, that are the prime generators of international terrorists.[13]

Some point out that the poorest and least educated do not become international terrorists, and argue that economic justice is unimportant for preventing terrorism. As *Just Peacemaking* (chapter 6) points out, however, it is those who have developed some *expectations* and then see their own or their fellows' conditions dropping *well below those expectations* who tend to turn to violence. We cite Ted Gurr, *Why Men Rebel*,[14] which won the American Political Science Association award for best book of the year. Based on transnational and longitudinal analyses of data, Gurr demonstrates that *"deprivation relative to expectations"* is the best predictor of rebellion, insurgency, civil war (and terrorism).

Another important study argues that the extent to which societal conditions lead to a sense of "indignation" might be the crucial factor for the decision to turn to terrorist violence. The objective conditions that face an individual are not as important as the perceived difference between what one has and what one deserves (in either material or political terms). Another work interprets this sense of anger as "an outgrowth of frustrated ambition, whereby upwardly mobile individuals are blocked in their attempts to translate their capabilities or assets into political power."[15]

Economists Alan Krueger and Jitka Malecková show that "when Palestinian college enrollment doubled in the early 1980s, coinciding with a sharp increase in the unemployment rate for college graduates," and "the real daily wage of college graduates fell by around 30%," then frustrated and angry Palestinians turned to the popular intifada of 1988. When "the Israeli occupation of the territories and lack of an effective capital market or banking system . . . prevented the labor markets in the West Bank and Gaza Strip from equilibrating," the violent intifada of 2000 broke out.[16]

The suicide bombers were disproportionately college graduates. Krueger and Malecková's data show similar disproportion of above average education and less rewarding economies among Jewish, Hezbollah, and Palestinian terrorists. This is not what they intend to prove, but it is what their data show, which makes it all the more impressive.

With the Israeli closures, unemployment increased to 80 percent in parts of the occupied territories of Palestine, and absolute poverty rose disastrously. Seventy percent of the population were living on less than

$2 per person per day. Levels of acute malnutrition reached 25 percent, hitting women and children the hardest. This drastic drop in basic economic sustenance correlates with intense suicide bombings in that period.[17]

Michael Radu seeks to divert our attention from just peacemaking's emphasis on the practice of *sustainable economic development*. He first shows that joblessness of educated Muslims, not poverty of uneducated Muslims, creates terrorists. Then from this he concludes that terrorism is not created by economic injustice. This is a *non sequitur*: the joblessness of educated Muslims is a problem of economic injustice. And their seeing their poor and uneducated compatriots also oppressed heightens the anger. Watch Radu's jump in logic:

> The known backgrounds of the September 11 terrorists suggest the same: leaders and recruits to the most fanatical terrorist groups are *not* the poor, unfairly treated, and marginalized masses of the Islamic world, but rather—just as in Latin America, Sri Lanka, and the Philippines—young and radicalized university graduates who have lost their traditional employment in government-paid universities and other public sector positions and find their career aspirations blocked. The same syndrome applies to unassimilated and unassimilable young, well-educated, usually second-generation Muslim immigrants in the West. . . . Nothing in the background of the Western-born or -based Muslim terrorists supports the widespread fantasy that Islamic terrorism can somehow be explained by injustice, poverty, or discrimination. On the contrary, terrorism on the scale of the September 11 attacks *requires* elaborate coordination by multilingual, adaptable, and highly educated people. No impoverished, ignorant victims of Western imperialism need apply. At bottom, therefore, international fundamentalist Islamic terrorism is not a social or economic, but rather a cultural, phenomenon."[18]

Surely it is also a cultural problem, including the culture of authoritarianism. That is why just peacemaking practices focus both on human rights and democracy, and on sustainable economic development. As Susan Thistlethwaite writes, "The spiral of violence will end only when justice is done. No amount of retaliatory violence will give us security in the age of terrorism."[19]

7

Zachary Abuza has written an impressive study of terrorist networks in Southeast Asia. He combines relative economic deprivation with authoritarian religion as causes of terrorist recruitment. In Southeast Asia, "radical Islam is growing for a variety of reasons. These include economic dispossession, the lack of political freedom, the spread of Wahhabism and Salafi Islam, the failure of secular education, and an increased number of religious students studying in Middle Eastern and South Asian *madrasses* (Islamic schools)."[20]

The growth of Islamic extremism around the world, since the Iranian revolution in 1979, has less to do with theology and more to do with the failure of the domestic political economies of respective Muslim countries. Increasing gaps between the rich and poor, inequitable distribution of wealth, poverty, a lack of economic diversity, unemployment, corruption, and the lack of a viable political alternative have all given rise to Islamic extremism. People literally have become so desperate that they have nowhere to turn except to extremist religious politics.[21]

Abuza's main theme is the intricate international interconnections of the international terrorists. It is an astounding web of financing, money raising, recruiting, teaching, organizing, encouraging, and inspiring that connects the terrorists together across the many countries in which they exist. The conclusion seems clear that combating terrorism cannot be the work of one powerful country with a large military force. It requires the just practice of international cooperation, rather than a unilateral policy that alienates other nations by what they perceive as "the arrogant empire."[22]

Declaring the struggle to prevent terrorism *a war* is one approach. Another is to declare terrorism *an international crime*. Seeing it as a war adds to the international attention that it gets, which is what terrorists seek, and adds to fear and disruption of basic rights and liberties. It tempts politicians to declare our side as righteous over against the injustice of terrorism. That then insulates us against self-analysis, against asking about logs in our own eye we might remove and thus be less an object of hostility. It tempts politicians to authoritarianism. Declaring terrorism an international crime and trying in court terrorists who are caught decreases its hero status among its frustrated constituencies. Identifying terror as a crime requires that actions against terrorists be directed against those responsible for terrorist acts as in a police action rather than using more indiscriminate force as in war.

In 2007 careful intelligence and police actions were successful in foiling terrorist plots in both Great Britain and Germany. Those responsible were caught without lethal violence, and the accused terrorists were brought before a court of law to be tried for their crimes. Trial and sentencing by the International Criminal Court or similar international courts clearly judges terrorism as illegitimate by international authority, not only by one country that terrorists have already delegitimized in their minds as the great enemy. It has the potential to bridge divisions between the West and Islam by identifying common norms in international law. It tempts politicians less to authoritarianism and self-righteousness, because it clearly declares that the law and justice are above what any one authority or authoritarianism desires. Furthermore, it strengthens *cooperation with the international networks* that is a major force in combating and preventing terrorism.[23]

WE NEED PACIFISM, JUST WAR THEORY, AND JUST PEACEMAKING THEORY

The thirty scholars who developed just peacemaking theory disagree on the important question, "When, if ever, are war and military force justified?" We are mostly just war theorists, believing some wars are just, but we also include some pacifists who believe we should witness against all war making. Just peacemaking won't always prevent wars, so everyone needs either pacifism to say their participation in war is never justified, or just war theory to judge whether a particular war is justified.

We could work together, and even reach consensus, because we were focusing on another question: "What practices of war prevention and peacemaking should we be supporting?" We believe that question is equally important, and that it usually gets slighted in debates between just war and pacifism. Public debates about war and peace need a definite paradigm of effective peacemaking practices so they can focus attention on those practices.

We ask our readers to see the importance of these two questions, and to separate them from each other. If you believe in the rightness of some wars, you still need an ethic that helps you think clearly about initiatives to make peace. If you believe "war is not the answer," you need to be able to answer the question, "then what is the answer?"

To the initial twenty-three scholars, we are pleased to add seven additional scholars for the third edition: Nicholas Read Brown,

Pamela Brubaker, James Burke, Meenakshi Chhabra, David Cortright, David Hollenbach, and Donald Shriver. Each has lent concepts to particular chapters, plus their important support to the whole of *Just Peacemaking*, though not all are co-authors of chapters.

The 9th Assembly of the World Council of Churches (WCC) in Port Alegre, Brazil (February, 14–23, 2006), adopted a statement titled "Vulnerable Populations at Risk" that shifts the language from the viewpoint of the interveners to the "responsibility to protect." "When there is a failure of that responsibility, whether by neglect, lack of capacity, or direct assaults on the population, the international community has the duty to assist peoples and states, and in extreme situations, to intervene in the internal affairs of the state in the interest and safety of the people." The focus should, first of all, be on nonmilitary preventive action, with attention to the root causes of impending humanitarian crises. In Rwanda, for example, warning signs were not heeded. Though the WCC document does not exclude the possibility of military intervention, it warns that we should not naïvely believe that force can solve intractable problems. It legitimizes force "only to stop the use of armed force and in order to reinstate civil means, strictly respecting the proportionality of means. It needs to be controlled by international law in accordance with the UN Charter and be taken only by those who themselves follow international law strictly."

In this book, chapter 8 on the United Nations (UN) affirms the use of military force in cases where it stops a massacre. Such a humanitarian intervention "may still be just even if its motives are mixed. For example, India's intervention in the former East Pakistan and Tanzania's in the Uganda of Idi Amin are often cited as unilateral interventions that nevertheless ended humanitarian disasters." This also applies to intervention that should have happened in time to prevent the massacre in Rwanda that killed 800,000 human beings, to the intervention with UN approval that deposed the dictators in Haiti, and to the intervention that stopped the chaotic war in Liberia. Our justification of such humanitarian interventions demands neither that the United Nations have the military force to perform the interventions (it doesn't), nor that all just interventions be approved by the United Nations (the veto can block them). But international approval provides a realistic check and balance against intervention for unjust reasons. The U.S. government claimed that its intervention to topple the dictator Saddam Hussein was justified by Iraq's possession of massive quantities of chemical, biological, and nuclear weapons. It was opposed by all but three members of the UN Security Council and by large majorities throughout the world. The result of making the war before the inspections were completed and without international approval greatly increased hostility against the U.S. government.

Because Mennonite pacifists as well as Catholic just war theorists, and many other diverse Christian ethics and faiths, are included in our team of thirty, we write in the introduction that "We do not all agree with Michael Smith's affirmation of humanitarian intervention, but we think it should be included." Some readers may believe that the one important question is whether we believe in the efficacy of military power. This leads them to the false assumption that peacemaking must mean offering no resistance to injustice. Yet many military veterans, returning from seeing the actual pain of war firsthand, are committed peacemakers. They are not renouncing military force as a last resort, but they are committed to just peacemaking practices to try to divert events from leading to the horror of yet another war. The ten practices we point to were developed in large part by veterans of World War II and subsequent wars who returned with the conviction that we must build practices and institutions that keep that destruction from happening again. Each practice is a realistic force in the actual world that we inhabit. Effective resistance against injustice is the point of *just* peacemaking: each one of these ten practices builds resistance against injustice into the system of nations and international networks.

REALISM

The original twenty-three scholars intentionally rejected ethics based on ideals about what the world might be "if only" people would act by ideals, and instead turned toward realism. Realism pays attention to what in fact is actually happening in empirical reality, with particular attention to the unpleasant, the sinful, the threatening dimensions of reality. Reinhold Niebuhr, the Christian realist, influenced us to be suspicious of cries of "peace, peace" as an ideal when there is no peace in practice. Niebuhr repeatedly asked what are the empirical power realities and interests, and what real steps of peacemaking are actually being taken now. Just peacemaking theory specifically rejects basing ethics on ideals outside of empirical history, and bases its ethics instead on what practices are actually proving to decrease the number of wars in real history. Furthermore, the description of each of the ten practices names real blocking forces that oppose the just peacemaking practices, and considers forces or strategies that help overcome those blocking forces. Hence just peacemaking theory seeks to be realistic in the sense that it focuses on what in fact works to prevent wars in real history, based on empirical reality.

We asked each other, "What realistically is working to prevent real wars?" We are Christian ethicists, international relations scholars, and conflict resolution practitioners with fairly diverse knowledge, experience, and perspectives. Based on our experience and the best empirical studies, we reached consensus on ten practices that do prevent wars, in reality. We wrote about those ten practices, paying attention to the data and the results of experience, of historical study, and of political science. The ten chapters describing these ten realistically effective practices represent our consensus. They are not merely ten separate essays; all of us reached consensus on the ten practices, and on the contents of the chapters. We are proposing a new paradigm, a third ethic, comprised of these ten practices.

We are not talking about peace as a utopian ideal. We are not predicting that there will be fewer and fewer wars. We are saying that conflicts of interest are strong and the instruments of destruction are now so devastating that the judgment of war can become a worldwide experience in ways too horrible to imagine. With all our beings we warn against the false optimism that has caused many to relax their peacemaking after the Cold War, precisely when our peacemaking is terribly needed and when it has the opportunity to spread peace widely and reduce the likelihood of local wars and global holocaust. We are not saying we can abolish war tomorrow. We are saying that these ten practices have in fact abolished wars in specific places and that they need our support to spread.

Some of us were students of Niebuhr, the realist. He taught us to be skeptical of major change in history, and instead to expect incremental change. He likely would have warned us about utopian expectations behind regime change based on U.S. military intervention, as he did when some were advocating U.S. military intervention in Indochina in the 1950s. Niebuhr said that utopian hopes are not helpful, but day-by-day practices can build changed relationships and structures that change reality and make peace. We now see the empirical evidence that practices of just peacemaking are incrementally changing the way nations relate. The combination of these various kinds of incremental change is adding up to a system change that is still insufficiently recognized.

We are pointing to such day-by-day practices. We are showing in our ten chapters that they are actually happening, spreading, and dramatically reducing the likelihood of war in major regions of the world. In places such as Serbia, Rwanda, Somalia, Sudan, Burma, and North Korea, however, these practices are absent or are only beginning to occur. In other places, they have begun but need much more support. The United States is learning too slowly that even a superpower with unchallenged military strength cannot achieve its objectives unilaterally, but must work cooperatively with other nations to achieve common goals of peace and greater security.

Classical realism in political science sees international relations as consisting of nation-states pursuing power and military and economic interest. The world lacks a governing power that could restrain the use of military force by these nation-states. Just peacemaking theory agrees that nation-states continue to be important for any foreseeable future. Yet the world is developing networks of relationships that nudge national interest in the direction of usually getting more results by cooperating with other nations. Realism is evolving in our time because of the strength of alliances, trade relationships, international networks, and the spread of human rights and democracy.[24] Furthermore, the usefulness of war is declining due to the destructiveness of weapons and the international opposition against unjustified warmaking. Realism is also evolving because terrorism tends to be perpetrated by groups that do not belong to any one nation-state. (There is also, of course, state-terrorism perpetrated by governments against citizens.) The transnational networks of terrorism need to be combated not by nations acting alone, but by international cooperation of nation-states as well as nongovernmental organizations.

If someone wants to debate about realism, we ask that person to discuss whether our evidence is right that each of these practices in reality does prevent some wars. Do not discuss our ethic as if we were proposing ideals, or proposing we have the magic package to abolish all wars; discuss the ethic on the basis of its claim to have empirical evidence that these practices do in fact prevent numerous wars and multitudinous misery and death.

Most people are stopped from doing terrorism by forces in their lives well short of the attack of an army. Just peacemaking is the steady strengthening of those forces of prevention. Regardless of what you believe about the efficacy of military force, you know that the degree of peace that exists on the street where you live comes from many forces of child-rearing, moral teaching, community organization, human networking, and habitual and societal restraint, so that no army needs to be stationed on your corner. This book does not argue about the need for armies; it argues that relying on armies is not enough; we need effective practices that restrain violence and create movement in the direction of justice.

THE HISTORICAL FORCES THAT CALLED FORTH
JUST PEACEMAKING THEORY

Several historical forces have come together as signs of our time to produce just peacemaking theory. After World War II, the world was stunned by the devastation of the war and the threat of nuclear weapons. The reality of that universally perceived threat persuaded people and institutions to develop new practices and networks to prevent another world war and the use of nuclear weapons. Now more than a half century has passed, and so far we have avoided these two specters. New practices are getting realistic results in ways many have not noticed. They are also important for combating terrorism. We believe we live in a moment of *kairos* (historical breakthrough given by the grace of God) when it can serve useful purposes to name these practices, to call attention to them, to support them ethically.

Now, after the Cold War and the beginning of U. S. dominance and increased attention to the threat of terrorism, as well as the threat of weapons of mass destruction, people lack a clear vision of what sort of just peacemaking is effective and is in fact preventing many wars. The threats are more diffuse. Hence, people are less clear about what they can contribute. The results are sometimes either inward emigration from effective and responsible involvement, or the submission to authoritarianism and militarism. Just peacemaking gives a roadmap for paths that do, in fact, prevent wars.

Paul Schroeder writes in chapter 7: "This makes just peacemaking into a task for action—a process in which ordinary citizens individually and in groups to sustain, criticize, goad, influence, reform, and lead the many kinds of voluntary associations—governmental and private—that can contribute to transcending the contradictions and managing and overcoming the conflicts of an anarchic international society. . . . It means exploiting, encouraging, and strengthening the concrete world trends that enable cooperation to fly."

In our time, there is a growing sense of the inadequacy of the debate between just war theory and pacifism. Debates dominated by those paradigms inevitably focus on whether or not to make war. That crucial question and those two paradigms will not go away if the just peacemaking paradigm succeeds.

But in that debate another question frequently is overlooked: What essential steps should be taken to make peace? Have they been taken, or should they yet be taken? The just peacemaking paradigm fills out the original intention of the other two paradigms. It encourages pacifists to fulfill what their name (derived from the Latin *pacem facere*) means, "peacemakers." And it calls just war theorists to fill in the contents of their underdeveloped principles of last resort and just intention—to spell out what resorts should be tried before trying the last resort of war, and what intention there is to restore a just and enduring peace. It asks both to act on their stated intentions.

Most of the church statements on peace issued by major Christian denominations during the 1980s call for developing a just peacemaking theory or a theology of peace. For example, in their pastoral letter "The Challenge of Peace," the U.S. Catholic bishops say:

> Recognition of the Church's responsibility to join with others in the work of peace is a major force behind the call today to develop a theology of peace. Much of the history of Catholic theology on war and peace has focused on limiting the resort to force in human affairs; this task is still necessary, . . . but it is not a sufficient response. A fresh reappraisal which includes a developed theology of peace will require contributions from several sectors of the Church's life: biblical studies, systematic and moral theology, ecclesiology, and the experience and insights of members of the church who have struggled in various ways to make and keep the peace in this often violent age.[25]

Official statements of the Presbyterian Church, United Methodist Church, and United Church of Christ proclaimed similarly that while the two predominant paradigms of limiting the resort to force, just war theory and pacifism, are still necessary, we also need a positive theory of just peacemaking. In addition, several Christian ethicists from different denominations, both just war theorists and pacifists, authored books calling for a just peacemaking theory. Key authors of all those statements and books participated in the project to develop a consensus just peacemaking theory.

Drew Christiansen traces the surprising evolution of Roman Catholic social teaching toward just peacemaking in the second half of John Paul II's pontificate (1991–2005). Christiansen proposes

> that the three most significant aspects of official Catholic peacemaking in this period were: (1) the articulation of a positive Catholic conception of peace and the development of new teaching on conflict with an accent on nonviolence; (2) an increased emphasis on international law and international institutions; and (3) the use of interreligious dialogue to counter violence and religious conflicts.[26]

By 2005, papal social teaching clearly evolved to "a more complex view embracing" both nonviolent struggle and a severely limited just war schema as well as the need for forgiveness in international politics.[27] In addition, the U.S. Catholic bishops in *The Harvest of Justice is Sown in Peace*, the tenth anniversary statement on their 1983 peace pastoral, called nonviolence "*a prima facie* public obligation of government officials and citizens."[28] This meant nonviolence was more than a vocational option of conscience for individuals. Given that in thirty-eight years of World Day of Peace messages (1968–2005) and their encyclicals, Paul VI and John Paul II also touched upon virtually all ten just peacemaking initiatives, one can fairly conclude Catholic teaching resonates deeply with just peacemaking. Yet, Catholic thought still wrestles with at least three questions about just peacemaking as a theory, a third ethic: Ought just war tradition be renewed through the integration of just peacemaking practices into its ethic? Can nonpacifist nonviolence ("strategic nonviolent conflict" in Peter Ackerman's parlance,[29] or "nonviolent struggle" in Gene Sharp's study[30]) be coherently integrated into a just war framework?[31] Can that just war framework, renewed by the integration of strategic nonviolent conflict, also draw upon the prophetic energies of just peacemaking to resist injustice and prevent war?

The worldwide peacemaking movement, linking together many groups with different emphases, provides the troops that support and implement just peacemaking theory. It is not merely an academic theory. It can provide overarching comprehension, guidance, and encouragement, showing how diverse actions weave together into a strong supporting web of peacemaking.

A THEOLOGICAL BASIS FOR JUST PEACEMAKING

We believe the practices of just peacemaking are ethically normative because they bring peace, they solve problems, they promote justice and cooperation in a world whose wars are immeasurably destructive. We see historical evidence for this. Therefore we were able to reach consensus on the ten practices of just peacemaking on pragmatic grounds. We purposely fashioned the wording of the ten practices of just peacemaking so they could be adopted by persons of many faiths or no official faith. We wrote *chapters explaining each practice* so its basis can be seen clearly in what is actually happening in our time to change the world. We *appeal to all people of good will* to adopt these practices and work for them, grounding themselves in a commitment to change our world (or at least their own little briar patch) to peace rather than war and oppression. Each person can base these practices on his or her own faith. A Muslim or Buddhist or simply a social scientist or human being whose experience has led her or him to care about making peace, not war, can say, "Yes, this is happening in ways I had not fully realized, and it is making a huge difference for good, and I want to support it." We hope many, from diverse perspectives, will make these peacemaking practices their own.

An exciting historical development is that now leading Muslim and Jewish scholars are saying they, too, support an ethic of just peacemaking with specific practices, not only an ethic about the rights and wrongs of war. We have been working together for several years on just peacemaking ethics among the Abrahamic faiths, at Fuller Theological Seminary, the Salam Institute, North Park University, Notre Dame University, and in conferences of the Abrahamic faiths led by Joseph Montville. The most recent meeting occurred at Stony Point, New York, June 13–15, 2007, with support from the U.S. Institute of Peace. Thirty prominent Muslim, Jewish, and Christian leaders and scholars, ten from each faith, reached unanimous consensus: "In the light of this urgent world situation, we have committed ourselves to continued conversation and to the development of practices of peacemaking that are an alternative to war. . . . We agreed to adopt the following consensus statement. . . . We all believe that Just Peacemaking is the best option to resolve human conflicts and actively working towards the elimination of the conditions that lead to violence. . . . We all agree to mine our own religious traditions to further develop the Just Peacemaking practices." The document is "Abrahamic Alternatives to War: Jewish, Christian, and Muslim Perspectives on Just Peacemaking" by Susan Thistlewaite and Glen Stassen. It may be found online at http://www.usip.org/pubs/specialreports/sr214.html. A consensus trifaith book on just peacemaking is in the offing. Ironically, the Christian scholars had based the ten practices primarily on pragmatic grounds and not only Christian Scriptures so that persons of other faiths could support them, but Jewish and Muslim scholars said: "We are text-based religions, and we should base them more explicitly in our Scriptures." All three faiths see basis in our texts for the practices of just peacemaking.

This gives great encouragement to the thirty scholars collaborating on this book, because most of us arrive at these normative practices of just peacemaking not only on pragmatic grounds, but from deeply held faith perspectives. With the eyes of faith, we give thanks to God that just peacemaking works, though we arrive at this historical perspective in different ways. Evangelicals among our group do our ethics with more biblical concreteness; mainline Protestants among us prefer more general theological grounding or middle axioms; two who do not identify themselves as Christian shy away from theological reasons; Roman Catholics among us work with natural law and natural rights in addition to scripture and church tradition; and peace-church members want arguments explicitly theological and faith-based. All of us appeal to persons and groups of various faiths to join with us in seeking specific, normative peacemaking practices.

In this introduction, we (James Burke and John Langan, S.J., Roman Catholics; Pamela Brubaker, Church of the Brethren; Duane Friesen, Mennonite; and Glen Stassen, Baptist) want to share something of the *specifically Christian faith perspective* that informs us. Our vision is grounded in three theological convictions:

1. *Initiatives*: A biblically informed concept of discipleship and peacemaking initiatives grounded in the life, teachings, death, and resurrection of Jesus Christ.

2. *Justice*: Churches committed to seek the peace of the city where its people dwell (Jer. 29:7); to further God's reign, not by withdrawal or quietism or by uncritical support of or reliance on the govern-

ment, but by engaging the issues of peace and justice—especially justice—actively within the brokenness of the world.

3. *Love and community*: Church communities as eschatological signs of God's love and reign in the world, embodied in a concrete gathering of persons who seek to discern together what just peacemaking means and to model peacemaking practices in corporate and individual lives.

These three theological convictions form, or correspond to, the three basic imperatives of peacemaking and to the basic divisions of this book: peacemaking initiatives (part 1), justice (part 2), and love-community (part 3). They provide a logical ordering for the ten essential practices of peacemaking.

Discipleship and Peacemaking Initiatives

Discipleship is based on an embodied or incarnational Christology, a view of Christ as representing a specific and concrete alternative way of life meant to be followed. We advocate an embodied Christology that is an alternative to views of Christ that, though they make Godlike claims for the Savior, fail to see Christ's way as the authoritative model for our ethical practice. We advocate Christologies that (a) see Christ as divine Sovereign of all of life, not only Sovereign over a "separate" sphere of life (the spiritual); (b) define the meaning of Christ in terms that include faithfully following Christ now; (c) interpret Jesus' teaching as related to concrete practices that can guide us to live in the real world, not merely as high and abstract ideals; and (d) are attentive to Jesus' humanity as one who modeled a way to be followed and saw himself as fulfilling the tradition of the Law and the Prophets, not a Constantinian tradition of alignment with political and economic power. We want to build our peacemaking on a Christology that stays close to the Jewish servant Lord of the Gospels who called his disciples humbly to follow his way of nonviolent love, community-restoring justice, and peacemaking initiatives.

A reexamination of an embodied Christology of Christ's way, an incarnational discipleship, requires a serious reexamination of how the Christian church has related to those of other faiths, most notably its relationship to Jews. Larry Rasmussen states the issue forcefully:

> Developments after the ecumenical councils, including the Reformation, only solidified the massive shift from the God-

19

centered Christology of an alternative servant community within the wider world to the Christ-centered theology of a universalizing empire. . . . This absorption of virtually all of God into the Jesus of imperial Christianity is at the greatest possible remove from the theocentric Jesus and his yeasty, salty, seedy community way. Deadly results for Jews, pagans, indigenous people and cultures would eventually follow.[32]

Our perspective should not be understood, however, as a simple claim about the historical Jesus. The Gospels and the other writings of the New Testament portray various images of the Christ of faith. The portrayal of Jesus in these accounts is what the early church believed Jesus to be in a variety of different contexts where they faced a variety of practical issues. The New Testament represents not one unified Christology but various images that suggest different nuances and emphases. But even the high logos Christology of the Gospel of John teaches Jesus' servant role as one who incarnationally and sacrificially embodies God's love for all of humanity, a model of love for all who follow him. Similarly, Paul's theology of justification by faith is integrally connected to his concern for the formation of an ethical community in which divisions between Jew and Gentile are overcome in Christ (as in Gal. 3:24f., where Paul says that in Christ there is neither Jew nor Greek, slave nor free, male nor female).

We can illustrate what an embodied Christology looks like by a brief examination of the *locus classicus* of Christian peacemaking, the Sermon on the Mount (Matt. 5–7). In Matthew's portrayal of Jesus' teachings, we see a way to confront evil—not through violent force but through transforming initiatives as an alternative to either passive withdrawal or violent confrontation. John H. Yoder's *Politics of Jesus*, Walter Wink's *Engaging the Powers*, and Glen Stassen's *Just Peacemaking: Transforming Initiatives for Justice and Peace* spell out this model in much more detail than we can here.[33]

The Sermon on the Mount has usually been interpreted with a dyadic structural analysis, such as (1) "you have heard of old, don't kill"; (2) "but I say don't even be angry" (Matt. 5:21, 22). In this schema, the focus is on not being angry, which is easy to dismiss as a high ideal or a hard teaching. In fact, the Sermon is organized as triads:

1. Traditional piety (e.g., "you shall not kill" [Matt. 5:21]).

2. Mechanisms of bondage (e.g., "nursing anger or saying 'you fool'" [Matt. 5:22]).

3. Transforming initiatives (e.g., "go, be reconciled" [Matt. 5:23]).

Matthew 5:21–7:12 consists of fourteen such triads. In each of them, the second member of the triad (the mechanism of bondage) does not use imperatives, but continuing-action verbs, realistically diagnosing the vicious cycles that we get ourselves into when we serve some other lord than God. For example, when anger rules us, we often fail to take the steps necessary to correct a problem. If we recognize the triadic structure of the Sermon on the Mount, we can see that the emphasis is on the concrete commands of Jesus, which are practical and doable (in this case, "go be reconciled").[34]

We see that the third element is always an initiative, not merely a prohibition. It is always a practical participation in deliverance from a vicious cycle of bondage, hostility, idolatry, and judgment. Each moves us away from the so-called hard-saying or high-ideal interpretation that has caused resistance, evasion, and a dualistic split between inner intentions of the heart and outer deeds in society. Each moves us instead into participation in God's grace, God's deliverance, God's reign.[35]

In preaching, teaching, and living this good news, Jesus modeled a way to confront evil in order to restore right relationships (righteousness or justice). We have a vivid picture or model in the New Testament, in images, stories, sayings, accounts of Jesus' life, and ethical exhortations, not only in the Gospels but in the ethical injunctions and practices expressed in other writings (the ethical exhortations of Paul, for example, in Rom. 12) of how the followers of Jesus envisioned what it means to follow him in a life of discipleship.

Therefore one basic imperative is *peacemaking initiatives*. A positive theology of peace is not simply reactive, but proactive. It takes initiatives. It creates peace. It sees peace not as something to be achieved merely by refraining from war, but by taking peacemaking initiatives. Peace, like war, must be waged. It must be waged courageously, persistently, creatively, with imagination, heart, and wisdom. Peacemaking is rooted in the heart of the biblical understanding of God's grace, which does not merely refrain from punishing but takes dramatic initiatives in coming to us, speaking in the burning bush (Exod. 3), pouring love into us in Jesus Christ while we were God's enemies (Rom. 5:1–21). New emphasis on the initiatives of God's grace is transforming our understanding of peacemaking in our time.[36] Four of our ten practices of just peacemaking follow the imperative of peacemaking initiatives: (1) strategies of nonviolent direct action enacted by millions of people taking inspiration from Gandhi and Martin Luther King, and (2) strategies of independent initiatives developed by Charles Osgood and spread by citizens' movements to governments follow Matthew 5:38–42; (3) strategies of conflict resolution now spreading widely follow Matthew 5:21–26; and (4) strategies of acknowledging responsibility, repentance, and forgiveness described by Donald Shriver in *An Ethic for Enemies* follow Matthew 7:1–5.[37] And they follow other biblical teachings as well.

These four practices embody the same seven essential ingredients of Christian peacemaking: (1) they are not simply passive withdrawal, but proactive ways of grace that empower us to take peacemaking initiatives; (2) they acknowledge the log in our own eye and take our own responsibility for peacemaking rather than simply judging the other; (3) they affirm the dignity and interests of the enemy, even while rejecting sinful or wrong practices; (4) they confront the other with an invitation to making peace and justice; (5) they invite into community in a way that includes, rather than excludes, former enemies and outcasts; (6) they are historically embodied or situated—they are in fact happening in our history; (7) they are empirically validated—they are making a significant difference in international relations and domestic conflict. Thus these practices are not simply unrelated items; they are parallel ways of embodying the historically embodied strategy of transforming initiatives.

We appeal directly to Christians for whom God's grace matters to join us in the sort of initiatives that God wills for us and takes for us in Jesus Christ.

Advance Justice for All

A second basic imperative is *justice*. Injustice is a major cause of war. To make peace, we must make justice. Two central sets of practices move nations toward justice and away from injustice. They are practices that (1) promote democracy, human rights, and religious liberty and (2) foster just and sustainable economic development.

Just peace spreads when human rights and democracy spread. But to flourish, human rights and democracy require a world economy in which extreme differences in wealth, power, and participation are progressively overcome. However, inequality has dramatically increased between and within countries in the past few decades. Many families around the world are increasingly living on the edge. Correcting economic injustices is crucial to the work of just peacemaking. The just peacemaking practice of sustainable economic development is an expression of this need and of Jesus' teachings about wealth, poverty, feeding the hungry, and covenant justice.

Justice is central to the biblical story, from beginning to end. The four basic words for justice in Hebrew and Greek are repeated 1,060 times in the Bible—more frequently than almost any other term. Time and again, the prophets teach that the way to avoid the judgment and destruction of war is to return to God and practice justice. Jesus identifies with the prophetic tradition and repeatedly criticizes those in authority who seek prestige for themselves, neglect justice, faithfulness, and mercy, and cover their sins with the temple sacrifices—just as the prophet Jeremiah had charged (Jer. 7). Jesus' peacemaking teachings in the Sermon on the Mount and elsewhere focus much attention on giving alms to the poor and seeking justice (righteousness) and God's reign.

Jesus taught and practiced a total devotion to God's reign that called into question the human devotion to acquisitive ends. Although Jesus does not deny the importance of material goods that sustain bodily well-being, the gospels severely condemn those devoted to the accumulation of wealth and the goods of this world. Walter Wink summarizes Jesus' teachings:

> Jesus . . . pours scorn on those who are clothed in soft raiment and dwell in king's houses (Matt. 11:8; Luke 7:25). He challenges creditors, not only to forgo interest, but to ask no repayment whatever. To those who wish to follow him, he counsels selling everything, and warns the rich that they have no access whatever to the new society coming. Those who hoard luxuries and neglect the poor at their doors are presented with the prospect of their own death and divine judgment (Luke 12:13–21; 16:19–31). To the religionist's dream of being able to be "spiritual" and still amass wealth within an unjust system, Jesus pronounces an unconditional no. "You cannot serve God and wealth" (Matt. 6:24; Luke 16:13).[38]

Compassionate presence is at the heart of the Christian faith. The New Testament portrayal of Jesus reveals a God who is not a detached sovereign ruling over the universe from a distance. The Greek word for compassion in the New Testament, *splagchnisomai*—a word that perhaps best characterizes Jesus—means to "let one's innards embrace the feeling or situation of another." Jesus as a compassionate presence with those who suffer is evident in many of the stories of the Gospels.

Jesus stands in solidarity with the marginalized. Those who are treated as outcasts within the social context of Jesus' time are those upon whom he has special compassion: the poor, widows, the sick, Samaritans, those labeled sinners. Jesus' attitude and behavior toward women and children is revolutionary in the cultural context of first-century Palestine.

The church is engaged in mission beyond its own borders. It does not exist simply for itself, but to participate in the liberating power of God's reign in the world. The Gospels portray Jesus as an agent of deliverance, God's anointed one (Messiah), who is commissioned to bring God's dominion or reign into the world. The vision of the dominion of God is not a sectarian model simply for the church, but a call to transform the world.

Though God's reign is still future in its full manifestation, it is present already where God's Spirit is breaking into history. It becomes present through Jesus when he gives sight to the blind, feeds the hungry, liberates people from demonic possession, and forgives sin so that people can live a life of wholeness.

Luke 4:18–19 (quoting Isa. 61:1–2) expresses the purpose of Jesus' messiahship:

The Spirit of the Lord is upon me,
because he has anointed me to bring good news to the poor.
He has sent me to proclaim release to the captives
and recovery of sight to the blind,
to let the oppressed go free,
to proclaim the year of the Lord's favor.

Christ's call to discipleship means the church will find itself frequently at odds with the dominant culture in which it exists. In some sense, like the Hebrews in Babylon at the time of Jeremiah, the church is an exile community. But exile does not mean withdrawal into a special enclave separate from the world. Rather, like the

Hebrews of Jeremiah's time, the church is called to "seek the shalom of the city where it dwells" (Jer. 29:7). The church exists not for itself, but for the world, to be God's body in the world. The advice of Jeremiah to pray to God on behalf of the city in which we live is not a call for passivity—to let God act while the church watches and waits. To pray genuinely to God for the welfare of the city is to yearn with all one's heart for its well-being. So, as David Hollenbach, S.J., writes:

> The 1971 Synod of Bishops of the Roman Catholic Church introduced its reflections on the meaning of justice in world society with a statement that has become the platform and legitimation for a whole series of new initiatives in sociopolitical life by Roman Catholics. The bishops stated: "Action on behalf of justice and participation in the transformation of the world fully appear to us as a constitutive dimension of the preaching of the Gospel, or, in other words, of the Church's mission for the redemption of the human race and its liberation from every oppressive situation."[39]

The worldwide push and pull for human rights for minorities and oppressed peoples since World War II, since the UN Declaration of Human Rights and the active work of many church groups as well as secular groups, has been a major factor in advancing justice and democracy and is a crucial practice for peacemaking. The push for human rights in the second half of the twentieth century contributed mightily to the spread of democracy and thus to the receding of the fires of war from half of the world's regions.[40]

Some, however, oppose Christian support of justice and human rights. They may be influenced by philosophical criticism of the possessive individualism of the eighteenth-century Lockean tradition. They may also be influenced (perhaps unknowingly) by authoritarian traditions that opposed historical struggles for civil rights, for the rights of Jews against Nazi racism, or for the rights of oppressed groups in the southern hemisphere.

We want to make clear that there are several quite different narratives of human rights. One is the eighteenth-century individualistic narrative shaped by John Locke. It emphasizes liberty as autonomy, rejecting monarchy and authoritarianism; and it emphasizes the pursuit of property, reducing the earth's resources to individual possessions once they are mined, used, or exploited. But the original narrative emphasizes community, responsibility, and basic human needs. It preceded Locke historically, being rooted in older Hebraic traditions of covenant justice, Catholic traditions of social responsibility, and early free-church Puritan traditions of religious liberty and covenant responsibility.

This more socially responsible tradition connects with the twentieth-century narrative of the oppressed and discriminated, seen in revulsion against Adolf Hitler's Third Reich; and in the drive of former colonies for independence, of those suffering from racial hatred, of Latin American people's movements, of movements for justice in the former Soviet Bloc, the Philippines, South Africa, and elsewhere. This is a narrative of rights to liberty (rejecting oppression and affirming participation), to life (including basic human needs), and to community (including membership and responsibility). It is expressed in the UN Universal Declaration of Human Rights; and it, not the possessive individualism of the Lockean narrative, is represented by the commitment of many churches and Christian movements to champion human rights.[41]

26 Thus John Langan, S.J., writes that a human right is, first,

> a right that a human person has simply by virtue of being a human person, irrespective of his or her social status, cultural accomplishments, moral merits, religious beliefs, class memberships, or contractual relationships. . . . Rights include economic and social rights such as rights to social security, to work, to education, and to a "standard of living adequate for the well-being of [one]self and [one's] family, including food, clothing, housing and medical care, and necessary social services." Economic and social rights were unknown to Locke and the eighteenth century natural rights theorists, . . . [and] this is a fundamental error.[42]

Langan clarifies that, within Catholic teaching, rights claims are situated in a social context where "rights are to be balanced with duties, and individual claims are to be integrated into the pursuit of the common good. . . . The duty [of] meeting basic human needs . . . falls on all human persons to the extent of their ability. . . . A fundamental commitment to human rights requires that one be critical of abuses of power and neglect of the needs of the disadvantaged, whether these occur under oligopolistic capitalism or state socialism or the national security state."[43]

Langan concludes with the emphasis on *community* that is found in the covenant community tradition of the Old Testament, the early free-church Puritan human-rights tradition prior to Locke, the Roman Catholic tradition, and the twentieth-century narrative to which we are pointing.

> Recognition of the social and economic rights of others constrains the free pursuit of interest. . . . [This] creates the basis of a comprehensive and nonexclusive form of community. For to acknowledge the rights of others is to enter into a form of community with them, a community which is both presupposed and realized by the common task of satisfying those claims that we recognize as universal moral rights.[44]

Yet those who are concerned about possessive individualism in our culture surely have a point. U.S. policy has been significantly shaped by narrow economic interests. The Policy Planning Staff of the State Department advised in 1948 that "we have 50% of the world's wealth, but only 6.3% of its population. In this situation, our real job in the coming period . . . is to maintain this position of disparity. To do so, we have to dispense with all sentimentality. . . . we should cease thinking about human rights, the raising of living standards, and democratization."[45] The U.S. role in coups in Iran, Guatemala, the Congo, and Indonesia—among others—was as much, if not more, about protecting the interests of U.S. capital as it was about fighting communism.[46] The Bush administration's desire to control Iraq's oil reserves is well known, but its economic interests in Iraq are much broader. Paul Bremer, as director of the Coalition Provisional Authority, issued orders that transformed "the very foundation of the Iraqi economy." These included orders suspending all tariffs, customs duties, and other protective barriers—part of the Trade Liberalization Policy imposed upon Iraq. Order #39 rewrote the rules for foreign investment, with provisions for 100 percent foreign ownership of Iraqi businesses, and unrestricted and tax-free remittance of all profits and other funds.[47]

Love and Community: Strengthen Cooperative Forces

The individualism of our culture has caused us to slight the gospel's emphasis on community. We need to recover the Hebraic emphasis on *covenant community*. We need to recover Jesus' emphasis that love includes enemies, outcasts, and the neglected. Otherwise, our peace-making ignores structural forces beyond interpersonal peacemaking. Essential to peacemaking is attention to those structural forces of co-operation that work steadily to build regular relationships and include enemies, outcasts, and the neglected in community with us. These forces bind nations together in ways that go beyond what any individual may do.

We put these *cooperative forces* last in our book. This is a sign of the way individualism in our culture narrows our understanding. Students who read the first draft told us that we should first point to forces such as conflict resolution and nonviolent direct action, because people readily grasp them. Structural forces of cooperation seem like a foreign language to the individualism of our culture. But these forces are changing the world dramatically in ways many have not noticed. They are hugely important for peacemaking. They need to be understood. And they need our support.

Cooperative forces may be seen as a dimension of love, if love is understood realistically rather than sentimentally. Love as a feeling for certain persons is not enough; love must mean building reliable community with others, and it must include enemies. This community-building love is central to the gospel.

So Judith Gundry shows how the Gospel stories of Jesus' encounters with the Samaritan woman and the Syrophoenician woman (John 4:1–30; Mark 7:24–30) are stories "about the inclusion of the 'other,' about crossing the boundaries caused by ethnic, religious, social and gender otherness and bringing about a new, inclusive community of salvation."[48] She tells of the history of hostility and avoidance, war and temple desecration, between Samaritans and Jews, as well as the male avoidance of mutual discussion with women. But in Jesus, the Samaritan woman found "a Jew who did not impose on her the Jewish stereotype of a Samaritan . . . a man who did not impose on her the stereotype of a woman. . . . The living water also overflows the boundaries dividing the figures in this story and envelops them in a new, inclusive [communion]." The woman had been alienated from her own Samaritan community, but through Jesus she "regains a voice in her community, her witness is heard and believed, and her key role in the salvation of the Samaritans is recognized." Because of her witness, the Samaritans press Jesus to stay with them, and "he accepts their offer and stays two days with the Samaritans." Similarly, Jews were oppressed politically and economically by Tyre and Sidon, "notoriously our bitterest enemies." The woman from Tyre and Sidon was excluded from Jesus' Jewish mission. But her clever appeal to the practice and experience of mercy over "both exclusivism and sequential priority in salvation based on ethnic identity" persuades him that his mission extends to Gentiles as well. He immediately goes to the Sea of Galilee, attracts great crowds of Gentiles, expresses compassion for them, and feeds four thousand of them. They are part of the community of compassion. God's mercy has triumphed over "the prejudice-based distance between nations and cultures."

So also Duane Friesen writes that Jesus gives the concept of trust in God a

> nonviolent interpretation by extending the meaning of who are God's people universally to include even God's enemies. Love is to be shown to enemies, for they are objects of God's saving activity, potentially members of the covenant community. . . . This universalization of the meaning of people-hood had already taken place in the Hebrew prophets. . . .
>
> The cross is both the negative consequence of Jesus' nonconformity to institutions threatened by his life and message, and also a positive demonstration of his radical love. The cross, above all, demonstrates his willingness to lay down his life for us. In demonstrating an alternative to revolutionary violence, Jesus introduces into the historical process the possibility of genuine reconciliation. Genuine reconciliation is possible because love overcomes all barriers, even the barrier between enemies. . . . The ethic of the kingdom extends beyond the narrow loyalties of nation, class, and race to the whole of humankind, even to one's enemies.[49]

And Lisa Sowle Cahill writes, "The New Testament makes it abundantly clear that to love and forgive one's enemies is not only intrinsic to the kingdom, but that a life of love and forgiveness is a concrete alternative now."[50]

The tenth practice of just peacemaking is "Encourage grassroots peacemaking groups and voluntary associations," which for us especially includes churches and church peacemaking groups. Political science and sociology are now discovering how crucial are grassroots groups, nongovernmental organizations, churches, meeting houses, mosques, and synagogues, and civil society to build the foundation for secure and peaceful societies, infrastructures of community solidarity, just relationships between people, and small-scale economic development within communities, thereby creating secure and safe environments that meet the basis needs of people. In other words, the actors of just peacemaking are not only governments, but those enduring relationships that are built up by churches and civil society. In fact, there is evidence that even in cases of severe humanitarian crises (Rwanda and Somalia, for example), existing civil structures were able to pick up the pieces and move on despite the failures of state structures. We need to pay more attention to the role of civil society in creating an orderly peace. John Paul Lederach, for example, has done effective work in building peace by recognizing the Somali clan structure (which lives within the "state" that failed). *The Battle for Hearts and Minds: Using Soft Power to Undermine Terrorist Networks*, although written by political science experts in government, emphasizes in almost every chapter how crucial are groups of civil society for combating terrorism and building healthy societies that do not produce or harbor terrorists.

American culture-conforming Protestant individualism needs correction by an understanding of churches as discerning communities. Discipleship is not primarily realized in the practice of heroic individuals, but is potent where it is embodied in the practices of a concrete community, in a social group which, by its very existence as an alternative community in the world, becomes a sign of God's reign, albeit in earthen vessels.

> To organized opposition, Jesus responds with the formal founding of a new social reality. New teachings are no threat, as long as the teacher stands alone; a movement, extending his personality in both time and space, presenting an alternative to the structures that were there before, challenges the system as no mere words could.[51]

The church functions as a community of memory and hope to nurture the paradigmatic story that orients the community in time and sustains a vision of God's reign. Deliberate attention to the nurture of churches, which keep alive the memory of paradigmatic stories (such as the Exodus or the parable of the good Samaritan [Luke 10:30–37]), is essential to the moral formation of people of character. Robert Wuthnow notes that there is widespread knowledge in

American society of the good Samaritan story:

> It provides a framework that helps us define—and therefore
> see—the possibilities for compassion in our own world. . . . For
> us the story of the Good Samaritan is fundamentally about the
> possibility of human kindness existing in a society of strangers.
> . . . The story of the Good Samaritan tells us that some basic
> element of our humanity can bridge the gap and create com-
> munity even among strangers. . . . It is also a story that reveals
> our diversity as a society—the divisions that ordinarily separate
> rich and poor, black and white, male and female, citizen and
> alien—and yet it shows that these divisions can be overcome.[52]

Churches structure a process of practical moral reasoning where
members of the community can listen to one another as they discern
together what discipleship means. If a church is a faithful community,
it embodies a conflict resolution process that assumes active participation by the entire membership (based on New Testament models
outlined in 1 Cor. 14:26–33 and Matt. 18:15–18). Commitment is not
primarily to a fixed system of ethics. Churches are gatherings of persons committed to speaking and listening to one another to discern
what faithfulness means in the light of the vision of life revealed in
Jesus Christ. This participatory model, when it functions well, can be
a school of learning for the participatory democracy that is a key practice of peacemaking. It has been such historically, and it can be so in
our contemporary setting.

It should therefore be clear why we strongly emphasize the tenth
practice of just peacemaking, "encourage grassroots peacemaking
groups," which we principally interpret as those churches, church
groups, and peacemaking groups that embody the peacemaking that
Jesus Christ of the New Testament taught and for which he died.

Our emphasis on churches as communities (as opposed to individualism) also influences us to see the importance of international community practices. These are cooperative forces in the international
system, including the United Nations and regional organizations that
not only function as deliberative bodies but encourage mutual admo-
nition, mutual understanding, communication, and common memories and narratives rather than simply national narcissism. Like
churches, these secular organizations have their own power struggles,
antagonisms, self-interests, inefficiencies, and internal conflicts. Yet

they do nudge nations, groups, and economic institutions into cooperative communities, even across lines of enmity.

We have learned from John Howard Yoder to notice that New Testament practices such as caring for the needy and including outcasts could be observed by nonbelievers, and could become models for analogous secular processes in the world. In fact, some secular processes such as hospitals and orphanages historically were set in motion or strongly supported by Jewish and Christian communities. Our correction of our own individualism by our appreciation of the importance of churches as communities opens our eyes to see the importance of processes of community that are transforming our anarchic world into a society. We see secular organizations such as the United Nations, international communication and treaties, and a hundred kinds of community-building processes as secular analogies to community-building love, which encourages nations, economic organizations, and people to build increasingly strong community with one another, often including those who are enemies or potential enemies. "Today the world is knitted together not just by the printed word, but by wires, cables, and satellite links buzzing with everything from breaking news to e-mailed Valentine's Day messages. What will such connectedness mean to the leaders of tomorrow?"[53] Thambo Mbeki in South Africa says that multiple international connections will make people much better informed and less dependent on political rulers for their information. Asked if there could have been apartheid in a South Africa connected to e-mail, international television news, and the like, he replied flatly, "There could not have been."[54] Empirical research shows that nations with many international ties and relationships are significantly less likely to make war with each other. Extensive and even surprising evidence of this will be presented in chapters 7, 8, and 9.

MODEST PARTICIPATION IN GOD'S GRACE IN OUR HISTORY

In our unprogrammed meeting/worship service on the last day of our working conference at the Carter Center, Susan Thistlethwaite read from Adrienne Rich's poem "Spider's Web." In weaving a web, a spider weaves over and over and over again, building a strong web despite the fragility of each strand. She called us to a similar modest hope, weaving our practices over and over and over again. Ted Koontz said he had moved from "this world is a mess and I need to fix it" to

"God is moving in history to do something, and I can join in." We are trying to describe what we see God doing in our history so that people can join in.

Some Christians resist, expressing fatalism. They cite the book of Revelation to support their belief that we cannot spread peacemaking. We should not hope to reduce or eliminate war, they say, because the Bible says there will be wars and rumors of war. We believe this misreads the message of the book of Revelation. Throughout the biblical drama, we are taught that though the powers and authorities seem in control, God is sovereign; and we are to be faithful to God's teachings. This is also the message of the book of Revelation: God is the real ruler; God is judging the powers, including the U.S. empire, who seem to be ruling for now and who are causing wars. God will redeem the followers of the Lamb; therefore, do not lose hope; follow the teachings of the Lamb. The followers of the Lamb do the deeds Jesus teaches. The same point is repeated again and again in varieties of phrasing, so often that one wonders how people could miss it: The followers of the Lamb are those who do the deeds Jesus teaches, who do God's will, keep God's Word, keep God's commandments, hold faithful to the testimony of Jesus, do the teachings of Jesus, follow God's teachings as given through Jesus, obey God's commands (Rev. 2:2, 23, 19, 26; 3:8, 10; 9:20–21; 12:17; 14:4, 12; 16:11; 19:10; 20:12–13; 22:11).

The book of Revelation does not teach that we should avoid taking peacemaking initiatives because God will do everything; it teaches that we should take the peacemaking initiatives that Jesus teaches: Do the deeds of Jesus. It does not teach that we cannot do anything about the future and so should fall back into fatalistic inaction; it teaches that when we do peacemaking deeds as Jesus commands, we are participating in the great drama of God's redemption of the world through the Lamb: Do the deeds of Jesus. The point is not that because things will get worse before they can get better, there is nothing we can do. The point is that things will not get better by trusting in the power of the violent beasts; we can expect violent trauma as judgment on their violence. Things will get better through God's delivering action, so we are to do the deeds of Jesus. God is working in our history to overcome the violence and injustice and to bring forth the New Jerusalem of Shalom. This will happen not by a simple belief in progress, nor by our own power, nor without suffering and trauma. It will happen by God's grace; we are called to believe in God's grace and to be faithful participants in it: Do the deeds of Jesus. The central question in the book of Revelation is whether we are followers of the Lamb or followers of the beasts who kill and destroy; whether we do the deeds of Jesus or the deeds of the evil rulers; our answer decides whether we are participants in God's present and eternal purpose and rule: Do the deeds of Jesus.[55] The deeds that Jesus teaches include deeds of peacemaking.

Churches can serve a special role in nurturing a spirituality that sustains courage when just peacemaking is unpopular, hope when despair or cynicism is tempting, and a sense of grace and the possibility of forgiveness when just peacemaking fails. A church nurtured by an eschatological vision of God's reign, grounded in a vision that the slain Lamb is the Sovereign of history, is particularly needed when popular culture fosters a mass spirit of hatred toward enemies and fans the flames of war. Peacemakers need to be sustained by a willingness to suffer if necessary, to overcome hatred of the enemy and the ability to endure abuse without retaliation, and to keep hope and patience alive during a long period of struggle. Churches can sustain trust in the possibility of the miracle of transformation when the evidence for change appears bleak, and joy even in the midst of suffering and pain. Just peacemaking will not long endure if its theological roots are based upon the assurance of success. We still need a realism about the depth of evil that guards people from disillusionment. Aware of the limits of our own ability to predict and control the future, we can still, through the gracious power of God, embrace our common humanity through simple deeds of kindness and charity.

PRACTICES, NOT PRINCIPLES

At our first working conference at the Abbey of Gethsemani, a form of the fact-value split arose. The question was raised whether we should emphasize moral principles or political strategies. That led us toward abstract, historically disembodied principles or ideals rather than historically situated practices. It led us away from concreteness and historical actuality. It was ironic—or providential—that this struggle between empirical description and moral imperative took place at the Abbey of Gethsemani, where right before our eyes the monks were actually, empirically, engaging in the normative practice of prayer, beginning at 3:20 each morning. A few of us participated in those early morning prayers, and the monks' normative practice may have been what led us forward into integrated embodiment.

We found our reintegration by explicitly turning to the ethics of normative practices. A practice is neither an ideal nor a rule, but a human activity that regularly takes place and that a sociologist could observe. Such activities include monks praying; churches worshiping by sharing bread and wine in Jesus' name and feeding, clothing, and housing the poor and hungry; Gentiles and Jews becoming one in the early Christian community; Jimmy Carter practicing conflict resolution; East Germans practicing nonviolent direct action while studying Martin Luther King; and Guatemalan women meeting together to struggle for human rights.

We have judged some practices to be ethically normative because they embody love, justice, and peacemaking initiatives and because they do, in fact, spread peace. But we have not simply derived our ten practices of peacemaking deductively from love, justice, and peacemaking initiatives; we have observed them inductively as actually happening in our history and then have judged them to be ethically normative. Some, of course, like nonviolent direct action and feeding the hungry, have arisen out of practices of faith; the relation between empirical observation and ethical assessment is a mutual interweaving.

Casting our just peacemaking theory in the form of normative practices brought together the empirical research of the international relations experts among us and the ethical arguments of the Christian ethicists and moral theologians. It brought together the realists and the advocates of a liberal-democratic peace, the empiricists and historians. Realism says the world is characterized by power struggles and conflicts of interest, and history does not take leaps; therefore, we have to learn to deal with the world as it is. Idealists say we should focus on ideals and imagine how we can move the world toward them. The practices of peacemaking that we are pointing to happen empirically in the real world, in the context of real threat, power struggle, and drive for security. They make power's expression in war less likely and peace more likely.

Casting our theory in the form of practices remedied the tension we experienced about the role of justice in peacemaking. When justice means historically actual practices that restore community, and we acknowledge our own complicity in injustice, then we can participate in modest and realistic ways that do lead to peace. When, on the other hand, justice is thought of as an absolute ideal or a truth that we already know, the result often is self-righteous crusading or postponing peace until the reign of God arrives in its fullness.

Focusing on practices grounded our normative recommendations in peacemaking processes that are taking place in our historical period and growing via positive feedback loops. When we notice that these ten practices are already happening, resolving conflicts, proving useful, and therefore spreading and making reliance on war unlikely in many regions, then we sense that ours is a historic moment in which we may be able to encourage a transition from war as normal to war as abnormal. We are calling all to notice what new processes of deliverance are happening among us and spreading globally. We are urging not disembodied ideals or ahistorical "oughts" to impose on an alien history they do not fit, but support for what is serving functional needs in the midst of power realities.

By no means are all practices in our time ethically normative. There are powerful economic interests and natural drives for national security that can work good or evil. There are interests that do not want to make peace, and interests that think they want peace but perceive things with such loyalties that their actions work at cross-purposes to peace. Some think the way to peace is to wipe out the enemy. There are enormous forces of evil: nuclear weapons and their delivery systems; chemical and biological weapons; international terrorism; devastating poverty and its offspring, population explosion; ecological devastation and nonrenewable energy consumption; ethnic and religious wars within nations such as Rwanda, Sudan, and the Congo. Whenever the peacemaking practices we point to work their way into areas where they are still foreign, each practice recognizes and seeks to resolve, lessen, discipline, or check and balance one or more of these evil forces.

Our focus on practices, and on churches and groups that encourage and foster those practices, means that we recommend to every individual and every church that they form groups to nurture such practices. Most church groups and denominations have a church peacemaking program. We urge each church to link up actively with its group's peacemaking program. We also urge linking up with networks that provide action alerts so we can know when to join with others in putting our shoulders to the wheel of peacemaking, so that in our numbers there is strength and in our timing there is effectiveness. Some will join

36

Peace Action (www.peace-action.org), Bread for the World (www.bread.org), Every Church a Peace Church (www.ecapc.org), Friends Committee on National Legislation (www.fcnl.org), Amnesty International, the Sierra Club, and/or www.creationcare.org.

In isolation is passivity; in working together is empowerment. The acting unit, for us, is not the isolated individual but the individual in a local group that is connected with a national network of peacemakers. Churches should have a peacemaker group, a Peace and World Hunger committee, or a Peace and Justice leadership group that will lead the church in peacemaking action. Denominational peacemaking programs and Every Church a Peace Church have suggestions for how to organize church peacemaking groups. Alone, as individuals, we lack the information, the group support, the sense of empowerment, and the ability to act in concert with other peacemakers to become a strong force for peace. Together, in groups, we can experience the fun of mutual support and friendship as well as the spiritual growth of the discipline of prayer.

CONSENSUS WITHOUT UNANIMITY

Churches and peacemaking groups, and governments and citizens, have an obligation to support these peacemaking practices in long-term work to build conditions that make peace more likely as well as in crises, where peacemaking initiatives can make war less likely. Whether a government employs these practices is a test of the sincerity of its claim to be trying to make peace. Whether a church supports these practices tests its sincerity in claiming to follow Jesus. We intend the new paradigm of just peacemaking to be used as a plumb line to measure whether churches and governments are doing what is right.

We ask: Does just peacemaking make new sense of our historical context, and point to faith-based, meaningful action and prayer in that context? Can these ten practices of just peacemaking help people participate in the peacemaking practices and forces that are changing our world? Do they grapple with realistic evils that cause war and destroy peace? How would you relate them to your faith or core beliefs and values? We are addressing all persons of various faiths or no claimed faith who are concerned about peacemaking, or who could become concerned if they had a map that would make sense of events and of peacemaking trends for them and that would indicate directions their participation can take.

Coming from diverse perspectives, we reached consensus. We celebrated; we were energized by our agreement. But we also recognized differences and omissions. John Cartwright observed that we had ideological differences in the essays, and he thought that was good; heads nodded in agreement. We need more on the nuclearized world; we believe many have relaxed too soon. We lack enough attention to racial-ethnic-religious conflict, but we have made efforts to emphasize this concern. We do not all agree with Michael Smith's affirmation of humanitarian intervention, but we think it should be included. We have definite disagreements over the international economy in its complexities, power realities, and injustices. We should say more about structural adjustment policies of the International Monetary Fund. Empirically, international trade decreases war, but the globalized economy is setting millions of the poor back further. The question of how we can make global corporations ethically and legally responsible in each country where they operate, despite their enormous power and their ability to leave any country, is one of the most crucial ethical questions for the next decades. We have not tried to answer it; we have only pointed to some effects on peacemaking. We should say much more about the global ecological crisis—issues such as global warming, and competition and conflict over scarce resources like water and nonrenewable energy. This can be a source of severe wars. We begin to point to crises over scarce resources and the critical need to practice conservation and to push governments and corporations for dramatic conservation policies in chapter 6 on *sustainable* economic development, but far more should be said. Conservation should be added as a just peacemaking practice in itself. We should add another book on that theme. All we can do here is strongly recommend Larry Rasmussen, *Earth Community: Earth Ethics*, which won the Grawemeyer Award for best book of the year in religion,[56] and the forthcoming book he is writing. Being based in members of the Society of Christian Ethics who have authored calls for just peacemaking, we lack Two-Thirds-World voices. Although we listen to voices from the developing nations, read books, visit developing countries, and seek to incorporate insights from those sources in what we have written, this book would be different if it had been written in Nicaragua or Uganda, El Salvador or the Sudan. From the perspective of our First World location, our practice should be confession and repentance for the injustice of the system, of international power, of economic practices.

Peace activists are located in the struggle for change, and this gives them a strongly critical tone toward present government policies, institutions, leaders, and other status-quo forces. Many members of established faith communities tend to be more a part of established institutions, more oriented toward gradual, incremental change, and often defensive in the face of more radical criticism of the status quo. We have become painfully aware of how difficult it is to stop a war once it has started. Iraq reminds us how much work we have to do in applying just peacemaking practices to prevent war, and how much work we still need to do in refining the practice of "transforming initiatives" to help extricate us from war. Study of opinion polls over the last century makes clear that a president can always manage to get initial majority support for a war that president is determined to fight, because of the forces of nationalism, fear of threat, and deference to presidential authority. Campaigns to say no to war always fail, and pushing for polling organizations to ask, "Do you favor taking military action to achieve some objective the president wants?" is to guarantee a loss in the polls. Only later do people realize the disaster the war has been, and decrease their support. Realism demonstrates it is far more effective to push for specific actions that can divert support for war. Polls prior to the Iraq War gave support two to one for letting the inspections for weapons of mass destruction finish their work before making war, and for obtaining UN support before making war.[57] In future crises energy needs to focus on preventive actions, just peacemaking alternatives to war, if we are to win the battle for public support.

Academics tend to be part of a would-be scientific and detached community, and so speak in distanced language. The distinctions are not airtight; many peace activists are deeply involved in faith communities; many academics are engaged in congregations, and many are more radically critical of the status quo. Most of us who have produced this just peacemaking paradigm are academics; many have been engaged in peace activism on the national, local, and church levels. Many of us are a synthesis: academic church peace activists.

The result is that, for some peace activists, we may not be critical enough of U.S. policies; for some church people, we may be too critical; for some academics, we may say too little about systemic theory. All we can say is that, yes, there are logs in our own eyes. We have those tensions in our group as well. But the more we have worked together, the more we have learned to appreciate one another's diverse perspectives, and the more we have become committed to the importance of these practices. We believe these practices are so important that we are genuinely eager for them to reach a wide audience. It has been fun to watch our enthusiasm grow out of initial skepticism as we have experienced the result taking shape. We ask you to focus on the sense the practices make; on how they can help you notice what is happening in our world, in our time; and on how you can be a part of them on the level of your personal practice, your group and congregational involvements, and your encouragement and criticism of governments. In Michelle Tooley's study of women working for human rights in Guatemala, she found that what empowered them was working together in groups with specific, shared practices of peacemaking.[58] We can do likewise.

PART ONE

peacemaking initiatives

One

SUPPORT NONVIOLENT DIRECT ACTION

John Cartwright
Susan Thistlethwaite

Nonviolent Direct Action came to the attention of most of us in the United States as the method used effectively by Martin Luther King Jr. and the civil rights movement; that application borrowed from the *satyagraha* campaign led by Mahatma Mohandas Gandhi for independence in India. And nonviolent direct action has been further refined through the nonviolent movement that ended dictatorship in the Philippines; the nonviolent campaign that ended rule by the shah in Iran; the recent revolutions in Poland, East Germany, and Central Europe; human-rights movements in Guatemala, Argentina, and elsewhere in Latin America; the nonviolent parts of the intifada campaign in Palestine; and the freedom campaign in South Africa. If we include its blocking the old Soviet rulers from their effort to squash the Yeltsin-led democracy, nonviolent direct action unseated two of the most powerful empires of the twentieth century (Britain in India and the Soviet Union).[1] It deserves to come first in the practices of just peacemaking.

Nonviolent direct action is a strategy that lances the festering boil of violence and produces healing without resort to war. Citizens and governments must support and work with such campaigns in situations of actual or potential conflict before the condition of "last resort" can be employed to justify violence. Hence the practice of nonviolent direct action is an obligatory norm where nonviolently it can transform festering injustice into constructive change.

Nonviolent direct action is designed to deal with injustice that is already happening. It becomes an action that transforms a situation from greater to lesser violence, from greater to lesser injustice, when it is employed out of an analysis of the violence and injustice that is currently underway. None of the nonviolent direct actions, taken out of this context, guarantees that greater justice and peace will automatically result. Any of these nonviolent direct actions can be and has been employed to increase violent confrontation for unjust ends.

As a general guideline, grassroots movements for peace and justice, nongovernmental organizations, or even government agencies and the military, when they are considering any of these practice norms, must engage in rigorous contextual analysis of the forces in the situation that are increasing violence and injustice and the current or proposed options for increased peace and justice. This analysis must be concrete and must be done in consultation with the many groups, agencies, or instrumentalities involved. Peacemaking is never simple. It always requires the broadest kind of consultation with *all* the parties involved, then a decision as to which practice norm, several norms, or none at all, best serves the interests of justice and peace in any given situation.

As Daniel L. Buttry says:

43

> The 1980s and early 1990s witnessed a transformation of the way people engage in struggles for freedom, justice, peace, and human rights. Wars, insurgencies, ethnic violence, and acts of terrorism still occur with horrifying frequency and tragic consequences, but for the first time in human history a global phenomenon of nonviolent movements shook up political powers, redrew national boundaries, and brought hope to millions of people ground down by oppression and poverty. . . . Through nonviolent action, ordinary people who had often been locked out of political decision-making processes became agents shaping their own destinies.[2]

As part of this global movement, the teachings and works of Gandhi and Martin Luther King Jr. spread around the world. Chinese students in Tiananmen Square quoted King. The movie *Gandhi* played in

Lithuania in 1987 just as the Sajudis independence movement was beginning. The International Fellowship of Reconciliation provided nonviolence training in Brazil, the Philippines, South Africa, Burma, Korea, and a host of other countries. Hildegard and Jean Goss-Mayr of the International Fellowship of Reconciliation were nominated for the Nobel Peace Prize for their efforts to disseminate nonviolence through their workshops. Adolfo Pérez Esquivel from Argentina received the Nobel Prize in 1980 for his work in linking together nonviolent movements as diverse as the Mothers of the Plaza in Argentina protesting the disappearance of their relatives, cement workers in Brazil striking for better working conditions, and Indians in Ecuador struggling for land reform. The theory and history of nonviolence has received more scholarly attention by people such as Gene Sharp, whose three-volume work *The Politics of Nonviolent Action* has become a classic in the field. These connections have helped to break down the walls of isolation that have aided repression, and have provided new insights, creative examples, and moral solidarity for people in a wide range of contexts as they struggle to better their lives and shape their destiny.

The practice of nonviolent direct action actually includes a set of practices, outlined in the sections that follow.

BOYCOTTS

A *boycott* is a concerted action designed to isolate an individual, group, or nation in order to express disapproval and to coerce change. The term "boycott" is taken from Charles Boycott, an English estate manager whose rent collection tactics in the 1880s so enraged Irish tenants that they refused to harvest crops for him. The withholding of labor was first used, therefore, on Boycott himself, and its success was demonstrated by his need for fifty volunteers from Ulster, working under an armed escort of nine hundred soldiers, to harvest his crops.

After 1880 the term soon came into common use, broadening to describe and include all forms of nonviolent intimidation. The nineteenth-century abolitionist movement, for example, was the first organized effort to change national policy in the United States through nonviolent means. Boycotting slave-made products was a common tactic in that endeavor. Indeed, product boycotts were common in the late nineteenth century when the nascent labor-union movement attempted to discourage the public from buying goods made by nonunion companies with unfair labor practices.

Numerous and varied examples of the use of the boycott pervade the twentieth century. In the 1930s, Gandhi encouraged Indians to boycott British textiles and to substitute their own homespun cloth, a significant factor in the success of the movement for Indian self-determination. The Montgomery bus boycott of 1955–1956 launched the Martin Luther King–led civil rights movement, and boycotts of stores and business districts that supported segregation were integral to the movement's success in many cities. César Chávez, who founded the National Farm Workers Association in 1962, organized national consumer boycotts of lettuce, grapes, and wines in order to protest the plight of migrant farm workers. In the 1970s and 1980s, organizations concerned about the abuse of infant formula marketing practices organized a successful global boycott focused on Nestlé, which resulted in new standards of marketing.

Although the boycott is most frequently used in labor disputes, it has had a much wider range of application and use. In recent history, perhaps the most impressive example of a global boycott that contributed to nonviolent political change was the action against South Africa. Boycotts of companies that invested in South Africa and economic sanctions against that state were a major force in persuading the government to drop apartheid and to enter into democratic elections and peaceful integration, when most observers had expected apartheid would end, if at all, only after very bloody violence.

That action demonstrated the increased ability of nonviolent activists to penetrate the complex corporate patterns of ownership and control. Activists were able to coordinate their research, confrontation, and publicity globally—a sophisticated model of boycott that has become easier with the increased availability of communication tools to activists around the world. This boycott was crucial in persuading the moderate (or, perhaps more accurately, amoral or morally ambivalent) parts of the South African business community of the eventual higher cost of resistance to change.

In the final analysis, all boycotts depend for their effectiveness on broad concerted action that is focused on a limited issue or problem. Since the purpose of a boycott is to change rather than annihilate the offending party, careful management of the boycott process is required. Furthermore, serious economic, political, and moral questions may arise from a miscalculation or disregard of the effects of a boycott on secondary parties or the community as a whole. This suggests a certain degree of control, foresight, and attention to both the manifest and the latent consequences of this type of concerted action.

In a thoughtful book, Mark W. Charlton concludes that international economic sanctions can produce corrections of systemic injustice without the violence of war, or they can violate basic human rights and even contribute directly to extensive loss of life. They must be evaluated not by abstract general principles but by an ethical framework of violence-reduction criteria that evaluate them in the context of specific policy situations:

1. The target country must have committed a grave injustice.

2. Less coercive measures must have been tried first.

3. A significant portion of the population must not already be living at a subsistence level and pushed over the brink by the sanctions; and neutral authorities—not the enforcers—must monitor the effects.

4. Humanitarian provisions must be included so that fundamental rights to food, medicine, and shelter are not violated.

5. Preference should be given to targeting the interests of those responsible for the wrongdoing, and to avoiding enriching them at the expense of the victims.

6. If domestic reform is the main objective, there must be widespread support for the sanctions within the targeted population.

7. Sanctions should be applied in a manner likely to lead to a long-term, just resolution: by upholding international law and widely accepted moral values; by being part of a broader political strategy to find a peaceful and just solution; by having clearly announced objectives that indicate what behaviors will result in lifting the sanctions; and by refraining from adding new conditions or objectives.[3]

However, one of the principle shortcomings of sanctions, as critics repeatedly point out, is that they are often too broad in scope and therefore tend to violate criteria 3, 4, and 5 above. This has led to the development of more calibrated "smart sanctions," which include steps like targeting and freezing financial assets, arms embargoes, restrictions on international travel, and other political and economic measures.[4] As Joseph Stephanides notes, such sanctions "enhance the prospect of achieving . . . stated objectives while minimizing unintended negative consequences," and therefore make smart sanctions an "effective means of conflict resolution" provided they are "integrated into an overall conflict resolution strategy and . . . complemented by other inducement measures."[5] Although still a relatively new instrument, smart sanctions have already enjoyed noticeable success in modifying the behavior of some of the world's most threatening and oppressive regimes, including North Korea, and Iraq prior to the U.S.-led invasion in March of 2003.[6]

STRIKES

A *strike* is a collective refusal by employees to work under the conditions required by employers. It can take the form of an outright walkout, a sit-down strike, a work slowdown, or a hunger strike. It is a practice norm in peacemaking when it is directed at noncooperation with unjust economic practice, or is combined with larger movements of noncooperation with unjust political and/or social orders. One could say that worker noncooperation with oppressive conditions is as old as history itself. Pharaoh experienced both a work slowdown on the part of the midwives and a complete walkout on the part of the Hebrews (Exod. 1:13).

Strikes as an organized effort of the labor movement date from the nineteenth-century Industrial Revolution in Europe and the early twentieth century in the United States. They were used as a tactic of labor organizing, particularly in Great Britain. Unions did not become legal in England until 1871, and not until 1935 did the National Labor Relations Act make labor organizing and collective bargaining legal in the United States. The Solidarity union in Poland achieved considerable social change through strikes in the 1980s. Local and national strikes as well as work stoppages and slowdowns formed a cornerstone of the struggle against apartheid in South Africa.

Strikes have often met with considerable violence on the part of both business owners and government. In Colorado in the early twentieth century, strikebreakers burned striking gold miners alive while they were gathered in a meeting hall. The leaders of striking Bolivian tin miners in 1977 were imprisoned, beaten, or exiled. Officials have called on police and even the National Guard, as Calvin Coolidge did in breaking the strike of the Boston police force in 1919. Owners have used scabs or nonunion workers to replace striking workers. Several states in the United States now have right-to-work laws that weaken unions by making closed shops—that is, only union shops—illegal.

Strikes and work slowdowns were used effectively in combination with consumer boycotts by a Mexican American, César Chávez. Chávez organized migrant farm workers in California, founding the National Farm Workers Association in 1962. Agricultural workers are among the most exploited segment of the U.S. labor force, being exempt from Occupational Health and Safety Standards and minimum-wage laws. Child labor still exists in farm work. Chávez gave these workers a sense of control over their own lives through this type of action.

Hunger strikes are sometimes a part of the strike effort. Certainly Gandhi elevated the hunger strike to a new level of spirituality. As he said in the Fast unto Death in January 1948, "My fast should not be considered a political move in any sense of the term. It is obedience to the peremptory call of conscience and duty. It comes out of felt agony."[7] Women leaders in the suffrage movement in England, such as Emmeline Pankhurst, effectively used hunger strikes as part of their struggle to secure women's right to vote. Arrested for her increased militancy in the struggle for women's suffrage, Pankhurst went on a hunger strike in prison in 1913. Hunger-striking prisoners had been force-fed in British prisons, and some had choked to death. The resultant public outcry had caused the government to release hunger strikers until they regained their health, after which they would be reincarcerated. Pankhurst was released and rearrested under this law twelve times in one year.

César Chávez used a thirty-six-day hunger strike to protest hazardous pesticide use. After the Bolivian tin miners' union leaders were killed, imprisoned, or exiled, four wives of imprisoned miners—Nellie Paniagua, Angelica Flores, Aurora Lora, and Luzmila Penmentel—began a hunger strike on Christmas Day 1977.

Archbishop Jorge Manrique allowed the women to hold the hunger strike in his own residence. On December 28, the Feast of Holy Innocents, which commemorates the children slaughtered by Herod, the women's children joined the hunger strike. When people protested, the mothers said they would release the children as soon as adults came to take their places. Soon almost fourteen hundred people had joined this hunger strike. As the tension mounted, international human-rights organizations, church representatives, and other non-governmental agencies tried to mediate. Negotiations broke down at one point, and some strikers and human-rights observers were arrested. The four women then began to refuse water as well as food.

The government acceded to the striking women's demands in full, providing amnesty for nineteen thousand political prisoners and exiles, reinstating jobs for union activists, and granting freedom to all arrested during the strike as well as the right to organize unions in the future.

The application of strikes as a practice norm is broad. Because unjust economic practice frequently is a form of institutionalized violence, strikes point directly to that often hidden form of violence. Strikes are particularly effective when combined with other practices such as public disclosure, since the reason for the strike will be obscured or distorted by the business or government leaders who oppose it.

Noncooperation is a historically effective nonviolent method of achieving social change. In the form of strikes, whether to organize a union or to call attention to widespread political and social injustice, noncooperation involves many people making a commitment not to participate, even for a short time, in the structures they wish to change.

Hunger strikes can be used separately from broader strike activity but are often used in conjunction with economic noncooperation to draw attention to the spiritual dimension of the effort.

MARCHES

A *march* is a mass public demonstration by a group or groups seeking to dramatize an issue, a concern, a point of view, or an injustice. Externally, its purposes may include one or more of the following: education, fund raising, a show of force (in terms of numbers), recruitment of new or marginal adherents, or engendering of so-called creative tension and crisis. Internally, the march serves to build group morale, to identify the sympathetic, and to foster cohesion among the participants with regard to the group's aims and goals. A march usually involves both a *parade* and a *rally*, the latter characterized by speeches and celebration.

Marches in the context of conflict resolution and peacemaking appear to be quite modern. In the United States, marches most often have been associated with dramatizing a particular issue or cause such as temperance, suffrage, labor-management conflict, civil rights, opposition to war, or gay rights. The celebrated March on Washington in 1963 and the Million Man March of 1995 have become particularly potent examples of the attention-getting effect of a well-executed mass demonstration.

King orchestrated the march to an art form. He saw that the nonviolent march should intentionally seek to create such a crisis and foster such a tension that a community that previously had refused to hear would now have to confront the issue in the form of living persons; such a live dramatization of an issue could no longer be ignored. As King stated in his classic "Letter from Birmingham Jail," conflict must be brought into the open in order to be healed:

> Actually we who engage in nonviolent direct action are not the creators of tension. We merely bring to the surface the hidden tension that is already alive. We bring it out in the open, where it can be seen and dealt with. Like a boil that can never be cured so long as it is covered up but must be opened with all its ugliness to the natural medicines of air and light, injustice must be exposed, with all the tension its exposure creates, to the light of human conscience and the air of national opinion before it can be cured.[8]

The march, therefore, is predicated on the faith that the exposure to truth creates its own dynamic and makes for resolution around the true issues rather than false or superficial ones.

In the United States, East Germany, South Africa, Argentina, and elsewhere, marches have brought dramatic nonviolent change that had been thought impossible without massive violence.

CIVIL DISOBEDIENCE

Civil disobedience is the act of disobeying or refusing to obey civil laws or decrees on grounds of moral, political, or religious principle. Persons who practice civil disobedience break the law because they consider the law unjust, want to call attention to its injustice, and hope to bring about its repeal or amendment. Although it adopts the tactics of nonviolence, civil disobedience is usually more than mere passive resistance. It often takes such active forms as illegal demonstrations or peaceful occupation of premises. As distinguished from other forms of rebellion, civil disobedience tends to invite a confrontation with civil authorities (most often leading to arrest) and willingly accepts the penalty for breaking the law.

Civil disobedience can be traced back at least to the Exodus of the Jews from Pharaoh's authority in Egypt and to the earliest Christians, who engaged in limited forms of civil disobedience on religious grounds. Religion often has been a basis for refusing to obey laws perceived as contrary to belief, as when the Doukhobors in Canada refused to send their children to state-operated schools. The Doukhobors then paraded nude in public to protest their prosecution for passive resistance to the school laws.

The classic exposition of civil disobedience is Henry David Thoreau's essay "Resistance to Civil Government" (1849), later retitled "On the Duty of Civil Disobedience." Thoreau said that when one's conscience and the laws clash, one must follow one's conscience. This stress on personal conscience and the emphasis on the need to act now rather than wait for legal change have become recurring elements in civil disobedience movements.[9]

Perhaps the most ambitious and most successful examples of mass civil disobedience were those of Mohandas Gandhi and Martin Luther King Jr. Gandhi called civil disobedience *satyagraha* (a term meaning "truth force") and taught it as an austere practice requiring great self-discipline and moral purity. With a versatile use of civil disobedience, Gandhi led the campaign for Indian independence in the 1930s and 1940s.

Also in the 1940s, blacks along with white sympathizers began to use forms of civil disobedience in order to challenge discrimination in public transportation and restaurants. The major movement, however, began in 1955 with the Montgomery bus boycott and the ensuing illegal sit-ins in support of boycotts of segregated public facilities. King was a disciple of Gandhi and became the chief advocate of nonviolent civil disobedience in the civil rights movement of the 1960s.

Civil disobedience has been practiced by pacifists and by individuals devoted to such causes as prohibition and women's suffrage. It also has been widely employed worldwide by oppressed groups that want to emulate the success of Gandhi and King. The tactic is often effective in changing laws and protecting liberties. It can take the form of refusal to serve in the armed forces (conscientious objection) or unlawful demonstrations such as those aimed at nuclear armament and the Vietnam War.

Civil disobedience has been shown to be a powerful political force when people have sought to liberate themselves from foreign domination within their own countries. In such cases, civil disobedience, when combined with mass withdrawal of cooperation in the form of strikes, boycotts, mass demonstrations, and the like, holds great promise of effectiveness.

PUBLIC DISCLOSURE

Public disclosure is publicizing the complete facts or events that are relevant to a conflict but that are being kept hidden or falsified due to deliberate strategies of disinformation. Violence loves the lie. Its operations are best done in secret and, where unavoidably visible, cloaked in justification and even glorification. Exposing the lie is as old as the first codes of moral conduct: "Thou shalt not bear false witness against thy neighbor" (Exod. 20:16). Yet the practice of public disclosure as a regular strategy of peacemaking is far more recent.

In a sense, public disclosure as a practice norm is a child of the information age. The forces of disinformation make excellent use of the modern ability to disseminate information quickly to large numbers of people, and their responsibility for distortions must be made public in order to check this misuse. Historian Margaret Miles has argued that the first use of the printed page was to stir up hostility and violence against witches.[10] The rise of anti-Semitism in Europe prior to World War II was led by a hysterical press. Lies about Jewish bankers ruining economies, controlling the media, and corrupting so-called pure societies flooded first the population of Germany and then, as the Germans swept across Europe, other populations.

Public disclosure as a deliberate practice norm for peace may be traced most directly to the thought and practice of Mohandas K. Gandhi. "I claim to be a passionate seeker after truth, which is but another name for God," wrote Gandhi in *Nonviolence in Peace and War.*[11] *Satyagraha*, the name Gandhi gave to nonviolent action, can also be translated as "passionate seeking of truth." Change in India resulted not only from the work of the *satyagrahas* in nonviolently resisting the British troops but also from the public disclosure of their resistance. And when Martin Luther King Jr. led marches in Birmingham and Selma and was met with firehose-wielding police, the lie that race relations were just fine was met with the force of public disclosure. It was surely the pictures of the body bags coming off the airplanes that accelerated resistance to the Vietnam War; and that was certainly the reason why, in the Gulf War, the phrase "body bag" was replaced by "human remains containers" and no photographs were allowed.

As with other nonviolent practice norms, the spiral of violence needs to be revealed.[12] Public disclosure of overt or covert violence usually leads the perpetrators of violence to produce yet more disinformation and increased violence. This becomes so obvious that they lose credibility, to the point where the violent will no longer be able to maintain the fiction that their course is honorable and justified.

Positively, public disclosure as a practice norm is rooted in the fact that an unacknowledged conflict cannot be mediated. Open communication regarding the existence of conflict and its contents is the first step in mediation.

Public disclosure has been effective where there are disinformation and denial that a conflict exists. Recent examples of the effectiveness of public disclosure include Karen Silkwood's disclosure of the dangers of nuclear power, the use of the Internet by Chinese students to get word to the international community about the massacre in Tiananmen Square, the witness of the COMADRES (Committee of the Mothers and Relatives of the Disappeared, Political Prisoners, and Assassinated of El Salvador), the demonstrations of the Mothers of the Plaza de Mayo in Argentina about their "disappeared," the coverage by CNN and Peter Arnet of the bombing of Baghdad during the Gulf War when the true extent of the violence was being hidden, and the witness of the Women of Greenham Common to the dangers of the impending installation of ground-launched cruise missiles.

ACCOMPANIMENT

Accompaniment is the practice of independent monitors accompanying those most exposed to potential violence. For example, during the civil rights movement, prominent citizens, members of the clergy, and many others participated in demonstrations and sit-ins in order to add their public witness and increase public attention to the injustices.

There are two major models of accompaniment. In the first model, human-rights monitors make third-party witnesses present and visible so that the potential calculus of violence must take into account public knowledge of the actions. The monitors remove the veil of secrecy. Even if the world is not particularly interested in the conflict at the moment, the monitors ensure that eventually the truth will be told. The genocide in Burundi and Rwanda sought not resolution of a competing claim but elimination of the competitor. The presence of monitors made this unjustifiable violence potentially more costly to its perpetrators. Monitors do not intervene and often are resented when they stand by taking notes in relative safety.

In the second model, a more interventionist accompaniment is pursued. During the Contra war in Nicaragua, thousands of unarmed volunteers placed themselves in harm's way, acting not just as witnesses but as a shield, calling themselves Witness for Peace. This interventionist form of accompaniment is especially effective in decreasing the likelihood of violence if potential perpetrators view those doing the accompanying as unacceptable casualties. In Nicaragua, the likely perpetrators were supported by the U.S. government, which made the deaths of U.S. citizen witnesses highly disadvantageous to their cause. In contrast, say, Belgian citizens would have had no such deterrent effect on those perpetrating violence in, for example, Rwanda.

The practice of accompaniment is a step of nonviolent defense that lessens the need for those facing attack to engage in defensive violence. It may be sought by a party for its defense or initiated by third-party peacemakers. Christian Peacemaker Team members have made a courageous and helpful witness in the West Bank of Palestine and elsewhere. It exposes peacemakers to serious risks and possible consequences by placing them in harm's way. It also challenges those who offer moral criticism of defensive violence by threatened groups to answer the question: "Do you so oppose violence that you are willing to accompany me and stand vulnerable with me before those I fear?" Hence it forces peacemakers to take a less abstract view of the relative risks faced by the parties involved.

The accompaniment option can be taken by neutral armed forces. But more often it is practiced by unarmed, and often unofficial, peacemakers. It need not be agreed to by both defender and attacker; it can be chosen by defenders to decrease violence.

SAFE SPACES

Safe space is used either to prevent conflict or during a conflict, when the physical and psychological safety of some is secured. Safe space finds its historical roots in the concept of *sanctuary*, which means "sacred space," set apart from the ordinary, profane world. Originally defined as natural locations, such as mountains or forest groves, sanctuary was extended to mean structures devoted to worship such as tabernacles, tents, lodges, or churches. Because such places were deemed sacred, and therefore the shedding of blood would profane them, they came to be regarded as asylums for those being threatened with violence, often criminals but also refugees.

In Christian law after the fourth century, the space of sanctuary free from violence was extended beyond the walls of the church structure to the surrounding area. Henry VIII abolished many church sanctuaries but established certain "cities of refuge." The practice of sanctuary survived in continental Europe until the French Revolution.

Sanctuary or safe space has been revived in several ways. During American slavery, abolitionists established the underground railroad, a network of safe houses linking transportation routes from the slave states of the South to the North. These safe houses, unlike earlier sanctuaries, were not respected by civil authorities.

In the twentieth century, when refugees from the wars in El Salvador and Guatemala began to cross into the United States, the Immigration and Naturalization Service (INS) began to deport them to almost certain death at home. This was being done despite the U.S. Refugee Act of 1980 and the United Nations Protocol Accords of 1967, which say that no persons can be deported who have a grave fear of persecution if returned to their homeland. A movement within the religious community to provide shelter for these refugees began along the U.S.-Mexico border and spread throughout the country. The U.S. government harassed churches, sanctuary workers, and peace advocates. Eventually eleven sanctuary workers, including two Catholic priests, a Presbyterian minister, and a Catholic nun, were arrested and tried in Tucson, Arizona. The judge refused to allow any evidence about conditions the refugees were fleeing to be entered into the trial. The sanctuary movement continued as long as the refugees were coming. It had a significant impact on U.S. public opinion, which eventually demanded and secured an end to U.S. government funding of the war by the Contras against the legally elected government in Nicaragua.

Another major locus of safe spaces is the battered women's movement, which began out of the women's consciousness-raising that took place in the 1970s. Prior to this movement, only a few safe spaces for women who were victims of domestic violence existed, such as Haven House opened by Al-Anon in California in 1964. In the 1970s, the extent of violence against women in the home was revealed. The tired question "Why doesn't she just leave?" was answered: Many of these women would leave in a minute if they had a place to go and the help they needed to get on their feet and live in peace. The earliest safe spaces for battered women were shelters opened in England and the United States during the late 1970s to respond to the degree of domestic violence. This movement is now worldwide. In Costa Rica, the degree of domestic violence is so high that now not only are there state-supported shelters but also women-run police stations. These stations were established because when battered women went to traditional police stations to report domestic violence, often they were sexually harassed by the police.

Safe space as a practice norm has been applied both at the domestic level in battered women's shelters and at the military level as a no-fly zone or safe zone. Between these two poles, several other applications are possible. In protecting civilian life in conflict, hospital areas have been recognized through the Geneva Convention and other treaties as safe spaces.

Domestically, much work needs to be done in our cities and towns to make schools safe spaces, free from weapons and from drug and gang violence. It might even be possible to extend the concept of "safe school zones" to parks and recreational areas used by children. Internationally, demilitarized zones have been used to separate warring parties and to reduce the chance of incidents that could escalate the conflict. In the war in Bosnia, safe spaces were used in an attempt to reduce the civilian casualties in a war where civilians had been the target of military attack and genocide.

A MENU OF INTERVENTIONS AND DEFENSIVE STRATEGIES

Nonviolent direct action represents an evolving menu of interventions and creative defensive strategies that forces those who easily drift toward violence to justify themselves. The technologies of violence are becoming more lethal and, in terms of just war theory, more unjust, due to the inevitable disproportionate scale of violence and the greatly increased tendency of such powerful and plentiful weapons to wound, maim, and kill innocents.

The technologies and techniques of nonviolent direct action are also evolving in ways that are more powerful and effective. Increasing access to communication tools makes it easier for organizers to coordinate participants, track the companies and governments opposing justice, and reach broad constituencies with the content and meaning of the action. The tools have evolved to the point where nonviolent direct action can be considered a norm that must be pursued before violence can be considered as a just last resort. Governments must make room for, must respect, such movements. And groups of citizens—including church groups, members of synagogues, mosques, and friends' meetings, and other groups united by religious faith, are challenged to engage in nonviolent direct action and thus to lance the boil of injustice before it festers and becomes increasingly violent.

Two

TAKE INDEPENDENT INITIATIVES TO REDUCE THREAT

Glen Stassen

The strategy of independent initiatives is a recent innovation in international relations. It was implemented successfully to achieve the Austrian State Treaty in 1955, by which the Soviet Union set Austria free and NATO agreed to Austrian neutrality and nonoffensive military force; by presidents Eisenhower and Kennedy to halt atmospheric testing unilaterally and eventually to achieve the Partial Test Ban Treaty of 1963; in the series of initiatives taken first by Soviet president Gorbachev and the U.S. Congress and then by U.S. president Bush to achieve dramatic reductions in nuclear weapons; and in small initiatives taken by Israel and its Arab neighbors and by adversaries in Northern Ireland to create the climate for peacemaking breakthroughs in the Oslo Accords. The strategy was named and affirmed in Catholic, Methodist, Presbyterian, and UCC statements in the 1980s but is not widely enough known. It needs to be understood more widely so that it will be noticed when it causes breakthroughs for peace and so that citizens can press governments to take independent initiatives.

In 1962, the social psychologist Charles Osgood proposed the peacemaking method he called "independent initiatives."[1] (I was at the time discovering the "transforming initiatives" structure of the Sermon on the Mount in Matthew 5:12–7:12, and somewhat like the brilliant flash of light that the Apostle Paul saw on the road to

Damascus, I immediately saw the uncanny connection between the teaching of Jesus and the strategy of independent initiatives. I kept digging further into the Sermon on the Mount while also studying peacemaking, and just peacemaking theory began to be born.) Over the next two decades, the strategy of just peacemaking was widely adopted by church statements and peace movements in Europe and the United States. Eventually, they persuaded governments to adopt it, with striking success. Osgood argued that in a relationship of distrust and heightened threat perception, nations are blocked from initiating peacemaking steps themselves, and misperceive peace initiatives from the other side as insincere manipulation.

The old strategy of building up military threats in times of tension increases threat perception and decreases flexibility. The opposite strategy of unilateral disarmament is politically unlikely. A new strategy is needed—independent initiatives. The strategy is to take initiatives to decrease the other side's distrust or threat perception, in order to induce them to take similar initiatives or to negotiate seriously to remove threats.

CHARACTERISTICS OF EFFECTIVE INDEPENDENT INITIATIVES

Effective independent initiatives are designed to decrease threat perception and distrust by the other side, such as Gorbachev's removal of tanks and river-crossing equipment from Central Europe, so that NATO would be less fearful of a sudden tank attack. Once NATO no longer feared a tank attack, it became more willing to negotiate reductions in medium-range nuclear missiles (see chapter 9, "Reduce Offensive Weapons and Weapons Trade").

1. They are visible and verifiable actions, so that the other side can see that they are, in fact, being taken. Mere words or invisible actions are insufficient to break through the context of distrust; they will be interpreted with disbelief.

2. They are independent of the slow process of negotiation. One side does not first negotiate what the other side will do if and when it takes this initiative, because that process takes too long; the point is to take surprising, transforming initiatives that create a climate where negotiation can succeed and make a difference, including ratifying and regularizing the initiatives that already have been taken.

3. They are designed to decrease the threat to the other side, but they should not leave the initiator weak. A feeling of weakness often increases distrust and threat perception.

4. Initiatives should be undertaken in a series; one initiative is not likely to decrease threat perception significantly enough.

5. If the other side reciprocates with some independent initiatives of their own, then the series of initiatives can continue in a major way. If the other side holds off from reciprocating, then relatively small initiatives should continue the series in order to keep inviting reciprocation.

6. The timing of each initiative should be announced in advance and carried out regardless of the other side's bluster: *Initiatives need to be on time.* To postpone confirms distrust.

7. There should be clear explanation of the purpose: to shift the context toward deescalation and to invite reciprocation.

HISTORICAL EXAMPLES

One of President Eisenhower's initiatives constitutes a historical example. In response to the worldwide movement against testing nuclear bombs by exploding them in the open air, he announced in 1958 that the United States would halt above-ground testing for one year. If the Soviet Union reciprocated, he continued, then the United States would halt for an additional year and perhaps more. The Soviet Union also halted such tests, and the halt lasted almost three years. Both sides already had a nuclear deterrent, and halting tests did not weaken them. After testing had resumed, a similar halt was again initiated by President Kennedy. This led to the 1963 Atmospheric Test Ban Treaty and the beginning of the thaw of the Cold War.

More recently, independent initiatives were a major factor in the peaceful end of the Cold War and the dramatic reductions of nuclear weapons. *Schritte zur Abrüstung*, the group of German political scientists and ethicists who advocated the strategy of independent initiatives, expressed surprise that the Soviet Union under Andropov and Gorbachev adopted the strategy more quickly than the Western governments did. They listed a dozen Soviet independent initiatives, including halting underground nuclear testing and inviting U.S. reciprocation; withdrawing from Afghanistan; destroying all SS-4 and SS-5 medium-range missiles; withdrawing half their tanks, all river-crossing equipment, and a large number of troops from central Europe; and accepting NATO's "zero-option" proposal, which eventually became the turning point in ending the Cold War. These initiatives did succeed, bit by bit, in changing Western perceptions of the Soviet Union, just as Congressional initiatives had given the Soviet Union hope of likely U.S. responsiveness to initiatives the Soviet Union might take.

In the 1980s, the peace movement (Freeze Campaign) persuaded the U.S. Congress to adopt the strategy bit by bit. The House voted to halt money for:

1. Any MX missiles beyond the fifty in the pipeline.

2. Any missile deployments exceeding SALT II Treaty limits.

3. One-third of the "Star Wars" program (officially named Strategic Defense Initiative or SDI).

4. Star Wars tests violating the Anti-Ballistic Missile Treaty.

5. Half of the chemical weapons program.

6. Contra aid for the war in Nicaragua.

7. Any increase in the military budget.

8. Flight testing of antisatellite missiles.

9. Underground nuclear testing.

The U.S. Senate agreed to all but halting underground testing (it finally approved a total halt in 1992).

Congress's initiatives interacted reciprocally with the Soviet Union's, encouraging yet further initiatives. The result was rapid removal of large quantities of threatening nuclear weapons. Citizen pressure stimulated by peace movements was crucial throughout the process for achieving the congressional initiatives.[2] It is crucial now for citizens' groups to learn the practice of independent initiatives, employ it in their own conflicts, and urge it on governments.

On September 27, 1991, President Bush senior took up the theme, stating that negotiations take too long (the START talks took ten years) and that the United States needed a sweeping initiative. He announced he would go along with Congress's canceling the mobile MX missile and the short-range attack missile and with the European governments' requests that the short-range missiles be removed. He would also remove shorter-range nuclear missiles from ships and attack submarines and relax the alert readiness of bombers. Gorbachev matched these and stopped nuclear testing. The outcome has been rapid reductions (see chapter 9). The strategy of independent initiatives has made an enormous contribution to our safety. We should push for its employment in other cases of hostility and threat.

During the buildup toward the Gulf War, Harold Saunders, the highly respected advisor on Middle East policy for several administrations, advocated that we try "a scenario of political steps that could lead to changes in the situation," spelling out independent initiatives designed to persuade Iraq to back out of Kuwait without war.[3] His initiatives were not tried.

The strategy of transforming initiatives has been studied extensively in experimental psychological research by Svenn Lindskold.[4] And Deborah Welch Larson has studied its effectiveness in achieving the Austrian State Treaty, peacefully freeing Austria from an East-West partitioning of the sort that Germany had to endure for forty-five years. Larson concludes that the parties did act as the independent-initiatives strategy predicts rather than as tit-for-tat strategy predicts —that the strategy did work to elicit reciprocating initiatives, to relax tensions, to defuse a potentially explosive area, to establish a buffer zone, and to produce "the most successful neutralization agreement negotiated during the postwar period. It prevented a dangerous confrontation between Western and Soviet troops over control of this strategic territory in the heart of Europe."[5]

A likely objection is that in order to deter an adversary from aggressive action, it is important sometimes to communicate firm determination to resist; thus, independent initiatives could weaken the perception of determination. Robert Jervis's book *Perception and Misperception in International Politics* is the preeminent study on the subject.[6] He describes this problem along with the opposite danger that the deterree will perceive signs of firm determination to resist as threats to attack and as intention to reject or take advantage of any moves toward deescalation and away from aggression. It is important to communicate firmness in resisting aggression as well as receptiveness to deescalation. Deterrence is persuasion, and it depends on perception—including the perception that if the adversary does back off, a better and more secure outcome is possible. For this, both firmness against aggression and independent initiatives pointing the way to deescalation are needed.

For example, during the Cuban Missile Crisis, President Kennedy not only communicated firmness, he also took initiatives to avoid confronting the first Soviet (non-missile-bearing) ship and to avoid retaliating when a U.S. spy plane was shot down. He agreed further to remove U.S. Thor and Jupiter missiles from Greece and Turkey.

We conclude that one essential step of just peacemaking is to take independent initiatives that point the way to deescalation, especially when distrust and threat perception are high. Governments that have not taken independent initiatives have not tried one essential resort to make peace. We call on persons of good will to explain the strategy of independent initiatives to others, to notice and point them out when they occur, and to urge governments as well as smaller groups and individuals to take independent initiatives where distrust and threat need a breakthrough.

CHURCH ADVOCACY OF INDEPENDENT INITIATIVES

The strategy of independent initiatives is advocated especially clearly by the statements of the United Church of Christ, the Methodist bishops, and the Catholic bishops.[7] In East and West Germany, it was a central feature of the strategy advocated by church and peace groups and was combined with the concept of security partnership: Our security depends on our adversary's perception of its own security.[8]

The U.S. Catholic bishops called for independent initiatives as obligatory, required, of governments:

> We believe the urgent need for control of the arms race requires a willingness for each side to take some first steps. . . . By independent initiatives we mean carefully chosen limited steps which the United States could take for a defined period of time, seeking to elicit a comparable step from the Soviet Union.
>
> In 1963 President Kennedy announced that the United States would unilaterally forgo further nuclear testing; the next month Soviet Premier Nikita Khrushchev proposed a limited test ban which eventually became the basis of the U.S.-Soviet partial test ban treaty. Subsequently, both superpowers removed about 10,000 troops from Central Europe and each announced a cut in production of nuclear material for weapons.[9]

Transforming initiatives are also urged by the United Church of Christ in *A Just Peace Church:*

Unexpected initiatives of friendship and reconciliation can transform interpersonal and international relationships and are essential to restoring community. . . . Each local church [should] become a community . . . willing to take surprising initiatives to transform situations of enmity. . . . We reject any use or threat to use weapons and forces of mass destruction and any doctrine of deterrence based primarily on using such weapons. We also reject unilateral full-scale disarmament. . . . We affirm the development of new policies of common security, using a combination of negotiated agreements, new international institutions and institutional power, nonviolent strategies, unilateral initiatives to lessen tensions, and new policies which will make the global economy more just. . . . We call upon the United States and the Soviet Union and other nations to take unilateral initiatives toward implementing [a mutual nuclear weapons] freeze, contingent upon the other side responding, until such a time as a comprehensive freeze can be negotiated. . . . All nations should . . . make unilateral initiatives toward dismantling their military arsenals, calling upon other nations to reciprocate.[10]

INDEPENDENT INITIATIVES DIFFER FROM GRUDGING CONCESSIONS

Robert Pape's study "The Strategic Logic of Suicide Terrorism" argues that suicide terrorist leaders are not merely fanatic: they have a rational strategy to achieve specific goals, and they often succeed. The sixteen suicide terrorist campaigns from 1980 to 2001, including Sri Lanka and the Tamil Tigers, Turkey and the Kurds, Russia and Chechnya, and the United States and the Saudi peninsula, as well as numerous campaigns between Israel and the Palestinians, all have had the objective of withdrawal of an occupying force from a national homeland and achievement of self-rule.[11] We have seen that in Iraq, as al-Qaeda in Iraq has sought to drive out what they see as the U.S. occupying force. Accordingly, Pape reports the facts of several time sequences in relations between Palestine and Israel, showing that times of terrorism were followed by limited Israeli withdrawals.

Looking at events from the perspective of the just peacemaking practice of independent initiatives, we notice another dimension of the same facts. In previous decades, Israel had made it illegal to negotiate with leaders of the Palestine Liberation Organization (PLO).

But in the early 1990s, Israel and its neighboring Arab countries engaged in small independent initiatives with each other, opening telephone communications between their people and opening some new trade relations. A bit of trust began to build—enough to allow secret negotiations to begin in Oslo between leaders of Palestine and Israel. Thus independent initiatives were followed by serious negotiations to give major areas of occupied homeland back to the Palestinians. The outcome in September 1993 was the Oslo Accords, in which Palestine promised to give recognition to Israel's right to exist in peace, and Israel promised to return first an A section, and then a B section, and then a C section, of the West Bank and Gaza to Palestinian self-rule by specified deadlines. Pape reports:

> In April 1994, Hamas [began] a series of suicide bombings in [retaliation] for the Hebron Massacre [in which an Israeli settler killed 29 Palestinians]. After two attacks, Israel decided to accelerate its withdrawal from Gaza, which was required under the Oslo Agreement but which had been delayed. Hamas then suspended attacks for five months. From October 1994 to August 1995, Hamas (and Islamic Jihad) carried out a total of seven suicide attacks against Israel. In September 1995, Israel agreed to withdraw from certain West Bank towns that December, which it earlier had claimed could not be done before April 1996 at the soonest. Hamas then suspended attacks until its retaliation campaign during the last week of February and first week of March 1996. . . .
>
> When Israel agreed to withdraw more promptly than expected, Hamas decided to forgo the remaining three planned attacks.[12]

Initiatives Need to Be on Time

Pape sees the efficacy of suicide attacks in persuading Israel to withdraw. Just peacemaking sees another dimension: the efficacy of Israel's withdrawal in persuading Hamas to end the attacks. But Israel failed to meet the agreed deadline for the withdrawals, thus violating a crucial rule in the strategy of independent initiatives designed to disconfirm distrust: Initiatives need to be on time, or they confirm distrust.

Pape reports:

> [In 1995] Hamas leaders deliberately withheld attacking during the spring and early summer in order to give PLO negotiations

64

with Israel an opportunity to finalize a withdrawal. However, when in early July, Hamas leaders came to believe that Israel was backsliding and delaying withdrawal, Hamas launched a series of suicide attacks. Israel accelerated the pace of its withdrawal, after which Hamas ended the campaign"[13]

Moreover, Pape continues:

Israel agreed on March 29, 1995, to begin withdrawals by July 1. Later, however, the Israelis announced that withdrawals could not begin before April 1996 because bypass roads needed for the security of Israeli settlements were not ready. Hamas and Islamic Jihad then mounted new suicide attacks on July 24 and August 21, 1995, killing 11 Israeli civilians. In September, Israel agreed to withdraw from the West Bank towns in December (Oslo II) even though the roads were not finished. The suicide attacks then stopped and the withdrawal was actually carried out in a few weeks starting on December 12, 1995.[14]

In four different presentations that he heads "The Facts," Pape recounts the following sequence of events each time: (1) Israel delayed beyond their announced deadline for withdrawing from one of the areas as per the Oslo Accords; (2) Hamas and Islamic Jihad engaged in a campaign of suicide terrorism rationally strategized to get Israel to carry out the promised withdrawal; (3) Israel finally carried out the promised withdrawal; and (4) the leaders of the suicide terrorists halted the attacks for months, until Israel was late again in a promised withdrawal.[15]

The strategy of independent initiatives sees the three-fold lesson clearly:

1. Never miss the announced deadline for taking the promised initiative.

2. The initiative strategy does work efficaciously to halt the attacks.

3. When the initiatives miss the deadlines, and the other side then takes coercive action, and the initiatives finally are taken late, the other side may believe the initiatives came grudgingly because of their coercive action and not because of any trustworthy intention to take the initiatives. They see their coercion as rewarded by the grudging late initiatives. So they take coercive action again the next time there is a delay.

Pape shows at length that the efficacy of suicide terrorism in achieving withdrawals is precisely the conclusion Hamas and many Palestinians reached. Although the Oslo Accords formally committed Israel to withdraw the IDF from Gaza and the West Bank, Israel routinely missed key deadlines, often by many months, and the terrorists came to believe that Israel would not have withdrawn when it did, and perhaps not at all, had it not been for the coercive leverage of suicide attack.[16]

Since Terrorism Is Purpose-Driven, Preventive Initiatives Make a Difference

The point of Pape's study is to demonstrate the rational-strategy character of the leaders of suicide terrorists: their objective is to get occupying troops withdrawn from their national homeland. We might expect this would lead Pape to conclude that the way to get the terrorism to stop would be to withdraw from their homeland as promised, and to do it on time: implement the Oslo Accords, continue the Wye negotiations at Taba rather than canceling them, accept the offer of peace from the twelve surrounding Arab nations with a two-state solution, implement the Roadmap for Peace, implement the Geneva Accords.

Pape does briefly suggest that what he calls the strategy of concessions can be effective in reducing popular support and recruitment for terrorism, and "improving the standing of more moderate nationalist elites."[17] But "concessions" differ from the strategy of on-time initiatives in key ways. First, Pape's "concessions" are responses to coercion by terrorists, giving in or conceding to their demands. Initiatives are creative actions to decrease distrust, and are designed to meet needs of the people, not necessarily of the terrorists. Second, Pape's "concessions" follow after the deadlines for initiatives were not met but were dragged out, and after terrorism was then used to get the concessions to occur. The strategy of on-time initiatives prescribes that the series of steps be carried out absolutely by the deadlines, never dragged out to appear as delaying tactics. Third, "concessions" are responses to terrorism; initiatives are not responses to terrorism but to one's own announced schedule. Fourth, "concessions" often carry a prior condition: for example, "We will give this land back only if you disarm your terrorists." That disempowers the conceding side from setting the timetable, and gives the power to the terrorists for the timing. Initiatives carry no prior condition, but invite some positive reciprocating action, to be rewarded by further initiatives. Thus the incentive is for reciprocating action, not for renegade terrorists to jam the process by doing a violent act. Fifth, "concessions" are often done grudgingly, with fear that one is rewarding terrorism, and so they are often accompanied by further assassinations or punishments to the terrorists, which removes the function of creating trust and inviting reciprocation. Initiatives are done graciously, if possible, with an explicitly stated hope for reciprocation and thus for additional future initiatives.

Pape states that six of eleven Palestinian terrorist campaigns did appear to lead to modest concessions, although in only three of the cases were the concessions clearly the result of the terrorism. I contend that only two of the Palestinian terrorist campaigns led to a real gain. Two of the six alleged successes were Israeli withdrawal from parts of occupied territory, which, as Pape concedes, Israel subsequently reoccupied in retaliation against further terrorism. One of these was the release of Sheikh Ahmed Yassin from prison, which was actually done not in response to terrorism but "in order to obtain the release of Israeli agents [who] were captured, and also was the product of American and Jordanian pressure." In the meantime Israel has increased settlements in the occupied territories several-fold and has assassinated Sheikh Yassin. Thus only two of the eleven campaigns achieved any results.

More clearly, the result of the terrorist campaigns has been to undermine Israeli voter support for parties that were willing to offer negotiated solutions, and to strengthen support for hawkish parties whose policies have been disastrous for Palestinians. Terrorism has *worked* to drive Israel to the right, to excuse massive assassination, invasion, and occupation actions by Israel, and the building of the Wall, which gobbles up additional Palestinian territory and cuts Palestinians off from necessary travel and former jobs. The first intifada, which was primarily nonviolent direct action, got much better results: the Oslo Accords and subsequent negotiations toward a two-state solution. Just peacemaking strategies work better than grudging concessions or terrorism.

TESTING THE THEORIES: WITHDRAWAL FROM THE SINAI DESERT

One way of testing the two theories is to ask if Israel ever withdrew from an occupied territory on time, and whether this led to more or less suicide terrorism. Israel had occupied the Sinai desert during the 1967 war. Egypt insisted that it be returned to Egypt. Israel insisted they needed it as a buffer zone to protect against Egypt's once again moving its tanks and weapons up to Israel's border. President Carter and the United Nations employed the just peacemaking practice of cooperative conflict resolution. They proposed the solution that Egypt would get the desert back and would promise not to move its tanks and weapons across the desert to Israel's borders. The UN would monitor the desert electronically and in person so that the world would know whether Egypt kept its promise. This brilliant conflict-resolution solution was agreed upon. Israel did withdraw from the desert by the deadline. The UN did monitor and still does. Egypt kept its agreement and to this day does not engage in terrorism against Israel, and does help work out some solutions with Palestine. The result is not a warm peace, but it is surely better than a hot war.

OSLO AGREEMENT, 1993

When the two sides signed the Oslo agreement in 1993 recognizing Israel and its need for security, and setting dates for stages of return of Palestinian land to Palestinian rule, there was some reason to expect that Israel might return the land as promised. Palestinian support for the agreement was initially 67percent in the key poll, and this rose to 80 percent as the first parts of land were returned. Support for violence against Israel plummeted to 20 percent, and actual violence was very low. Prime Minister Netanyahu took office in 1996 and postponed the return of land indefinitely. Expectations of a permanent peace settlement in polls of Palestinians dropped from 44 percent to 30 percent in Netanyahu's first year, to 24 percent under Prime Minister Ehud Barak (with settlements expanding twice as rapidly than previously), and to 11 percent under Ariel Sharon, with his canceling of the negotiations at Taba that were following up the Barak offer of a two-state solution. Support for violence against Israel increased inversely, both in the polls and in actuality.[18] "Polls by the Jerusalem Media and Communication Centre indicate that increased coercive measures by Israeli forces during the Second Intifada (fall 2000–present) are positively correlated with Palestinian popular support for attacks. Support for suicide attacks, in turn, directly correlates with increased support for the radical Islamic groups, decreased support for the Palestinian Authority, and decreased Palestinian readiness to support the peace process toward a negotiated solution."[19]

Embittered leaders of Hamas say they will not stop until they have driven Israel completely out. But the poll data above depict huge majorities of Palestinians supporting peace when they see Israel giving back most of their land. And the PLO and the twelve surrounding Arab countries say they will accept Israel within its borders.

Ehud Barak announced that Israel would remove itself from the morally unsupportable occupation of Southern Lebanon, and Israel met that deadline. Peace with Lebanon followed until the disastrous Israeli re-invasion in 2007, in response to Hezbollah's capturing two Israeli soldiers, after Israel had re-invaded Gaza.

U.S. DISENGAGEMENT FROM JUST PEACEMAKING PRACTICES

The Bush administration announced from its first days that it was disengaging from efforts to do conflict resolution in the Middle East. This left a weak Palestine with a powerful Sharon-led Israeli government. Sharon canceled the negotiations in Taba that were seeking to work out agreement on the offer of previous prime minister Ehud Barak to return Gaza and most of the West Bank to Palestine. Further, Sharon invaded the Muslim Holy Place, the Temple Mount, with hundreds of troops, and in response to Palestinian suicide attacks began a policy of assassinations of Palestinian opponents. The most shocking assassination was carried out in August 2001. Israel sent two rockets through the office window of Abu Ali Mustafa, assassinating the much loved leader of the Popular Front for the Liberation of Palestine. President Bush gave the assassination his blessing in a public statement, and Arab calls for revenge filled the e-mails and streets from then until the September 11, 2001, attack three weeks later. The 9-11 Commission report says al-Qaeda made its final decision to proceed with the 9-11 attack on about September 1, 2001. Had the U.S. administration been engaged from January through September in pressing Israel to take the initiatives of continuing negotiations at Taba, halting the assassination attacks, and halting expansion of settler occupation of Palestine, we do not know if al-Qaeda would have proceeded with the 9-11 attack or would have held off. But with the dashing of hope for negotiations and return of land, and with the United States doing nothing to press Sharon to engage in peacemaking, Israel as well as the United States experienced a huge increase in terrorism.

By any measure 2002 was an astonishing year for Israel in terms of suicide bombings. An average of five attacks a month were made, nearly double the number during the first fifteen months of the second intifada—and that number was itself more than ten times the monthly average since 1993. Indeed, according to a database maintained by the National Security Studies Center at Haifa University, there were nearly as many suicide attacks in Israel [in 2002] (fifty-nine) as there had been in the previous eight years combined (sixty-two).[20]

During the time of strong Arab anger at U.S. support for Israeli occupation in Palestinian territory and the Israeli assassination policy, British Prime Minister Tony Blair persuaded U.S. President George W. Bush to announce that his administration and he personally were committed to support the Roadmap for Peace. The Roadmap for Peace was an independent initiative strategy: Palestine and Israel each took several initiatives: Palestine chose a prime minister with whom Israel could negotiate and halted suicide attacks in Israel for three months. Israel withdrew from occupation of Bethlehem and the northern part of Gaza and returned some Palestinian prisoners. Israel, however, violated the strategy of independent initiatives by repeatedly assassinating persons they named as leaders of Palestinian terrorist organizations. Israel continued its assassinations throughout the period of the Roadmap, and Palestine did not disarm the terrorist organizations or extend the suspension of terrorist attacks. The Bush administration did not press effectively for implementing the strategy of the Roadmap to Peace, and, in fact, disengaged from the Roadmap. The inconsistent implementation of the strategy of independent initiatives failed. *Just Peacemaking* urges subsequent administrations to reengage in practicing just peacemaking.

Three
USE COOPERATIVE CONFLICT RESOLUTION

Steven Brion-Meisels,
Meenakshi Chhabra
David Cortright
David Steele
Gary Gunderson
Edward LeRoy Long Jr.

Cooperative conflict resolution (CCR) emphasizes active coworking by parties in conflict; they attempt to develop creative solutions that each can affirm and support. They take on the process of conflict resolution as a shared enterprise, an active partnership in problem solving, in order to devise mutually beneficial outcomes.[1] The goal is to transform one's view of possible solutions to any given conflict from inevitable deadlock to multiple possibilities and to transform one's view of the other party from adversary to partner. Theologian Jürgen Moltmann states the aim well when he calls for a provisional peace in which fighting enemies can become "quarreling partners" and deadly conflict can become "non-lethal controversy."[2]

Under many different names, cooperative or transformative conflict resolution has been a core peacemaking practice for centuries, and it has increasing urgency for intra- and international conflicts in the future. CCR contrasts sharply with the unilateral, win-lose strategies used by the U.S. government in its tragic reactions to terrorism after the attacks of September 11, 2001—especially its approach to Iraq, Afghanistan, and then Iran.[3]

The cooperative conflict resolution process is transparent as well as transformative. It involves self-critical honesty, yet is nonjudgmental toward others. Therefore, it requires risk-taking and spiritual awareness. Its historical roots, in fact, draw deeply from many religious traditions that teach followers to respect and value all persons, even enemies, and that teach healing and forgiveness as crucial to the quest for fullness of life. It highlights the importance of often neglected aspects of conflict—the historical, spiritual, cultural, emotional, individual, and social elements of our experience. Writing about what she calls "the great transformation" among religious and ethical traditions that emerged in Europe and Asia in the period between 1600 and 200 BCE, Karen Armstrong says:

> Each tradition developed its own formulation of the Golden Rule: do not do to others what you would not have done to you. As far as the Axial sages were concerned, respect for the sacred rights of all beings—not orthodox belief—was religion. . . . The Axial peoples all found that the compassionate ethic worked.[4]

TEN PRINCIPLES OF COOPERATIVE CONFLICT RESOLUTION

1. Those involved in cooperative conflict resolution (CCR) must seek to understand the perspectives and needs of adversaries, even when they may personally disagree. They work to understand the problem from the others' point of view. They see cultural differences as resources rather than deficits. They recognize that creative approaches may challenge their own cultural practices and ways of seeing. They use personal and group histories, stories, and emotions to discover basic needs hidden behind surface positions and strategic interests.

   Mohammad Abu-Nimer criticizes Western practices of conflict resolution that overlook cultural diversity and faith, reducing all to "rational interests."[5] *Just Peacemaking* makes the same criticisms; its *cooperative* conflict resolution explicitly emphasizes active cooperation of the parties, with their local customs, their different religious and cultural understandings, not blocked out, but included as assets that we can use cooperatively to seek resolution.[6]

2. Participants in CCR listen carefully for content, feeling, and meaning, before judging or offering solutions. They make space for the voices of all involved, both victims and perpetrators. They withhold judgment even as they are clear about their own principles, positions, and stances.

3. Participants in CCR distinguish judgments about behavior and actions from judgments about persons or cultures. They follow Gandhi's advice to "hate the sin, not the sinner." They may need

to oppose or condemn particular actions, but their strategies for resolving conflict do not dehumanize or demonize the "other." Rather, all participants hold out the possibility of mutual solutions and mutual survival.

4. Participants in CCR acknowledge their own involvement in creating or escalating conflict and work to facilitate personal and social transformation. They are willing to examine basic attitudes and values self-critically. A religious way of saying this is that participants confess their sin, both personal and corporate. As Reinhold Niebuhr wrote, "Our own sin is always partly the cause of the sins against which we must contend."[7] A more secular formulation is that all participants must admit their own responsibility, both general and particular, in the history of the conflict. Therefore, facilitators must help adversaries examine their accountability and seek forgiveness as well as repentance—knowing that with acknowledgment and transformation come a basic honesty that encourages all parties to avoid arrogance, hubris, and domination (see chapter 4).

5. Cooperative conflict resolution is transparent and honest in all aspects of its practice. Goals are clearly stated yet open to negotiation. Strategies are democratic, with negotiators respecting the right of all parties to know and participate in the process. They recognize and help others to affirm that giving up some individual power increases the likelihood of a potentially transformative collective power.

6. Participants in CCR generate and support a partnership approach to problem solving. They seek to use power *with* rather than power *over*—cooperation rather than domination—in order to confront a mutual problem. They attempt to reconcile underlying interests or needs, rather than remaining focused on fixed positions, in order to remove parties from rigid stances. They encourage brainstorming multiple options before attempting to select the best solution. They advocate criteria for decision-making that are both fair and transformative, representing the full vision of shalom.

7. If force is necessary, it is used to separate, restrain, and create space so that an alternative to violence and injustice can be found through reflection, negotiation, healing, and a partnership approach to problem-solving.

8. Those who seek to resolve conflict cooperatively take risks in order to find common ground. They are willing to make themselves vulnerable, in order to create safe spaces for resolution and in order to encourage others to do the same.[8]

9. Participants in CCR seek long-term solutions that help prevent future conflict. They look for prevention strategies, even as they work to heal and resolve conflict through a just peacemaking intervention.

10. They perceive both peace and justice as equal core components. They understand that the pursuit of peace without justice leads to appeasement, while the pursuit of justice without peace leads to a crusade mentality.

HISTORICAL AND CONTEMPORARY CASES

The principles of cooperative conflict resolution were at the center of many movements for social change in the twentieth century, with important interpersonal, community, and international outcomes. Although best known for his successful campaign to liberate India from British domination, Gandhi also persevered in efforts to abolish the caste system and reconcile Hindus and Muslims in India. He always attempted to treat the opponent as a partner. Boycotts, marches, public disclosure, and civil disobedience were strategies designed to bring adversaries to the negotiating table where the parties could find a just and peaceful solution to the problem. Gandhi himself took part in negotiations with the British government during the famous roundtable discussions in London in 1931 and in the final stages of the Indian independence movement in the 1940s.[9]

Martin Luther King's six steps for nonviolent social change included reconciliation and negotiation. He even pressed his followers to look for ways in which the opponent could also win. King understood and communicated to his colleagues that civil disobedience is a means to accelerate and strengthen the negotiation process in order for justice to be accomplished peacefully. There are many examples of Cooperative Conflict Resolution in the campaigns of Gandhi, King, César Chávez, Dorothy Day, Barbara Deming, and Saul Alinksy, and in historic movements such as the Nuclear Weapons Freeze Campaign, the Polish Solidarity struggle, and the Burmese democracy movement.[10]

Interpersonal and Interethnic Cases

In the past three decades, cooperative conflict resolution strategies have been effective at several levels. In the 1970s, President Jimmy Carter helped create the first Neighborhood Justice Centers (soon to be called "community mediation programs"). These were democratic and often volunteer-driven alternatives to courts in dispute-settlement processes. The practitioners who worked in these programs sought resolution instead of judgment or punishment, shared a set of problem-solving skills, and saw themselves as facilitators for community members.

A decade later, a number of community mediation programs sought to extend their work into schools. They saw conflict as a normal part of school life and resolution skills as essential for young people's long-term success. Most importantly, they believed that, with teaching and guidance, most students could learn to resolve their own conflicts—acting as peers within a democratic and voluntary partnership process.[11] Successful peer mediation programs address many of the issues that a just peacemaking framework seeks to resolve—including situations that cross lines of race, gender, culture, class, age, and even inequitable power. These practices have been used successfully to squash violence resulting from rumor or other kinds of incomplete or manipulative communication; to deal with issues where one group seeks to exclude another; to address issues of racial or cultural intolerance; and to quell threats and intimidation over property, turf, or zones of control in urban gang warfare. Research shows that teaching students in the early grades to practice mediation and conflict resolution not only reduces violence in schools, but throughout the rest of their lives.[12] It is much more effective than waiting for high school, when students have already formed their patterns.

In recent years, these programs have been combined with restorative justice approaches to CCR that draw on Native American and other multicultural roots. Peer mediation (a European-rooted tradition) and restorative justice (a Native American and in some cases African tradition) have contributed to peacemaking in both interpersonal and intergroup conflicts; their potential for international applications needs more attention and support.

Peer Mediation

In peer mediation, each disputant works to understand the perspective of the other, with active listening rather than judgment or punishment. The focus is on concrete behavioral change rather than on counseling or changing deep-seated psychological patterns, or sweeping judgments of others. Peer mediators see themselves as members of the community with a role in the history, as well as the solution, of the problem. Therefore, rather than heaping all blame on one person, they help each disputant own or acknowledge her or his role in the problem. The processes of peer mediation are laid out before the actual mediation begins. They are transparent and open to being shaped by the disputants at any time. Rules are established, including rules about the threat of force, in order to create and maintain a safe space for reflection, listening, and resolution. Effective mediators do not seek power for themselves but share the power of the process with the disputants, thereby amplifying the power of peacemaking for all involved. The process seeks and encourages alternatives—devoting a good deal of time to brainstorming possible solutions even when one solution emerges early as a "favorite." All involved in the mediation agree to take a risk in order to seek common ground; the mediators

76 risk failure and in some cases physical threat. The disputants risk by agreeing to let go of comfortable patterns of conflict (for example, fight or flight) and by standing against peer pressure to escalate the conflict. The focus is on prevention—on the future rather than the past—and the emphasis is on building a community that supports peaceful conflict resolution. Finally, peer mediation, when it is successful, pays attention to institutional factors that often fuel any individual conflict—for example, unfair or undemocratic discipline policies, the absence of culturally sensitive avenues for dialogue, pedagogy that frustrates students who have different learning styles, and so forth. Thus, effective peer mediation addresses fairness as well as violence reduction, justice as well as peace.

Until very recently, the dominant approach to peer mediation in the United States was drawn primarily from an Anglo American legal framework. In the past decade, however, new models of peer mediation have been evolving that are more culturally literate, reexamining assumptions of universal applicability of Western terminology (such as "win-win"), patterns of nonverbal communication, and understandings of conflict and its resolution. New strategies are developing to transform conflict instead of merely manage it, so that the results are peace and justice rather than compliance, and empowerment rather than "keeping things under control."[13]

A typical peer mediation case can help clarify this paradigm shift. Conflict in a high school between a star athlete and a Portuguese Creole–speaking recent immigrant threatened to escalate into a fight, with classmates taking sides. Crucial to successful resolution were a trained mediator who spoke Portuguese Creole and a prior training program designed to enable the culturally dominant "American" peer mediators to function sensitively with cultural minorities. The use of peer mediators helped to reduce the power inequities so that *power over* the students was replaced by *working with* them. Finally, the goal of the mediation shifted from establishing a judgment of right or wrong to formulating a shared agreement. It then became possible to view the "irreducible conflicting interests" in new ways. Both students were able to save face with peers (rather than having to back down), and agreed to coexist (rather than having to become friends), thereby enabling both to stay out of trouble.

Restorative Justice between Groups

In the past two decades, restorative justice circles have been increasingly effective ways to integrate crosscultural values with alternative dispute resolution methods. Restorative justice is deeply rooted in Native American traditions that emphasize the power of community, the role of elders, and the metaphor of circles, as ways of understanding human relations.[14] Crimes (including violent ones) are seen as violating the community, not only the law. Therefore, the goal of the *justice* process is to *restore* relations between the perpetrator and victim, the criminal and the community, and in the community itself. Restorative justice circles are gaining increasing support and popularity in the legal process, and among community groups, to resolve interpersonal and intergroup conflicts.[15]

Restorative justice incorporates all ten principles of CCR, but it also increases the power of CCR because of its clear commitment to cultural competence and to the interdependence of individual members within the community; both of these components thereby strengthen the potential of CCR in larger-scale, international conflicts.

Restorative justice and CCR have been part of a broader set of strategies to heal and transform American society's historic patterns of racism. CCR can be effective in this context because it integrates personal and institutional change; it emphasizes power *with* instead of power *over*; it recognizes the importance of personal as well as historic pain, transgression, and healing; it opens doors for transformation rather than simply management of conflict; and it includes both peace and justice in its core principles.

Terms like "stereotype," "prejudice," and "racism" mean different things to different people—depending on their historic and cultural contexts. Furthermore, terms like "affirmative action," "quotas," and even "multicultural education" have been used by demagogues to obscure rather than inform, divide rather than heal, and incite rather than resolve. Community workers and scholars have begun to develop languages and strategies that can help translate shared ideas across barriers of race, culture, and class. One good example of this progress is the "Ten C's" framework, developed by Ulric Johnson and Patti DeRosa in their antiracism projects.[16]

Our experience suggests that interweaving the ten principles of CCR with a real commitment to multicultural competence helps to sustain lasting change in interpersonal and institutional levels.[17] For example, restorative justice addresses *cultural barriers* and helps groups who are unfamiliar with, or marginalized by, the dominant legal system to find a voice and a path toward reconciliation. Restorative justice also addresses cultural barriers when it is applied to gang mediation, some forms of gender-based violence, and even intercultural conflict. Restorative justice practices have been effective in conflicts where there is *deep damage or pain*—including examples where the victims of violent crime have been reconnected to their aggressors. The same practices have been used in cases where *power inequities* are present (for example, with gender-based violence) or when there appear to be *irreducible conflicting interests* (for example, in the work of the Family Circle group that bridges Israeli and Palestinian families whose children have been killed in the violence there). All of these situations suggest the possibility—and the power—of CCR strategies applied beyond the individual, to *large-scale* conflicts.[18]

CCR in the former Yugoslavia

The carnage, genocide, and cultural destruction in the former Yugoslavia were of such a scale as to challenge any model of conflict resolution. They took an immense toll on all levels of society—personal, family, community, national, and transnational. In the midst of the violence, individuals and groups used CCR to prevent and reduce the impact of violence, as well as to heal and restore community connections. As David Steele has reported, neighbors and civic leaders in Bosnia stepped across religious and ethnic lines to create safe havens, heal the wounds of war, and begin the process of reconciliation during the violence. For example, at the start of Muslim-Croat fighting in central Bosnia, two Franciscans and an imam succeeded in mediating an agreement that kept certain troops on each side out of the fighting. Braving initial threats from both armed forces, they met one another and convinced the two commanders to meet for negotiations. The subsequent agreement lasted throughout the Muslim-Croat fighting: these troops never fought each other.[19]

CCR seminars encouraged people at the grassroots level to work together to overcome the stranglehold of ethnic and religious division on the individual and the collective spirit; to develop constructive ways to handle grievances and differences; to equip people with the tools for promoting healing and social reconstruction; and then to build a critical mass of support for peace-building.

The first-level seminars were focused on building trust through intrapersonal, interpersonal, and intergroup reconciliation. Building toward reconciliation in the aftermath of war requires special attention to expressing and acknowledging others' grievances and encouraging a self-critical honesty. The trainers must themselves listen carefully before judging or offering solutions and they must distinguish judgments about behavior and actions from those about persons or cultures. Participants must be encouraged to listen carefully and empathetically to one another's pain. Starting with the common experience of suffering and designing an environment in which each group can begin to feel safe helps to develop cross-group bonds.

Near the site of the worst massacre in the war in Croatia, Serb refugees from other regions of Croatia, but now living in the Vukovar region, shared their stories of pain with Croats, some of whom were themselves refugees from Vukovar. Refugees listened and cried with fellow refugees. Although the primary strategy in this seminar was storytelling by participants, it was interspersed with interpretive material on the grief process, drawn from Old Testament laments and such contemporary theorists as Elizabeth Kübler-Ross. Contemporary laments patterned after those in the Psalms, as a ritualized catharsis within a community framework, ensured that victims were heard, and vindictive responses were limited.[20] At a seminar in Banja Koviljaca, Serbia (on the Bosnian border), in May 1997, Serbian Orthodox priests, together with Catholics, Muslims, and Protestants, used lament writing to build bonds of trust. In this way, people's deep pain, rather than being a barrier, became a bridge upon which they could engage together in self-critical honesty.

Weaving in theological reflection gave added legitimacy for religious people. For example, awareness that the later stage of the lament motif in the Old Testament prophets incorporates confessing sin into the grief process resulted in profound discussion at each of two Serbian seminars held close to the Bosnian border in 1996 and 1997. When Serbian Orthodox priests began discussing the complicity of their church in the Bosnian war, a very big step had been taken toward reconciliation and implementation of CCR principles 4 and 5, acknowledging one's own responsibility and being transparent and honest.

The second-level seminars focused on changing attitudes and clarifying perceptions. Conflict always involves some degree of misperception and, therefore, requires a concerted attempt to understand the perspectives and needs of adversaries (CCR principle 1). In cases of intense conflict, the experience of victimization usually has contributed to such a threatened sense of identity that bias and stereotyping begin to function as a group survival mechanism. These biases become entrenched, distorting and contaminating one group's perception of another. Even in such deep-rooted, identity-based conflicts, it is possible to acknowledge one's own unhealthy prejudices and resulting manipulative behavior. Participants were asked to step into the shoes of another ethnic, religious, or national group while examining the nature and dynamics of the conflict. By watching others, including members of one's own ethnic group, successfully role-playing another persona, the blocked persons started to listen more carefully and began to replace distorted attitudes with accurate perceptions.

In addition, the second-level seminars introduced participants to problem-solving skills that require acceptance of everyone's basic needs and concerns, as well as creating alternative approaches to resolving the conflict. It is absolutely crucial to legitimize people's most basic concerns (CCR principle 1), by which we mean the need for recognition, well-being, security, belonging, and control over one's life. Fear that such legitimate needs may be denied creates a desperation, an intransigence, and all too often violence. It is also important to distinguish these basic needs from the positions, demands, or strategies by which a group insists that its needs be met. Assisting people to look behind their positions to the underlying needs frequently leads to a recognition that the basic interests are compatible, thus providing an element of trust that can become the basis for mutual problem solving. One very poignant example of this occurred as a Muslim imam from Sarajevo, at a seminar held in 1995 during the war, shared his own soul-searching attempt to comprehend what was happening to his people. During an exercise designed to map the needs and fears that underlay all sides of the war in Bosnia, he shared how he was led, through meditation, to recognize that beneath some of the Serbians' brutal actions lay an understandable fear for survival, a legitimate need based on a history of Ottoman oppression. His moving description of the way God opened his eyes, despite the terrible struggle of his own people for survival, powerfully created trust and opened dialogue, especially with the Serbs who were present. By the end of the exercise, members of all three ethnic groups were able to identify numerous mutual needs within their supposedly incompatible entities. This demonstrated that, despite the difficulties still apparent in bringing lasting resolution to the Bosnian conflict, a presumption | 81 of completely irreducible conflicting interests was unfounded.

Once people have addressed relational problems and identified compatible needs, they are more able to create solutions for resolving conflict. The aim is to generate a partnership approach to problem solving (CCR principle 7) that seeks both peace and justice (CCR principle 10). Participants in such a process must be willing to take risks (CCR principle 8) in the search for long-term solutions that will help prevent future conflict (CCR principle 9).

These examples illustrate that CCR can be applied successfully to deep-rooted conflicts between large groups. Educators working with the United Nations and the Hague Appeal for Peace have institutionalized CCR as part of a "culture of peace" project in schools and communities throughout the former Yugoslavia. These constitute a crucial step toward developing civil society and realizing a critical mass of support for peace-building efforts. Interethnic work teams trained in conflict resolution skills have begun to develop both physical and social structures in that war-torn society.[21]

FROM INTERPERSONAL TO INTERNATIONAL

Especially powerful examples of the ways CCR can promote just peacemaking can be seen in the violent conflicts in Israel/Palestine and India/Pakistan, because they have had intrapersonal, interpersonal, interethnic, interreligious, and in many ways international consequences.

Israel/Palestine

The first example involves a tree and a house. *The Lemon Tree* tells the story of a forty-year relationship between individuals and groups in deep conflict, facing the major challenges often described by political realists: cultural barriers, a high degree of pain, problems of scale and power inequities. Bashir Khairi's Palestinian father built a home and planted a lemon tree in the village of Al-Ramla, Palestine, in 1936. In 1948, his family was forced to flee from the interethnic violence between Jewish settlers and indigenous Palestinians—a conflict fueled in no small part by British colonial rule, anti-Semitism in Europe, and an emerging international recognition of the role that petroleum would play in world politics. Into their home in the town now renamed Ramla in Israel moved a Jewish Bulgarian child, Dalia Eshkenazi, herself a refugee from Nazism. After the 1967 war, they met—in the garden, near the lemon tree.[22]

The story of their friendship, struggles, disagreements, and shared hopes suggests ways in which CCR can bring together peoples whose lives seem shaped by irreconcilable differences. Over the course of forty years, they worked persistently and patiently to understand each other's perspectives. They listened and judged slowly. They separated judgments about behavior and policy from judgments about culture. They acknowledged their own involvement and accountability, as individuals and as members of warring groups. They were transparent and honest, even when it was painful or frightening. They set limits and boundaries in their communication when the tension threatened to undo their friendship. They took deep risks, personally and culturally. And they understood that peace and justice are intertwined. They formed a partnership that led to the creation of Open House—a child care and educational institution that brings together Israeli children from Jewish, Christian, and Muslim faiths. Forty years later, they continue to seek long-term solutions.

The principles of CCR also appear in other programs that seek understanding and reconciliation in the Middle East—including Israelis who monitor human rights violations at border crossings (the Machsom Watch mothers) or who accompany Palestinians to medical care, and the growing number of peace camps for young people in the United States and elsewhere.

One well-known example of how the principles of CCR can help with international conflict is the work of the Family Circle Project—documented in the 2006 documentary film called *Encounter Point*. This project brings together families who have lost members (mostly children) to the violence in Israel and Palestine—whether they have been killed by suicide bombers or members of the Israeli Defense Forces. Family Circle members explicitly work to change the politics of the situation. They apply what they have learned in their work with Jewish Israeli groups who see all Palestinians as terrorists, as well as in their work with young Palestinians whose anger draws them toward violent resistance. The Family Circle participants represent a range of stories and backgrounds, from former IDF officers, to former settlers, to Palestinians working in the tradition of Gandhian resistance. Across these differences, their shared commitment to the principles we identify as CCR have allowed them to work for peace with justice in the face of all the realistic challenges: cultural barriers, a high degree of pain and loss, power inequity, and irreducible conflict interests.

India/Pakistan

Since the partition that created Pakistan and India, the region has been the site of interpersonal, interethnic, and international violence that has included significant damage to civilian populations especially in the border areas—what has come to be called the "Line of Control." In the midst of this violence, individuals and groups have consistently applied the principles of CCR in order to rebuild bridges among the peoples of the region. Supported by international groups like Seeds of Peace, young people from India and Pakistan meet in the United States to learn about each other, to exchange views and (in many cases) lamentation about the loss their families have faced, and to begin to learn how to live with each other. The summer work is continued "back home" in Mumbai, Delhi, and Lahore, as groups of young people meet with Seeds of Peace allies. Countless numbers of small groups have managed to cross the boundaries between the two warring nations—and their work moves people on both sides of the border to develop support for the governments to do likewise.

This work embodies many of the principles of CCR. Participants in these dialogue groups seek to understand the perspectives of "the other." In the process, they discover that what they are saying about the other is what the other says about them. Participants are often curious, just as they are fearful, because "the other" is always in their consciousness—in the stories told by elders (many of whom had to flee across the border) as well as the material put out by each nation's media and political leadership. Participants discover that they can speak their own truth and at the same time begin to understand that there are more similarities between Pakistanis and Indians than there are differences—in fact, the similarities in language, food, cultural practices, and music have been masked by religious and territorial divisions. With support from trained facilitators, participants in these dialogues learn to listen carefully before judging others, separate judgments about government policies from judgments about persons or cultures, and acknowledge the role of each nation in the current conflict. Participants take significant risks in talking openly and transparently about their hopes and their pain; they agree to create and sustain safe contexts for the difficult work of reconciliation; and they often leave prepared to expand the circle of this work. In a recent interview, one Indian participant said:

> There was a time when there was no acceptance of Pakistan. Families who had fled Pakistan to India said "One day we will be back." We saw the story from one side only. Partition was simply about loss. When we began to learn about and understand the mistreatment of Pakistanis, I began to understand their need for their own nation. This shift can only happen if you take the risk, the step of talking.[23]

Kashmir, the site of terrible violence in the past fifty years, Muslim and Hindu individuals have reached across barriers and borders to create bridges that are beginning to force both governments to change their patterns of threat and retaliation.

LEARNING FROM HISTORY: THE WISDOM OF TALKING VERSUS NOT TALKING

In many cases CCR prevents wars, and in many cases it achieves better justice without the destruction of war. Citizens and governments are therefore obligated to engage in CCR, both as a war-preventing action, and as a conflict-transforming and justice-achieving practice. Let us review some history in order to see the obligation of talking with an adversary.

The Munich Myth

Those who oppose talking often refer to the experience of British Prime Minister Chamberlain in talking with Hitler at Munich prior to Hitler's invasion of Poland, which started World War II. The truth in the Munich myth is that Chamberlain underestimated Hitler's evil—both in terms of Hitler's plans for international domination and his genocidal plans for Jews and other minorities. Chamberlain's error was not that he talked; it was what he did not say. He should have warned with unmistakable clarity of the realistic consequence if Hitler continued his aggression: war with England, France, and the United States, and also with Russia, and terrible devastation for Germany. Hitler was deceiving himself, and was not listening to his own foreign policy experts, who were clearly warning that attacking Poland would cause war against Germany by the Allied Powers.

The Gulf War

When U.S. Ambassador April Glaspie talked with Saddam Hussein prior to Iraq's attack on Kuwait that set off the first Gulf War, she should have been instructed to make clear that attacking Kuwait would bring about war with the United States and its allies. The U.S. Defense Department analysts had told the administration on three separate occasions that Iraq was massing its tanks on the Kuwaiti border and was about to attack Kuwait. Yet the U.S. administration never told Iraq the consequence would be war with the United States. Ambassador Glaspie should have been instructed to say just that. And she should have urged Iraq and Kuwait to practice CCR in resolving Iraq's claims that Kuwait was stealing Iraqi oil, owed payments to Iraq, and was blocking Iraqi access to its seaport. Furthermore, the administration refused to talk with Saddam Hussein about withdrawal from Kuwait prior to the U.S. initiation of the Gulf War. France and the Soviet Union did talk with him, and he told them he would get out. But the United States attacked anyway. It was that war that convinced Osama bin Laden to turn to terrorism and organize al-Qaeda.[24]

Israel and Palestine

There have been few successes for Israel's and its neighbors' need for peace, security, and justice. The major exception occurred when they finally were persuaded to talk. Egyptian President Anwar Sadat took a dramatic independent initiative, traveling to Israel to address the

Knesset. U.S. President Jimmy Carter persuaded Sadat and Prime Minister Menachem Begin of Israel to come to Camp David and practice CCR. This resulted in the Camp David Accords, which made lasting peace between Egypt and Israel, and then between Jordan and Israel. Until then, no Arab leader was willing either to travel to Israel or to make peace with Israel. Since then, no violence has occurred between Israel, Egypt, and Jordan, and Egypt has worked to help soften conflicts between Israel and Palestine.

Carter's practice of cooperative conflict resolution has continued through his personal intervention in conflicts throughout the world, including in Haiti, North Korea, Nicaragua, Sudan, and Bosnia. Carter is one example of a spiritually motivated citizen-diplomat who practices CCR. His efforts to understand each side sometimes have led to accusations that he cozied up to tyrants. Yet his commitment to CCR has led to successes where others have failed.

By contrast, when President George W. Bush took power in 2001, he immediately announced the U.S. administration was ceasing efforts to make peace between Israel and Palestine, and between the United States and North Korea. The result, of course, was that no peace initiatives succeeded. Almost seven years later, as his last year in the presidency approached, he announced a policy reversal, engaging in active support for negotiations between Mahmoud Abbas and the Israeli government. Along with his administration's reversal in finally talking with North Korea and its finally talking with Iran about peace in Iraq (but not about nuclear enrichment), this signals a dramatic realization that refusing to practice CCR has worked badly, and CCR is needed.

In the first years of this century, the Israeli government and the Bush government declared that negotiations with the Palestinian government in the West Bank could not succeed unless the Hamas government in Gaza agreed to it. Yet they refused to talk with the democratically elected Hamas government, because it supported terrorism. Unless this changes, prospects do not look good for getting Hamas or the Israeli Knesset to agree to the negotiated outcome, if there is one.

The Iraq War

Prior to the decision of the administration of George W. Bush to initiate the Iraq War, the U.S. government's approach stood in opposition to every principle of Cooperative Conflict Resolution. No attempt was made to understand the perspective of adversaries—within

Iraq or the broader international community.[25] Fed by the mourning and fear that followed 9/11, and fueled by a U.S. administration eager to demonstrate its military power, negative judgments about the Iraqi people were quick to develop and became the major focus for U.S. public statements. Motives and strategies were cloaked in secrecy. All attempts at international collaboration were rejected with language that created two sides (those with us and those against us; the United States versus the Axis of Evil). Force was used to threaten, bully, conquer, and humiliate ("shock and awe") rather than to restrain or separate. Risks were minimized, and long-term solutions were considered irrelevant in the face of short-term political exigencies. Neither peace nor justice was achieved.

Tragically, the work of the United Nations Special Commission, which applied several CCR principles, was ignored and denigrated in the march toward war. The intrusive weapons-monitoring efforts of the UN Special Commission (UNSCOM) 1991–98, and the UN Monitoring, Verification, and Inspection Commission (UNMOVIC), December 2002–March 2003, proved to be far more successful than was generally recognized at the time.[26] As former chief weapons inspector Hans Blix wrote, "The UN and the world had succeeded in disarming Iraq without knowing it."[27] In its nearly eight years of operation, UNSCOM identified and dismantled nearly all of Iraq's vast store of prohibited weapons. In its brief four-month effort, UNMOVIC thoroughly monitored and confirmed the depleted state of Iraq's capabilities.

Most of the headlines of the early 1990s focused on the Baghdad government's attempts to stall, evade, and obstruct the work of UN weapons monitors. Yet the record shows that UNSCOM and UNMOVIC mounted a highly successful disarmament effort. Even Vice President Dick Cheney called the UN disarmament program "the most intrusive system of arms control in history," although he dismissed its utility.[28] Rolf Ekéus, Blix, and their inspectors stayed focused on the behavior of the Iraqi government rather than making judgments about the intentions of that nation's leaders. They were transparent and honest in their dealings and reports. They sought international collaboration, and took into account the legitimate needs of the Iraqi people for security and international respect.

UN sanctions contributed to the disarmament process by pressuring Iraq to accept (however grudgingly) inspections and monitoring.

The comprehensive trade sanctions imposed against Iraq caused severe humanitarian suffering and should have been adjusted as the hardships became evident in the early 1990s, but the arms embargo and financial controls that were part of the sanctions were effective in preventing the regime from rebuilding its armed forces and blocking the import of vital materials and technologies for producing weapons of mass destruction.[29]

Along the road to war, the U.S. administration had multiple opportunities to choose another path that included international collaboration. Beginning in 2001, the Bush administration launched a major diplomatic initiative that succeeded in lifting the remaining sanctions on civilian trade with Iraq and tightening the embargo on weapons and military-related imports. As the purpose of sanctions narrowed to preventing weapons imports rather than blocking civilian trade, international support actually increased. The divisions within the Security Council that had surfaced in the late 1990s gave way to a new consensus. By the fall of 2002 the administration had constructed the core elements of an effective international program for containing the military ambitions of Saddam Hussein.[30] Rather than utilizing these mechanisms of cooperative control, the administration opted for war and military occupation.

North Korea and Libya

Initially, neither the Clinton nor the George W. Bush administration agreed to talk with North Korea. Instead they relied on threats. North Korea responded during 2002–2006 by building what they called a nuclear deterrent against possible U.S. attack. They produced enough plutonium for perhaps ten nuclear bombs and tested one bomb in October 2006. Wiser heads in both administrations saw that refusing to talk was not working. Former President Jimmy Carter in 1994 and U.S. Assistant Secretary of State Christopher Hill in 2007 each talked directly with North Korean negotiators. They quickly worked out solutions. Secretary of State Condoleezza Rice and President Bush affirmed the result of the 2007 talks. North Korea's Yongbyon reactor is closed down, international inspectors are monitoring it, and removing the plutonium may be in prospect.

Similarly, Libya continued its pursuit of chemical, biological, and nuclear weapons for several years. Only after quiet, direct engagement with U.S. and British officials for more than a decade, and offers of normalized trade and diplomatic relations, an end to sanctions, and increased foreign investment, did Libya agree in December 2003 to renounce these weapons.

Iran

Ever since the Iranian hostage crisis during the Carter administration, the U.S. government has refused to talk with the Iranian government. But in May 2006, President Bush and his aides reached the decision "that the approach they had once publicly described as successfully 'isolating' Iran was in fact going nowhere. Mr. Bush's search for a new option was driven, they say, by concern that the path he was on . . . would inevitably force one of two potentially disastrous outcomes: an Iranian bomb, or an American attack on Iran's facilities."[31] Therefore, U.S. Secretary of State Condoleezza Rice announced on May 31, 2006, that the United States would join multilateral talks with Iran on its nuclear program "once Iran suspends disputed nuclear activities." Kazem Jalali, spokesman for the Iranian parliament's Foreign Policy and National Security Committee, said the U.S. move "might be viewed positively in Tehran *if preconditions were dropped*."[32]

To give in to the U.S. demand that they suspend enrichment of uranium even before talks would begin is very difficult in a culture that values honor. It would mean giving up the right to enrich uranium for generating electricity—a right universally recognized for other nations. David Isenberg writes in *Defense News:* "After all, nearly 30 years after the 1979 revolution, we need to consider what the policy of no official U.S. dialogue with Iran has achieved in terms of influencing Iranian behavior. In a word: nothing."[33] Howard Baker, secretary of state in the first Bush administration, pointed out that despite major disagreements, the United States and the Soviet Union talked directly many times, helping us avoid nuclear war and achieve a peaceful end to the Cold War. Former U.S. foreign policy officials, both Republican and Democratic, including Howard Baker, Zbigniew Brzezinski, William Perry, Henry Kissinger, Madeline Albright, Richard N. Haass, and Richard L. Armitage, support direct U.S.-Iranian unconditional negotiations. In a 2006 poll, 59 percent of Americans supported negotiations even if Iran refuses to suspend enrichment.[34]

In the spring of 2003 Iran offered to grant formal recognition to Israel, to cut off assistance to Palestinian armed groups and pressure them to halt terrorist attacks within Israel's 1967 borders, and a "stop of any material support to Palestinian opposition groups (Hamas, Jihad, etc.) from Iranian territory" along with "pressure on these organizations to stop violent actions against civilians within [Israel's] borders of 1967." Even more surprising, they offered to take "action on Hezbollah to become a mere political organization within Lebanon." They offered to accept much tighter controls by the International Atomic Energy Agency (IAEA) in exchange for "full access to peaceful nuclear technology," with access to any facility IAEA inspectors would request, making cheating much more difficult.[35] Is this offer real? The only way to tell is to sit down and talk, and then verify the results. "Trust but verify," as President Reagan used to say.

Realism—Nations Need Help Facing Reality

We need a realistic understanding of human nature and of governments. A rational-interest, utility-maximizing model of human nature, according to which all we need to do is to manipulate the other side's interests and then they will "rationally" do what we want, overlooks the realistic fact that others often do not act according to their interests *as we see them*. They have loyalties, pride, defensiveness, bureaucratic inertia, ideologies, and different cultural perception patterns than utility-maximizing models of rationality predict. Oddly, *they see us* as driven by peculiar ideologies as well. They are stuck in a perception that does not see their interests as we see them. And we are stuck not seeing what they see. CCR can function as reality testing for both sides.

Sometimes national elites refuse to talk because talking could suggest some change they are not eager to make. Hence, for example, President Reagan's advisors urged him to refuse to talk with Gorbachev, because they feared he might agree to arms reductions. Then when Congress refused him arms increases unless he would talk, he finally agreed to the first Summit meeting. Sometimes national elites put their trust in their ability to dominate, whether by military or economic power. Sometimes they are driven by resentments of the other, and by self-righteousness about their own superiority. Sometimes they misperceive.[36]

Now in a time of encounter between different religions and different national cultures in our globally interacting world, we are becoming more aware that different people, different cultures, different traditions, and different nations see things differently and do not see much of what others see. Furthermore, people and cultures often prefer not to face realities about their own limitations and errors. Talking often needs to be realistic, helping all of us to face realities we would rather not face. We all need some reality testing.

CHALLENGES, CONCERNS, AND LIMITATIONS

An examination of any conflict situation must consider three factors that have complex interpersonal, cultural, historical, and political dimensions. First, we need to understand the *relationships among the people* involved in the conflict. Second, we need to understand the *sources and dynamics of the particular dispute.* Third, we need to understand the *social structures*—how they continue the conflict and how they offer openings for resolution. CCR has demonstrated success in addressing the first two factors. However, some have criticized CCR for lack of attention to the structural dimension with its inherent power imbalance and complex network of historical, socio-anthropological, economic, military, and political factors that shape the conflict.

Does the complexity of this broader context exceed the capacity of CCR? The first answer is that just peacemaking has precisely the advantage that it is a multilevel approach in which CCR practices are only one part, and justice within nations as well as international structures are also key parts. Beyond that, CCR is now being deepened by attention to structural contexts.

Cultural Barriers

Transplanting a conflict resolution method across cultural, racial, or ethnic lines may either distort the process or supplant indigenous alternatives that would work better. *Culture,* expressed through traditions, stories, rituals, religion, and language, provides identity for a society. Verbal and nonverbal expressions are likely to take on different meanings when crossing cultural lines. Many who practice mediation in school and community settings are now beginning to look to non-Western practices as resources or models for more culturally literate approaches to mediation. In the transnational arena, an elicitive approach has begun to influence training for conflict resolution in non-Western cultural contexts.

Degree of Damage or Pain

The degree of damage or pain is often much more complex at inter-community and transnational levels than at the interpersonal level.

Can expressions of confession, repentance, and forgiveness lead to reconciliation between races or enemy nations? This question is addressed directly in chapter 4 by Alan Geyer and Donald Shriver, and by former U.S. diplomat and current theorist of citizen diplomacy Joseph Montville, who calls for acknowledgment of historical guilt as a prerequisite for conflict resolution.

Problems of Scale

Face-to-face problem-solving strategies work best when disputants are few in number, know each other well through daily interaction, and expect to have an ongoing relationship after the dispute is resolved. Close to 90 percent of those involved in school peer mediation, for example, report satisfaction with the agreement and willingness to honor their agreements over time. In contrast, peer mediation with large groups is often less effective. A different kind of training and support is needed when mediators take on the structural issues underlying racial or ethnic clashes and a large number of disputants.

Power Inequities

Neoconservatives contend that an approach based on CCR is likely to fall into the trap of *appeasement*, as in the Munich myth—a negative relational dynamic in which the more powerful party is allowed to dominate. To balance the power relationship in order to create the conditions in which meaningful negotiation can take place, they believe the use of threat and coercive force is likely to be indispensable. Furthermore, they claim that power asymmetry constitutes the more typical state of affairs. Therefore, they depend on a coercive approach to virtually all situations of conflict, a confrontational stance that utilizes position-taking to address systemic dominance and intransigence.

CCR advocates agree that power relationships must be considered. Often, as in the sanctions on Iraq, power-pressure can lead to a willingness to negotiate. But if then we refuse to talk, we throw away the opportunity that the pressure has offered us. Furthermore, CCR procedures seek to improve the balance of power by identifying nontraditional sources of power, by providing either party with the option to refuse agreement, and by reaching agreements that include checks against power domination. What we argue against is reductionism. Economic and military power factors are not the only factors that shape outcomes. Other structural factors and ways of relating are also important. CCR can help create a context where conflict can be resolved without the costs of violence, and where solutions depend on the power of persuasion and public opinion as well as on other forms of power. At issue here also is the need to unmask the often hidden power inequities and to empower the weaker party so that, in the end, a lasting reconciliation as well as a just resolution might be possible. Looking to the New Testament for guidance, we find that, even in situations of significant power inequity, the evidence weighs heavily in favor of trying a nonviolent confrontation designed to convert or transform one's adversary. In the Sermon on the Mount, Jesus calls us not to seek revenge by violent or evil means, but to take transforming initiatives that confront injustice and call for peacemaking relationship.[37]

In Gandhi, we find a similar nonviolent methodology. He called upon people in India to produce salt and disregard the British colonial monopoly, as a metaphor of resistance and a tactic for mobilizing the masses. This empowered the people and thwarted British domination. Later in the twentieth century, the American activist and author Barbara Deming integrated Gandhi's approach with a keen awareness of the role that resistance can play in addressing inequities of power. Deming wrote: "To resort to power one need not be violent, and to speak to conscience one need not be meek. The most effective action both resorts to power and engages conscience." Deming argued for forceful, active resistance, including civil disobedience, that she called revolutionary nonviolence.[38] When the response to this kind of resistance is positive, adversarial relations can be both unmasked and eliminated without dominance or assimilation by the more powerful.

Irreducible Conflicting Interests

Another criticism of CCR centers in the conviction that in many conflict situations, especially deep-rooted ones, parties are locked in irreducible conflicting interests that limit them to competing for a zero-sum outcome in which one's gain is always another's loss. There is only so much oil in the Middle East, for example. Since, from this perspective, interests are irreducible and the limited number of options are usually well known, any serious attempt to resolve the conflict in one's favor must rely on firming up a position that will protect one's sphere of interest in the inevitable struggle.

CCR makes no claim that it will always work; some cases are indeed highly resistant. Nevertheless, the pluralist school of political thought contends that it is usually possible to alter the perceived reality, especially in deeply rooted ethnic and ideological conflicts where one's perceptual lens or viewpoint is all-important. Like other proponents of CCR, pluralists expand the number of actors in the international system to include nonstates, and maintain that a relationship of interdependence exists among them. Furthermore, they affirm that different parties' basic interests, such as identity and security, do not ultimately conflict because, by nature, they increase in distributable size as each actor has more of them. When Palestinians have their state and a negotiated reduction in occupation, Israelis will have increased security and peace. All this allows expanding the pie and adopting a negotiating style based on interdependence, integration, and cooperation—a stance they claim is much more desirable in a world where violence has become too dangerous and is often counterproductive.

A realist critique often characterizes international relations as similar to the "prisoner's dilemma" in game theory. In the game, two accomplices in a crime are imprisoned and separated so they cannot communicate and cooperate in their defense. Although refusing to betray each other would be in their mutual interest, each calculates that accusing his/her accomplice is the best defense against the likelihood of being accused by the accomplice. The claim is that participants in transnational conflict, like the ones in this game, lack the necessary trusted communication that might motivate them to cooperate.[39]

However, even in the midst of an intractable transnational conflict, chances are significantly enhanced when the parties know they will be interacting repeatedly over the long haul, a factor that is more present in transnational relations than in the single-interaction prisoner's dilemma. Yet due to the lack of communication and mutual distrust that characterize many transnational conflicts, it may be necessary to involve a third-party mediator who can begin a problem-solving process. If both sides see progress in resolving the conflict, they invest more trust in the mediator, leading to greater trust and communications between the adversaries.[40]

Second, the likelihood of developing cooperative strategies is enhanced if actors in the conflict become aware of the importance of mutual interests. If a narrow, competitive, individualistic view of self-interest prevails, negotiations inevitably lead to deadlock. But if actors come to see the benefits to themselves in pursuing the common good, this can change. Therefore, it is in their ultimate interest to develop cooperative, rather than competitive, strategies. At the very least, this common self-interest can be pursued by announcing and acting on rules of mutual restraint. By eliciting such reciprocity, along with adequate mechanisms for verification, one can affirm mutual self-interest even when there is no friendship.

Third, morality, especially if embedded in a framework of ethics, "can supply additional reasons for restraint."[41] Although realism rightly argues that morality, when it is in strong conflict with self-interest, cannot alone govern transnational relations, it can alter the terms of interaction by encouraging people in conflict to value each other's needs and concerns. Once one engenders a sense of shared morality, affirms mutual collective interests, and builds in repeated interaction between the parties, then the door is open to CCR.

Cooperation theorists have emphasized the power of positive reciprocity. Robert Axelrod and others found that the most stable basis for cooperation is the simple tit-for-tat process, in which one party responds in kind to the gestures of the other.[42] Game theory experiments show that the most successful strategy for gaining maximum benefit for both parties is to open with a cooperative move and thereafter respond in kind to the other player's actions. Cooperative gestures regularly generate the most favorable outcomes for both parties.

The costliness of the opposite scenario is seen in interpersonal tragedies (like spousal abuse), inter-group conflicts (as in the Congo and Bosnia), and international conflicts (like the current tragedy in Iraq). During the Cold War, the pursuit of narrow self-interest spurred many decisions to increase weapons rather than negotiate test-ban and arms-reduction treaties. Prior to Gorbachev's initiatives in the late 1980s, the result was continual escalation of the nuclear threat, wasting billions of dollars, and endangering innocent lives.[43] Again, there is a strong moral obligation for governments to try CCR before embarking on such a costly course.

CONCLUSION AND RECOMMENDATIONS

Because of their moral authority, churches, synagogues, and mosques should take the lead in advocating and modeling noncoercive conflict resolution strategies. From the great religious writing of ancient times to modern-day peacemakers like Martin Luther King and Thich Nhat Hanh, many religious traditions provide us with people who have pointed the way. As agents of God's message of love, healing, and reconciliation for all humankind, congregations need to be in the forefront of the struggle to replace violence with at least a provisional peace, and to change the adversarial nature of relationships into a partnership approach.

Training in cooperative conflict resolution should become a core component of the educational program for a broad range of civic leaders. Efforts to teach these skills should begin early and become a universal component of civic education for children and young adults—so that they can apply these principles in their local lives, understand their usefulness in larger community settings, and advocate for their use as citizens.[44] Training in CCR should be a core component of training programs for diplomats and national political and military leaders. The absence of these skills in the junior Bush administration has been a key contributor to their reliance on unilateral (and often militarist) strategies—with dire consequences for civilians around the world, as other governments began to follow their U.S. lead, as well as for the health of our nation's democratic institutions.

Funding for these kinds of approaches needs to be dramatically increased at all levels of society because the connections among interpersonal, intergroup and international conflicts are increasingly clear. Local funding can include support for conflict resolution, peer mediation, restorative justice, and community policing. National funding can include support for federal institutions designed to promote CCR and just peacemaking, as well as support for nonlegislative efforts to heal and reconcile. International funding should begin with a commitment to a healthy, reformed United Nations—whose effective role in conflicts described in this chapter might have reduced the human loss as well as improved the opportunities for peace with justice.

Policy and practice should emphasize prevention. One of the key lessons from public health is that prevention is more cost-effective than intervention: strategies like draining swamps, childhood vaccination, public education, clean water, and accessible health care are more successful and less costly than treating the victims of preventable problems. And these approaches support the principles of CCR: they emphasize prevention over judgment, they are transparent, they require and support collaboration and partnership, they focus on long-term solutions—and they address the importance of economic and social justice as a core prevention strategy.

Finally, we need to disseminate and celebrate the kind of work done by individuals and groups that appear in this chapter. They are but a small sample of a growing worldwide recognition that the old ways of win/lose and demonizing the enemy are not only ineffective— they are suicidal for cultures, nations, and the human community. Recognizing and publicizing these efforts will help teach these skills, starting with young children and stretching into the institutions that train world leaders. By writing, talking, and teaching about these (and other) efforts, we can also provide financial, political, and spiritual support for the courageous people who are using CCR strategies in the most violent contexts or the most humble ones. As Dr. Martin Luther King Jr. has said,

> We still have a choice today: non-violent coexistence or violent co-annihilation. We must move past indecision to action. Now let us begin. Now let us rededicate ourselves to the long and bitter—but beautiful—struggle for a new world. The choice is ours and, though we might prefer otherwise, we must choose in this crucial moment of history.

Four

ACKNOWLEDGE RESPONSIBILITY FOR CONFLICT AND INJUSTICE AND SEEK REPENTANCE AND FORGIVENESS

Alan Geyer
Donald W. Shriver

Peacemaking, whether in personal, group, or international relations, requires a variety of capacities for self-transcendence:

- Transcendence of one's own interests and perspectives for the sake of understanding the interests and perspectives of the other side calls for the capacity for *empathy*.
- Transcendence of one's human desire for retaliation-in-kind calls for a capacity for *forbearance from revenge*.
- Transcendence of one's temptation to exist in permanent isolation and animosity towards the other calls for a capacity for at least envisioning the possibility of *future reconciliation*.

Not to be transcended, however, is a search for the facts of possible moral wrongdoing on one or both sides of the conflict, and this presupposes the element of *moral judgment*. Fully defined, forgiveness is an act that synthesizes at least these four elements. An acknowledgment of wrongs clears the way for the development of empathy, forbearance, and reconciliation. Were judgment of wrong to be abandoned in attempts to resolve human conflicts, the moral core of forgiveness would be abandoned. Were there no real wrongs committed, there would be, morally speaking, nothing to forgive. Honesty in a process of forgiveness requires the motto, "Remember and forgive," not "forgive and forget."[1]

But this analysis recalls an old issue in discussions of these four ingredients of forgiveness: Is it really possible for nations or their governments to practice such virtues?

SHOULD NATIONS EVER APOLOGIZE?

The authors of this volume have engaged one another in the most spirited disagreements as to how to answer that question, disagreements concerning the very nature of theological discourse about politics. An enduring maxim in "political realism" (of a sort) insists that nations cannot and must not live by such personal dispositions—in particular, that nations should not apologize, lest the gesture be taken as a sign of weakness. Such realism holds further that because nations always seek to maximize their power, expressions of repentance and forgiveness are to be regarded as inappropriate if not irresponsible moralisms.

Politicians and generals are not alone in doubting the place of repentance and forgiveness in political conflict. In his early but still influential writings, the premier American theologian (and also the dominant political ethicist) Reinhold Niebuhr discounted severely the relevance of Jesus' gospel of love and forgiveness to the realities of world politics and even of interpersonal conflict.[2] Niebuhr defined political responsibility in terms of a power-compromised ethic of justice that typically has to reject the counsels of love.

But Niebuhr's political and ethical legacy on this matter is ambiguous and even contradictory. For no one has more to say about the follies of American pride and pretension than Niebuhr, whose works are a constant summons to repentance and humility. His incurable ambiguities are reflected in such statements as "Only a forgiving love, grounded in repentance, is adequate to heal the animosities between nations. But that degree of love is an impossibility for nations. It is a very rare achievement among individuals; and the mind and heart of collective man is notoriously less imaginative than that of the individual."[3] Sixteen years later, in *The Irony of American History*, Niebuhr sounded a similar note, but then qualified it ever so slightly:

> Nations are hardly capable of the spirit of forgiveness which is the final oil of harmony in all human relations and which rests upon the final recognition that our actions and attitudes are inevitably interpreted in a different light by our friends as well as foes than we interpret them. Yet it is necessary to acquire a measure of this spirit in the collective relations of mankind.

Nations, as individuals, who are completely innocent in their own esteem, are insufferable in their human contacts.[4]

These passages from Niebuhr are all from his postpacifist, "realist" years. They were implicitly challenged in the title of a 1953 book by Andre Trocmé, the French Huguenot pastor in the village of Le Chambon whose nonviolent resistance to Nazi tyranny was followed by service as European Secretary of the International Fellowship of Reconciliation. That title, *The Politics of Repentance*, reflected Trocmé's pacifist political witness, similar to that of John Howard Yoder's *The Politics of Jesus*. And what to Trocmé is the political relevance of repentance? The repentance of Christians "has very definite consequences in the social and political order. . . . People convinced of their own innocence cannot be reconciled. Only repentance can [reconcile]. . . . As long as [the State] is abandoned by the church, it knows nothing of repentance. But the church in its midst does know repentance, and it knows *only* that, and it bears witness of that before the State, for the healing of the State."[5] Thus, Trocmé, like Niebuhr, seems to suggest that repentance and forgiveness are unnatural acts for government, but he holds to the hope that the church may lead the state to repentance and forgiveness.

To regard this as basically a pacifist-nonpacifist controversy, however, would be a mistake. Shriver's 1995 book, *An Ethic for Enemies: Forgiveness in Politics*, puts the issue sharply: "Can whole nations repent? Forgive? Engage in processes that eventuate in collective repentance and forgiveness?" He puts off a theoretical answer in deference to Kenneth Boulding's principle, "If it has happened once, it must be possible." The book turns to some happenings in the history of twentieth-century conflict, all three involving the United States: the aftermaths of its wars with Germany and Japan and its unending internal struggle for racial justice. Throughout these case studies, evidences of secular versions of forgiveness are documented, sometimes in collective gestures that go by other words than those usually associated with religious versions of the concepts.[6]

This chapter proceeds on the assumption that acknowledgments of wrongdoing on all sides, empathy, forbearance from revenge, and overt hope for reconciliation are necessary practices in the work of peacemaking. When faithfully practiced in combination, these practices over time can yield genuine collective forgiveness. Moreover, they are unique forms of power rather than expressions of weakness, as exemplified in laws ancient and modern that locate the power of amnesties and commutations of the death penalty in presidents and prime ministers. In the experience of nations and other social entities, repentance and forgiveness have been and may be the preconditions of genuine reconciliation. Indeed, they may be preconditions of the maintenance of society itself. Robert Frost put it succinctly: "To be social is to be forgiving."[7]

REPENTANCE AS AN ORIENTATION AND AN ATTITUDE

Repentance and forgiveness share both an orientation to history and an attitude toward the future. The year 1995, punctuated with so many fiftieth anniversaries of the climactic events of World War II, posed these issues with an emotional intensity that many persons born after 1945 found difficult to understand. In particular, remembrance of the liberation of the death camps of the Holocaust and the atomic bombing of Hiroshima and Nagasaki provided occasions for discussions of repentance and forgiveness.

101

U.S. Remembrances of World War II

It proved exceedingly difficult for many Americans to acknowledge any national responsibility for the Holocaust, Nazism, and the other horrors of history's most terrible war (the so-called "good war" because the Axis enemy was so obviously evil, the American people were rallied to such a high pitch of unity, and the lives of so many Americans were materially enhanced by the wartime economy and its affluent aftermath). Little recollection in 1995 was made of the ways in which the allies' demands after World War I contributed to the ascendancy and aggression of Nazism in Germany and militarism in Japan—or of the likelihood that World War II and the Holocaust could have been prevented, but for American isolationism, repudiation of the League of Nations, the collapse of parliamentary institutions in Germany and Japan in the wake of the North American Depression, Western anti-Semitism, and the racist exclusion of Japanese immigration. Even when confronted in 1939 with a thousand Jewish refugees aboard the *S.S. St. Louis* as it attempted to dock in American ports, our government sent them back to Bremerhaven, the vast majority to almost certain death.

Some German and Japanese leaders have found it possible to acknowledge their nations' war guilt and to offer words or gestures of repentance. In Germany, Dietrich Bonhoeffer wrote a powerful acknowledgment of guilt on behalf of himself, the churches, Germany, and the West in the manuscript for his *Ethics* in 1941.[8] The churches exerted early leadership in the Stuttgart Declaration of the Evangelical Church in Germany (EKD) in October 1945 and two years later in its Darmstadt Declaration. Neither of these statements mentioned the Holocaust, however, which finally in 1950 appeared in the statement of one of the territorial church bodies of the EKD. These and other movements in the German churches, however, did prepare some ground for the single most important German initiative to repair the damages of the war to neighboring countries: Chancellor Willy Brandt's *Ostpolitik*. The essence of that policy was the restoration of the 1939 borders of Poland at the Oder-Neisse line, some forty thousand square miles of territory once inhabited by many Germans. An elite group of scientists, church leaders, and academics called for this action in their "Eastern Memorandum" of 1965. They thus prepared ground for Brandt's initiatives as chancellor. Poland was the first country to be blitzkrieged by the Nazi war machine and the country with the largest number of Holocaust victims (perhaps three million). In December 1970, Brandt courageously (with no guarantee of parliamentary approval) signed a treaty accepting the Oder-Neisse frontier, a decision personally dramatized by his kneeling silently at the Warsaw Ghetto Memorial as an act of atonement for German offenses against the Polish people. That Brandt, of all people, should assume such a posture of repentance was especially remarkable in view of his own anti-Nazi credentials and his exile in Norway throughout the war. It was an extraordinary, winsome, powerful, long-lasting act of personal leadership. It made peace possible.

102

Fifteen years later, on the fortieth anniversary of the end of World War II in Germany—May 8, 1945—Bundespraesident Richard von Weizsaecker addressed the Bundestag with one of the most eloquent confessional statements of the century. Shriver writes: "The speech achieved international acclaim almost overnight. . . . What impressed the world about this speech was its lengthy, unflinching, excuseless enumeration of Nazi crimes and many degrees of association with those crimes by millions of Germans in the years 1933–45."[9] Among many other stunning passages, von Weizsaecker offered these confessions:

> We cannot commemorate the 8th of May without making ourselves aware of how much conquest of self the readiness for rec-

onciliation demanded of our former enemies. Can we really identify with the relatives of those who were sacrificed in the Warsaw Ghetto or the massacre of Lidice? . . . Who can remain innocent after the burning of the synagogues, the looting, the stigmatizing with the Jewish star, the withdrawal of rights, the unceasing violations of human worth? . . . As human beings, we seek reconciliation. Precisely for this reason we must understand that there can be no reconciliation without memory.[10]

Von Weizsaecker profoundly understood that conquest of self, or self-transcendence—whether by victors or vanquished—is the prerequisite of forgiveness and its goal of reconciliation. Having been a participant in the life of the EKD and the World Council of Churches, von Weizsaecker is an example of a Christian politician who learned to translate some of the fundamentals of theology into political speech.

In some contrast, as the Hiroshima anniversary approached in August 1945, certain officials of the Japanese government acknowledged deep remorse for its aggression in World War II, but never with the concreteness of the von Weizsaecker speech. The mayor of Hiroshima, Takashi Hiraoka, who in 1991 had laid a wreath at Pearl Harbor's battleship Arizona memorial, came to Washington to help open a Hiroshima exhibit at American University after veterans' groups had effectively protested the scheduling of such an exhibit at the Smithsonian Institution. At the time, many lively forums reviewed the A-bomb decisions, but the U.S. government made no official statements of remorse or regret for the two bombs or for the firebombing of Japanese cities which killed more civilians than died in Hiroshima and Nagasaki. In this the U.S. government paralleled the resistance to apology and statements of regret that seemed endemic to the cultures of both countries. Most Americans probably sympathized with the Japanese view that it is best to "let the past flow under the bridge like a river."

As a result, it is safe to say that reconciliation between Germany and the United States is probably deeper than that which prevails between Americans and the Japanese, especially among survivors of the war of 1941–45. Resentments still linger among the latter, the more so because leaders of neither nation have seen fit to confess to excessive uses of violence by some of our ancestors.

More Recent Episodes

In our first edition we wrote that the issues of war crimes and genocide raised so horrendously by World War II and the Holocaust have reappeared in the 1990s, particularly in the context of escalating ethnic strife in many countries. Former Yugoslavia and Rwanda were the most publicized cases, each with hundreds of thousands of victims. At this writing, prospects for acknowledgment of historic responsibility and offers of forgiveness are not promising in either case. Now, after his death, we remember that, in his long trial for war crimes in the Hague, Slobodan Milosevic only blamed others. But his trial and Serbia's successful shift to democracy (practices 5 and 8) helped assuage the thirst for revenge stirred in many victims of his decisions in Serbia's wars in the 1990s with the Croatians and Bosnians.

One example of American repentant attention to longstanding grievances for our actions in Central America came during the Clinton administration with the president's apology for U.S. support of dictatorship and overthrow of an election in Guatemala in 1954.[11]

104

Clinton also went to Rwanda, as did UN Secretary General Kofi Annan and the British prime minister, to apologize for failure to intervene for stopping the massacre of eight hundred thousand people. Rwandans report that this helped pull the thorn of post-massacre resentment that could easily fuel another outbreak of revenge. That same apology came from some leaders of the Rwandan government in the mid-1990s, for example, the Rwandan ambassador to the United States, who in a forum at the Riverside Church in New York confessed his shame at how little the Christians of his country had done to stem the carnage or to refuse to participate in it.

Analogously, also in the 1990s, South Africans made extraordinary efforts to overcome the brutal legacy of the apartheid era in the work of the Truth and Reconciliation Commission chaired by Archbishop Desmond Tutu. The moral authority of a Tutu and a Nelson Mandela offer a powerful example of how political leaders can help their countries to transcend the burdens of their history. Their collaboration with other South African leaders in devising the TRC will rank among the most moral and most political achievements of recent history. Above all, as a contribution to peacemaking in one violence-torn country, the TRC was an example of citizen courage in undertaking a struggle with the complexities of political forms of the justice, forbearance, empathy, and hope for reconciliation inherent in the definition of forgiveness offered at the beginning of this chapter. As a justice of the South African Constitutional Court, Ismail Mohamed, in turning down a suit aimed at abolishing the TRC, described the Commission as

> A difficult, sensitive, perhaps even agonizing, balancing act between the need for justice to victims of past abuse and the need for reconciliation and rapid transition to a new future; between encouragement to wrongdoers to help in the discovery of truth and the need for reparations for the victims of that truth; between a correction in the old and the creation of the new. It is an exercise of immense difficulty interacting in a vast network of political, emotional, ethical, and logistical considerations. . . . The results may well often be imperfect and . . . support the message of Kant that "out of the crooked timber of humanity no straight thing was ever made."[12]

THE UNITED STATES' CLAIMS OF INNOCENCE

Repentance may be peculiarly difficult for a country like the United States, which has conceived itself, as Reinhold Niebuhr put it, as "the darling of Divine Providence." One of the more vicious consequences of such a metaphysical nationalism is a chronic difficulty in viewing history from an adversary's perspective. The naïve habit of many, if not most, Americans has been to confront every international conflict reactively, as if it had no history at all, or at least no American implication in it.

This posture of historical innocence helps to explain the insensitivity with which the public has responded to recent events in Vietnam, Iran, the Persian Gulf, Lebanon, Mexico, Nicaragua, and Somalia. In each case, American power has produced a heavy legacy of contributing to the eruption of conflict. The cultures of Asia, Africa, and Latin America tend to sustain much longer historical memories than most Americans exhibit. One American historian has remarked that for most of us the past is so much dust kicked up in the wake of a moving vehicle. We keep our eyes out for the future. By contrast, the Maori of New Zealand see themselves as backing into the future, with their eyes fixed on the known past for directing themselves into the largely unknown future.

The Gulf War of 1991

The Gulf War, so widely believed to be an exemplary U.S. military triumph, was largely the consequence not only of Saddam Hussein's dictatorial rule and blundering aggression but also of the United States' lack of meaningful political memory of its past policies and actions that contributed to the hostilities. That past included the CIA's overthrow of Iran's nationalist revolution in 1953; complicity in the Shah's oppressions and corruptions, which led to the Khomeini regime, against which the U.S. then proceeded to help build up the power of Saddam Hussein's regime in Iraq; incoherent U.S. diplomacy vis-a-vis Iraq; a persistent anti-Arab tilt in the Arab-Israeli conflict; an undisciplined domestic energy policy that made the U.S. excessively dependent on Middle East oil and disposed to intervene militarily for the sake of oil; and a longtime U.S. lack of will to help construct an effective UN crisis-intervention force that might have prevented Iraq's invasion of Kuwait.

The actual U.S. conduct of the war, moreover, involved violations of humanitarian laws of war (especially in the pitiless slaughter of retiring Iraqi troops) and enormous civilian casualties and suffering in Iraq. In short, the 1991 war ought to have been an occasion for national repentance rather than triumphalism. In their case study of the Gulf War, Alan Geyer and Barbara Green conclude their analysis with the comment:

> A truly foundational ethic of war and peace must begin by taking the fullest possible account of the moral burdens of history that weigh upon any conflict within and among nations. Because historical responsibility for the causes of conflict typically is shared, a keen sense of the ambiguities of justice will help prepare conflicting nations for every prospect of peaceful settlement. Such a sense is spiritually nurtured especially by acknowledging the necessity of repentance as the precondition of reconciliation. The incapacity of nations and their leaders to admit even the possibility of repentance is often more a sign of weakness than of some real strength beneath their proud belligerence. That incapacity may also reflect profound historical ignorance or forgetfulness.[13]

The Cold War

Owning up to the moral burdens of history is also required in coping with the numberless human consequences of the Cold War, a half-century global conflict in which not only the Soviet Union but the United States, the American people, their economy, and all their social institutions were heavy losers. As Ambassador George Kennan re-counts: "Nobody 'won' the Cold War. . . . It greatly overstrained the economic resources of both countries, leaving them both, by the end of the 1980s, confronted with heavy financial, social, and . . . political problems neither had anticipated and for which neither was fully pre-pared. . . . All these developments should be seen as part of the price we are paying for the Cold War."[14]

Many other countries were dragged into the Cold War, however, and continue to suffer its consequences. The United States has largely washed its hands of the chaos in Somalia after the October 1993 inci-dent of spray-and-slay gunfire in which U.S. forces killed hundreds of Somalis in Mogadishu while suffering eighteen deaths of our own troops. The United States showed little memory of the fact that the Soviet Union and the United States had once sought to make Somalia a client state. In the process, the superpowers bequeathed the heaps of weapons that fueled Somalia's domestic violence and the continuing breakdowns of its basic institutions. U.S.-UN intervention, originally a TV-driven humanitarian relief mission in a situation of desperate human need—a mission that undoubtedly saved several hundred thousand lives—climaxed with an unwarranted scorn of the Somalis' capacity for self-government and a continuing presumption of American innocence. On every continent today, the UN system is burdened with the human, institutional, and environmental wreckage of the Cold War. As is often observed, the resistance of the Clinton administration to assembling a coalition of UN members for bringing the Rwanda massacre to a halt in the spring of 1994 owed much to the perception in Washington that the American public, after Somalia, would not tolerate another loss of a soldier's life in another humani-tarian intervention in Africa. Thus do democratic publics share some of the blame for the faults of their leaders.

THE NEED FOR NATIONAL SELF-RESPECT

Whatever the possibilities of repentance and forgiveness as discrete acts in particular cases, they must ultimately be deeply grounded in the dis-positions of a political culture and the spiritual resources of a religious faith. American comprehensions of history are more myopic than some nations, less than others. Because of our power and leadership, our re-sponsibility is greater. Our schools, colleges, and churches share with our political leaders a heavy responsibility in cultivating a much better-tutored historical consciousness. That does not mean wallowing in national self-hate and humiliation; it does mean appealing to our national self-respect by willingness to recall the flaws in our favorite accounts of history. A study of changes in American high school history books over a half century reveals some progress in this historical honesty: not all of the current books skim over details of the darker sides of American history, for example, slavery and the near genocide of Indians.[15]

Indeed, there remain vast treasures of heritage in international policy that must be recalled when the nation needs to summon "the better angels of our nature" in the face of brutal conflict: the foundation of human rights and the vitality of civil liberties; the endurance of democratic, constitutional government; the relentless, if episodic, struggle for multiracial justice and harmony; the overcoming of isolationism in creating and sustaining the United Nations (notwithstanding much backsliding); the Marshall Plan and innumerable other works of relief and reconstruction.

Occasions of U.S. Self-transcendence

Also instructive is to recall those moments, few though they may be, when American leadership has reached for words and acts expressing (or even hinting at) repentance or forgiveness.

- Abraham Lincoln's second inaugural address, in 1865, which before concluding "with malice toward none [and] charity for all," acknowledged that both sides in the Civil War, while reading from the same Bible and praying to the same God, shared guilt for "the offense" of slavery—and must remember that "the judgments of the Lord are true and righteous altogether."

- President John Kennedy's "Strategy for Peace" address at American University in June 1963 (reportedly inspired by Pope John XXIII's encyclical, *Pacem in Terris*), which confessed "We must re-examine our own attitude" toward the Soviet Union and its legitimate security interests—followed in a few weeks by the Partial Test Ban Treaty prohibiting atmospheric nuclear tests. Quite evident in these words were Kennedy's experience in the previous October in restraining both the USSR and the USA from catapulting the world into nuclear war.

- President Gerald Ford's 1976 proclamation revoking Executive Order 9066 (1942), which interned Japanese Americans in concentration camps. Ford declared that an "honest reckoning . . . must include a recognition of our national mistakes as well as our national achievements. . . . We know now what we should have known then—not only was that evacuation wrong, but Japanese Americans were and are loyal Americans."[16] More than another decade passed, however, before Congress finally approved twenty thousand dollars in reparations payments to each of the sixty thousand internees still alive in 1988, after protracted lobbying by the Japanese American Citizens league. Two more years would pass before President Bush dispatched letters with the twenty-thousand-dollar checks, acknowledging: "A monetary sum and words alone cannot restore lost years or erase painful memories. . . . We can never fully right the wrongs of the past. But . . . in enacting a law calling for restitution and offering a sincere apology, your fellow Americans have, in a very real sense, renewed their traditional commitment to the ideals of freedom, equality, and justice."[17]

- President George H. W. Bush's 1991 address on the fiftieth anniversary of Pearl Harbor, as he spoke to an audience largely of Pearl Harbor survivors and their families: "I have no rancor in my heart toward Germany or Japan. . . . This is no time for recrimination. World War II is over. It is history. We won. . . . We reached out, both in Europe and in Asia, and made our enemies our friends. We healed their wounds and, in the process, we lifted ourselves up."[18]

WHAT IF REPENTANCE HAD BEEN ENACTED?

The eminent historian Gordon Craig remarks that "the duty of the historian is to restore to the past the options it once had."[19] Rejected here is the notion that the past comes down to us as mere "happenings" rather than the results of decisions made by human beings facing both constraints and alternatives in how they behave. On a similar track, John Paul Lederach, longtime student of human conflicts, pleads for more leeway for the role of *imagination* in the search for ethical alternatives to violence. This suggests an important discipline for all of us who believe that the future does not have to imitate the mistakes of the past: the past itself could have been different.[20]

This study concludes, then, with a "what if" case study. What if acts or signs of repentance had been forthcoming in a severe foreign-policy crisis in 1980 that virtually destroyed a presidency and thereby contributed to a perilous breakdown in U.S.-Soviet-Iranian relations and nuclear diplomacy? This case remains controversial in participants' memories, including that of one of us, Alan Geyer, who was recruited to assist in its hoped-for resolution.

The context was the U.S. hostage crisis in Iran, which lasted 444 days from November 4, 1979, until inauguration day 1981. In February 1980, there was an unpublicized effort to signal a penitent U.S. attitude as a step to facilitate the release of the sixty-three U.S. hostages. The effort eventually failed, not because of intransigence in Iran but because of White House rejection and bureaucratic resistance within the churches. Yet many elements of potential success were present and, if allowed to be put into action, might have had profound effects not only in U.S.-Iranian relations but in presidential politics and across the entire agenda of both domestic and foreign policy.

Throughout 1980, Jimmy Carter's presidency was traumatized and increasingly enfeebled by apparent American impotence in the face of the captivity of the Americans in Tehran. However, within weeks of the militant Muslim students' seizure of the U.S. embassy, there were intimations that they wanted a face-saving way out of their unanticipated difficulties in managing prolonged belligerent operations. But the militants clearly saw themselves as defenders of a nationalist revolution, which, first, had been overthrown by a U.S.-engineered coup in 1953 and, second, had been brutally repressed by the corrupt tyranny of the Shah, whose military and secret police were regarded as extensions of American power.

An American Methodist leader, John P. Adams, was on temporary service in Tehran to help facilitate a mail-exchange project for the hostages, a project led by John Thomas of the International Indian Treaty Council. Adams, a resourceful specialist in conflict resolution employed by the United Methodist Board of Church and Society, sent word to Geyer from Tehran that the militants would probably respond favorably to a high-level (preferably presidential) U.S. acknowledgement of the legitimacy of Iranian grievances. Preparation for such a statement might include expressions of repentance by American churches. The Adams initiative was strongly backed by the United Methodist Bishop of Washington, James K. Mathews.

Adam's presence in Iran was cut short by apprehensive Methodist board members in Washington and by the advice of UN Secretary

General Kurt Waldheim to the National Council of Churches that nongovernmental efforts might hamper UN negotiations. (Waldheim's personal diplomacy in this case ended with a highly publicized, hapless trip to Tehran, from which he hastily departed.) A denomination staff colleague of Adams opposed his initiative, citing a recent passage from denominational editor Arthur Moore, who had taken the "realist" line that repentance was inappropriate for a government. Moore insisted: "We should always be re-examining the results of our foreign policies whether they turn out well or ill, but to call such an examination national repentance is extremely poor theology. . . . The concept of *metanoia* [repentance], of turning about, rightly applies only to religiously committed individuals, as it does in the New Testament. It is a religious, not a secular, experience."[21]

However, Adams and Geyer had received alternative counsel from two veteran professionals in the field of conflict resolution, Roger Fisher of Harvard Law School and James Laue of a conciliation center in St. Louis. Their advice was precisely that an unofficial channel might be just the key to ending the crisis, and they doubted Waldheim's capacity to do so. Their advice was seconded by a former U.S. delegate to the United Nations. Here glimmered the practical importance of negotiations that diplomat Joseph Montville would one day label "Track Two." Informal and largely unpublicized, such negotiations can sometimes lead to understandings and strategies that governments may not be able to imagine or propose.

Accordingly, the Adams initiative proceeded on two tracks. At the request of Bishop Ralph T. Alton, president of the United Methodist Council of Bishops, and Bishop Mathews, Council secretary, Ash Wednesday, February 20, 1980, was widely observed as "a day of repentance and intercession" for the United States and Iran. A background paper on U.S.-Iranian relations was prepared to be distributed at Ash Wednesday services and throughout the churches. That piece concluded: "Our deepest concern for the welfare and release of American hostages, as well as for the principle of diplomatic immunity, is not likely to find effective expression unless and until those Iranian grievances are better recognized and understood."[22]

But the prospect for success of this unofficial initiative ultimately depended upon official words from the U.S. government. Meanwhile, the Iranian government was also publicly seeking a signal of contrition as a catalyst to end the crisis. On January 29, 1980, the Iranian ambassador to the United Nations, Mansour Farhang, had urged President Carter to say something like this: "Yes, we made some policies in Iran that were not in the interest of the Iranian people. . . . We want to change that perspective, and we are sorry for the mistakes or misperceptions or the wrongness of the past."[23]

"A Proposal for a Presidential Statement on U.S.-Iranian Relations" was drafted in consultation with Fisher, Laue, and Bishop Mathews and also with Congressional leadership and interested officials of the State Department. The majority leader of the House of Representatives forwarded it to the White House with his endorsement. That draft statement said, in part:

> We are eager to restore our friendship with the Iranian people. We know that grievances on both sides must now be heard. As Americans, we cannot accept the seizing of hostages as an act of social justice, whatever the record of wrongs in years past. . . . Wherever our own policies may have given offense, even when their purpose has been our mutual peace and security, we shall seek to understand and rectify.[24]

No such statement was ever made by President Carter or any U.S. official. When Carter was asked at a press conference whether some acknowledgment of the U.S. role in overthrowing the nationalist government in 1953 might help resolve the crises, he dismissed the reference as "ancient history." On the Iranian side, however, it was anything but ancient history. To them, the wisdom of William Faulkner was only too relevant: "The past is not dead and gone; it isn't even past." The weeks went by. Carter was under mounting pressure to do something forceful to save the hostages. On April 24, 1980, an ill-conceived and ill-fated military rescue effort ended at Desert One south of Tehran. The effort was abandoned after mechanical failures and the deaths of eight Americans, with five more wounded and with good reason to fear discovery by Iranian personnel. As all the months of that national election year passed, President Carter seemed increasingly powerless to cope with either Iran or double-digit inflation. His presidency was overwhelmingly repudiated in the Reagan electoral vote landslide, 489 to 49. When the hostages were finally released on Reagan's inauguration day, Carter's humiliation was compounded. Yet the defeated president was justifiably commended for his protracted restraint in favor of negotiations—that is, after the disaster at Desert One.

As it happened, the 1980 election led to momentous changes in American politics, both domestic and foreign policy, and the public role of the churches. The Iranian hostage crisis offered one of the more important "what if" moments in the late twentieth century. Now there is no way to know whether words of repentance and forgiveness might have made all the difference—but history shows time and again that the lack of such expressions merely sows the seeds of future conflicts. A notorious illustration is the Versailles Treaty of 1919, when allied thirst for vengeance against Germany laid the foundations of Hitler's subsequent popularity with aggrieved Germans.

Among other "what if" cases has to be that of the atomic bombing of Hiroshima and Nagasaki. What if such a bomb had been dropped on an island military installation off the coast of Japan as a demonstration to its government that the power it now faced was overwhelming? Most modern Japanese scholars believe that by 1945 Japan was already virtually defeated. Even today, the popular feeling in Japan is that the atomic devastation of two cities was unnecessary for ending the war.

The 1962 Soviet-American crisis over missiles stationed in Cuba is a positive, historically momentous "what if" case: What if John F. Kennedy and Nikita Krushchev had yielded to the advice of many of their military leaders that an all-out nuclear war was worth risking? In the midst of the crisis, Kennedy emerged from a military conference with the troubled reflection, " I wonder if those men know that we are dealing with the deaths of millions?" Had nuclear war been adopted in 1962 instead of the patient, restrained negotiations finally carried on between the two national leaders, human history right now would be different. Some of us would not be alive to write these paragraphs. Shakespeare's words, in the mouth of Hotspur, an aggressive soldier, apply to the Cuba Missile Crisis: "Out of this nettle, danger, we pluck this flower, safety."[25] Millions of Americans, Russians, and Cubans can be thankful for the stewardship of their lives undertaken by leaders on both sides of this event. The greatest responsibility of the politician is not for making war but for making peace. And peace, in every conflict, must emerge from all sides as they listen, respect, and seek the good of each other.

PART TWO

justice

Five

ADVANCE DEMOCRACY, HUMAN RIGHTS, AND INTERDEPENDENCE

Bruce Russett

As World War II drew to a close, leaders of the great powers drew up a set of documents, including the Charter of the United Nations and the foundations for the Bretton Woods financial institutions. The inspiration for these documents stemmed primarily from the democracies, notably the United Kingdom and the United States. They were determined to do what they could to avoid repeating the causes of World Wars I and II. To do so, they created new international institutions that would potentially have the military means to restrain aggressors. But more than military strength was at issue, and the new structure for international relations encompassed much more. It promoted trade, economic assistance, and foreign investment, both as direct means to prosperity and indirect means to a peace resting on prosperity and economic interdependence. It also promoted democracy and human rights as expressed in the Universal Declaration of Human Rights and advocated by instruments of cultural influence like the U.S. Information Agency and the BBC. A key feature was that it was not a unilateralist policy, but multilateralist. Its multilateral instruments ranged far beyond NATO and the rest of the alliance system to depend heavily on regional trade arrangements like the OECD, the World Bank, the IMF, GATT, and many UN specialized agencies. Central UN institutions were also vital.

Initially, the hope was that the Soviet Union would be fully inside this structure. But the rise of the Cold War meant that some of the institutions were ineffective and many operated without the active participation of the Soviet Union. Thus, it was only in part a fully global structure and, in important ways, principally a structure for managing and strengthening relations among the Western allies. For that purpose, on the whole, it worked well. More recently, the end of the Cold War provided an opportunity to broaden the earlier structure to encompass a much larger proportion of the earth.

Contemporary policy formulation needs a similar central organizing principle. To promote its acceptance, that principle would be best rooted in the earlier experience. It should build on the tripod of principles that underlay the rhetoric and much of the practice—principles rooted in beliefs about the success of free political and economic systems. The first of these principles is democracy and institutionalized respect for human rights. The second (now buttressed by increasing evidence that economic interdependence promotes peace as well as prosperity) is interdependent markets. The third is international law and organization. These ideas remain as strong as ever.

Consider a puzzle about the end of the Cold War. The question is not simply why did the Cold War end, but rather, why did it end before the drastic change in the bipolar distribution of power, and why did it end peacefully? In November 1988, Margaret Thatcher proclaimed, as did other Europeans, that "the Cold War is over." By spring 1989, the U.S. State Department stopped making official reference to the Soviet Union as the enemy. The fundamental patterns of East–West behavior had changed, on both sides, beginning even before the circumvention of the Berlin Wall and then its destruction in October 1989. All of this preceded the unification of Germany (October 1990) and the dissolution of the Warsaw Pact (July 1991). Even after these latter events, the military power of the Soviet Union itself remained intact until the dissolution of the USSR at the end of December 1991. None of these events was resisted militarily.

Any understanding of the change in the Soviet Union's international behavior before its political fragmentation, and in time reciprocated by the West, demands attention to the operation of the three principles.

1. Substantial political liberalization and movement toward democracy (*perestroika* and *glasnost*) in the Soviet Union, with consequent improvements in free expression and the treatment of dissidents at

home, in the East European satellites, and in behavior toward Western Europe and the United States.

2. The desire for economic interdependence with the West, impelled by the impending collapse of the Soviet economy and the consequent perceived need for access to Western markets, goods, technology, and capital, which in turn required a change in Soviet military and diplomatic policy.

3. The influence of international law and organizations, as manifested in the Conference on Security and Cooperation in Europe (CSCE) and the human rights based on the Helsinki accords and their legitimation and support of dissent in the communist states. Whereas the United Nations itself was not important in this process of penetrating domestic politics, the CSCE as an international organization most certainly was, as were the many citizens' groups and international nongovernmental organizations devoted to human rights.

A vision of a peace among democratically governed states has long been invoked as part of a larger structure of institutions and practices to promote peace among nation-states. In 1795 Immanuel Kant spoke of the possibility of perpetual peace based partially upon states sharing "republican constitutions." His meaning was compatible with basic contemporary understandings of democracy. As the elements of such a constitution he identified freedom, with legal equality of subjects, representative government, and separation of powers. The other key elements of his perpetual peace were "cosmopolitan law," embodying ties of international commerce and free trade, and a "pacific union," a confederation established by treaty in international law among sovereign republics.

By the twentieth century, some progress had been made in actualizing these principles. Woodrow Wilson expressed the vision forcefully. In his famous Fourteen Points, he did not explicitly invoke the need for universal democracy, since not all of America's war allies were democratic. But his meaning is clear if one considers the domestic political conditions necessary for his first point: "Open covenants of peace, openly arrived at, after which there shall be no private international understandings of any kind but diplomacy shall proceed always frankly and in the public view." Point three demanded "removal, so far as possible, of all economic barriers and the establishment of an equality of trade conditions among all the nations consenting to the peace and associating themselves for its maintenance." The fourteenth point was "A general association of nations must be formed under specific covenants for the purpose of affording mutual guarantees of political independence and territorial integrity to great and small states alike."

The Wilsonian application of this vision failed, but later in the twentieth century it was picked up again. Konrad Adenauer, Jean Monnet, and other founders of the European Coal and Steel Community (now the European Union) sought some way to ensure that the great powers, who had repeatedly fought dreadful wars over the previous century, would finally live in peace with each other. To do so, they supported restored democratic institutions and protections for human rights in their countries, built a network of economic interdependence to make war unthinkable on cost/benefit grounds, and embedded their relationships in new structures of European organization.

DEMOCRACIES RARELY FIGHT ONE ANOTHER

The following discussion will necessarily be merely an overview with references to detailed research. I will discuss evidence supporting all three elements of this vision here, although I focus more on democratization than on the other two elements. That is also appropriate because the most extensive and elaborated evidence is for the proposition that democracies do not make war on each other. Much of it is addressed in my first book on this topic, although far more has accumulated since then.[1] In the contemporary era, "democracy" denotes a country in which nearly everyone can vote, elections are freely contested, the chief executive is chosen by popular vote or by an elected parliament, and civil rights and civil liberties are substantially guaranteed. Democracies may not be especially peaceful in general (we all know the history of democracies in colonialism, covert intervention, and other excesses of power). Democracies may be involved in as much violence—often but not always in self-defense—with some authoritarian states, as are authoritarian states toward each other. But the relations between stable democracies are qualitatively different.

Democracies are unlikely to engage in militarized disputes with each other or to let any such disputes escalate into war. In fact, they rarely even skirmish. Over the years since 1885 democratic states have been far less likely to use or even threaten to use military force against each other than against dictatorships, or than dictatorships against each other. Established democracies fought no wars against one another during the entire twentieth century. (Although Finland, for example, took the Axis side against the Soviet Union in World War II, it engaged in no combat with the democracies.)

The more democratic the states are, the more peaceful their relations are likely to be. In their disputes with each other, democracies are more likely to employ democratic means of peaceful conflict resolution. They are readier to reciprocate each other's behavior, to accept third-party mediation or good offices in settling disputes, and to accept binding third-party settlement. Democracies' relatively peaceful relations toward each other are not spuriously caused by some other influence such as sharing high levels of wealth, or rapid growth, or ties of alliance, as has been established by statistical analyses of the behavior of pairs of states in the international system. Pairs of states that are democratic are more peaceful than others, even controlling for these influences. The peace between democracies is not limited just to the rich industrialized states of the global North. It was not maintained simply by pressure from a common adversary in the Cold War, and it has outlasted that threat.

The phenomenon of democratic peace may be explained by the pervasiveness of normative restraints on conflict between democracies. That explanation extends to the international arena the cultural norms of live-and-let-live and peaceful conflict resolution that operate within democracies. The phenomenon of democratic peace can also be explained by the role of institutional restraints on democracies' decisions to go to war. Democratic institutions help hold democratic leaders accountable to their people, so a leader who starts a war that imposes great monetary or human costs on the voters is likely to be thrown out at the next election. So presumably democratic leaders choose their fights carefully. The leaders of two democracies, knowing each others' incentives to choose carefully, will be reluctant to get into war with each other. A dictator, on the other hand, has the opportunity to enrich self and cronies by a successful war and runs less risk of being overthrown in a losing fight by being able to forcefully suppress popular opposition.[2]

Nonindustrial societies, studied by anthropologists, also show restraints on warfare among democratically organized polities that typically lack the institutional constraints of a modern state. Despite that ab-

120

sence, democratically organized units fight each other significantly less often than do nondemocratic units. And political stability also proves an important restraint on the resort to violence by these democratically organized units. Finding the relationship between democracy and peace in preindustrial societies shows that the phenomenon of democratic peace can extend far beyond contemporary Western democracies.

The end of Cold War ideological hostility was particularly significant because it represented a surrender to the force of values of economic and especially political freedom. To the degree that countries once ruled by autocratic systems become democratic, the absence of war among democracies comes to bear on any discussion of the future of international relations. By this reasoning, the more democracies there are in the world, the fewer potential adversaries we and other democracies will have and the wider the zone of peace.

The possibility of a widespread zone of democratic peace in the contemporary world exists. To bring that possibility to fruition, several fundamental problems must be addressed: the problem of consolidating democratic stability, the interaction of democracy with nationalism, the role of economic development and interdependence, and the prospects for changing basic patterns of international behavior.

STRENGTHENING DEMOCRACY AND ITS NORMS

The literature on the conditions under which democracy can develop and flourish is vast. Most but by no means all of the influences on the successful consolidation of democratic transitions are largely domestic, within states. Some of the international influences, along with the domestic ones, can have a great effect.

Among the international influences that played significant parts in producing the latest wave of recent transitions to democracy, Samuel Huntington notes changes in some religious institutions (including transnational ones) that made them less defenders of the status quo than opponents of governmental authoritarianism; a more activist policy by states, international organizations, and nongovernmental agents to promote human rights and democracy; and snowballing or demonstration effects, enhanced by international communication, as transitions to democracy in some states served as models for their neighbors.[3] Among his list of conditions that favor the consolidation of new democracies is a favorable international political environment, with outside assistance. While internal influences are certainly prominent, the international conditions are impressive also. Favorable international conditions may not be essential in every case, but they can make a difference, and sometimes a crucial one, when the internal influences are mixed.

Citizens' groups and nongovernmental organizations have often been vital to this process. For example, in the Helsinki negotiations, human-rights organizations prodded Western governments to insist on the human-rights plank. The resulting agreement put a strong lever in the hands of many different movements in Central Europe and the Soviet Union, which pushed for actualization of the guarantees that had been officially endorsed. The Solidarity movement in Poland, the nonviolent "revolution of the candles" in East German churches, the Czechoslovakian human-rights movement led by Vaclav Havel—all were human-rights movements that added pressure for democracy. They were, in turn, part of a larger international movement for human rights and democracy that changed almost all the military dictatorships in Latin America into various stages of democratization. Their efforts were echoed with substantial success in South Korea, Taiwan, and South Africa. The indigenous movements were aided by a shift in U.S. government policy, beginning with the Carter administration, to monitor human-rights performance and require governments to show progress in observing those rights as a condition of economic assistance. They also drew on transnational support from churches, groups like Amnesty International, labor movements, cultural leaders, the influence of the U.S. civil rights movement, and the impetus for human rights reflected in the international conventions adopted on various human-rights and nongovernmental organizations' participation in UN conferences.

The culture of human-rights organizations and their allies requires a network of persons who are ready to serve as independent and articulate reporters of abuses perpetrated by governments and who have confidence in others' reports. They must be ready to engage in protests and collaborative action; to spend considerable amounts of time, energy, and money to gain public attention for their protests and for the people they are trying to protect; and to incur the risk of retaliation by their governments. Human-rights organizations require from their members compassion for the victims and toughness in the face of the practices relied on by governments and groups that routinely violate human rights.

With economic conditions still grim in much of the developing world and in some former communist countries, and the consequent dangers to the legitimacy of new democratic governments, external assistance is especially important. New democracies will not survive without some material improvement in their citizens' lives. As a stick, aid can surely be denied to governments that regularly violate human rights, for example, of ethnic minorities. Clear antidemocratic acts, such as a military coup or an aborted election, can be punished by suspending aid. As to the carrot of extending aid on a conditional basis, broader goals of developing democratic institutions require creation of a civil society and are less easily made conditional. The aid may come from a particular foreign government, or from the European Union or an international organization. Recipients may see multilateral aid, with conditions of democratic reform attached, as a less blatant invasion of their sovereignty than aid from a single country.

ETHNIC CONFLICT AND THE HUMAN RIGHT
TO CULTURAL EXPRESSION

A special complication, hardly unique to the current era but felt acutely now, is ethnic conflict. With its lines of inclusion and exclusion, nationalism readily conflicts with the quasi-universalistic ethos of "democracies don't fight each other." Hatreds, long suppressed, emerge to bedevil any effort to build stable, legitimate government. An irony is that the initial creation of democratic institutions can contribute to the explosion of ethnic conflicts by providing the means of free expression, including expression of hatred and feelings of oppression.

Even if stable and established democracies are generally at peace with one another, the process of democratization is not always a peaceful one. A country struggling toward democracy but still only part way in transition from dictatorship may be unstable and may face fierce problems of restructuring its economy and satisfying diverse interests and ethnic groups. Under these perhaps temporary circumstances, nationalism and domestic problems may sometimes lead to conflicts with neighboring states. Nearby autocracies may attack such a state because they see its shift to democracy as endangering the legitimacy of authoritarianism, or its period of transition as a moment of potential weakness to be exploited. But, importantly, only those democracies that have autocratic states as neighbors are likely to get into military conflicts. One piece of good news is that democratizing states from the former Warsaw Pact have been substantially peaceful with democratic or democratizing neighbors. Furthermore, liberalizing transitions from dictatorship or autocracy toward democracy are no more dangerous to international peace than are failed liberalizing efforts that revert to autocratic rule. The problem is one of incomplete democratization, not of new democracies.[4]

Any solution does not lie in less democracy. Rather, it requires measures, including external assistance and protection, to assist and speed the transition. It also requires attention to devising institutions, and nurturing norms and practices, with respect for minority rights. Minority rights are rightly thought of largely in terms of the rights of ethnic, racial, and linguistic minorities. More broadly, however, they reflect tension between the legitimate needs of the state to build common loyalties to a nation versus the basic rights of individuals and groups to the preservation and expression of cultural diversity. In this respect, rights to religious liberty, as specified in the UN Charter and the Universal Declaration of Human Rights, are central and often help define ethnic identity.

124

Current Western principles of religious liberty did not, of course, evolve quickly or easily even in the West. Catholics and Protestants learned painfully the costs of trying to impose their beliefs on each other, coming belatedly to see freedom of religion not merely as a matter of prudence but as an essential moral and ethical principle and peacemaking practice. That principle still is strained by some fundamentalist groups in democratic countries and is highly contested in countries not sharing the Western experience of difficult learning about democracy and religious liberty. The alternatives, however, may be either civil war and attempted secession of minorities or vigorous repression of them.

The creation of institutions, norms, and practices to protect minorities and human rights has never been easy. If incomplete democratization is temporarily a problem, the establishment of stable democracy is vital to the solution. But it presents the fundamental challenge of world political development in this era. It is worth remembering that the most terrible acts of genocide and state-sponsored mass murder in this century (from Turkey's slaughter of the Armenians through Hitler, Stalin, Pol Pot, and others) have been carried out by authoritarian or totalitarian governments, not democratic ones.[5]

ECONOMIC INTERDEPENDENCE AND
INTERNATIONAL ORGANIZATIONS

Ties of economic interdependence—international trade and investment—form an important supplement to shared democracy in promoting peace. Here is the second leg of the tripod for peace, representing the role of a high level of trade and commercial exchange.
Economic interdependence gives countries a stake in one another's
well-being. War would mean destruction, in the other country, of one's
own markets, industrial plants, and sources of imports. If my investments are in your country, bombing your industry means, in effect,
bombing my own factories. Just the threat of war inhibits international
trade and investment. Economic interdependence also serves as a
channel of information about one another's perspectives, interests, and
desires on a broad range of matters not the subject of the economic exchange. These communications form an important channel for conflict management. Interdependence, however, is the key word—mutual dependence, not one-sided dominance of the weak by the strong.

The expansion of interdependence over the past century has importantly contributed—above and beyond the influence of joint
democracy, wealth, and alliances—to reducing conflict among states
so linked. When countries' trade with each other constitutes a substantial portion of their national incomes, violent conflict and war between them are rare. Democracies trade more with one another than
with nondemocratic countries. The combination of democracy and
interdependence is especially powerful. States that are both democratic and economically interdependent are extremely unlikely to initiate serious military disputes with one another.

New democracies and freer markets should be supported finan-
cially, politically, and morally. Successful transitions in some countries
can supply a model for others. A stable and less menacing international system can permit the emergence and consolidation of democratic governments and peaceful economic growth and interchange.
International threats—real or only perceived—strengthen the forces
of secrecy, authoritarianism, and autarky in the domestic politics of
states involved in protracted conflict. Relaxation of international
threats to peace and security reduces the need and the excuse for repressing dissent and centralizing control of the economy.

Reliance on international law and institutions, and the need for
strengthening them, constitutes the third element of this structure for

peace. As expressed in former UN Secretary General Boutros-Ghali's *An Agenda for Peace,*[6] the United Nations has a new mission of peace-building, attending to democratization, development, and the protection of human rights. It is newly strengthened and, paradoxically, also newly and enormously burdened.

International organizations, like other institutions, may serve a variety of functions. Their occasional role in coercing norm-breakers (for example, by the Security Council) is only one. In addition, they may mediate among conflicting parties, reduce uncertainty in negotiations by conveying information, expand material self-interest to be more inclusive and longer term, shape norms, and help generate narratives of mutual identification among peoples and states. Some organizations are more successful than others, and in different functions. But overall, as Michael Smith will demonstrate in chapter 8, they do make a difference.

An extension of the quantitative empirical analyses referred to above makes the point. The same kind of analysis that first established an independent and significant influence of democracy in reducing conflict among countries, and then added evidence for an additional meliorative influence of economic interdependence, has been carried out on the effect of international organizations. We have collected information on the number of intergovernmental organizations (IGOs) in which both of any pair of countries are members. This "density" of IGO membership varies from zero for some countries to over one hundred for some pairs of European states. Adding this information to the previous analysis, we find that it too contributes an additional, independent, statistically significant effect in reducing the probability of international conflict. The thicker the network, the fewer the militarized disputes.

Most important are those regional international organizations in which most of the member countries are democracies. Examples include the European Union, NATO, and the organization of American States in the western hemisphere. They can make continuing membership in their organizations contingent on remaining democratic and can act to reinforce democratic forces and democratic procedures, such as free elections, in their members and in countries that aspire to membership. They can also insist that aspirant members first settle any border disputes with other members, as the European Union did very effectively in central Europe.[7] These results represent good evidence for the third and final leg of the structure underlying peaceful international relations.

DEMOCRATIZATION AND THE ROLE OF INTERNATIONAL ORGANIZATIONS

Understanding that democracies rarely fight each other, and why, has great consequence for policy in the contemporary world. It should affect the kinds of military preparations believed to be necessary and the costs one would be willing to pay to make them. It should encourage peaceful efforts to assist the emergence and consolidation of democracy. But a misunderstanding of it could encourage war-making against authoritarian regimes and efforts to overturn them—with all the costly implications of preventive or hegemonic military activity that such a policy might imply.

The post–World War II success with defeated adversaries can be misleading if one forgets how expensive it was and especially if one misinterprets the political conditions of military defeat. The Allies utterly defeated the Axis coalition. Then, to solidify democratic government, they conducted vast (if incomplete) efforts to remove the former elites from positions of authority. The model of "fight them, beat them, and then make them democratic" is no model for contemporary action. It probably would not work anyway, and no one is prepared to make the kind of effort that would be required. Not all authoritarian states are inherently aggressive. Indeed, at any particular time, the majority are not. A militarized crusade for democracy is not in order.

External military intervention, even against the most odious dictators, is a dangerous way to try to produce a democratic world order. Sometimes, with a cautious cost-benefit analysis and with the certainty of substantial and legitimate internal support, it might be worthwhile—that is, under conditions when rapid military success is likely and the will of the people at issue is clear. Even so, any time an outside power supplants any existing government, the problem of legitimacy is paramount. The very democratic norms to be instilled may be compromised. At the least, intervention cannot be unilateral. It must be approved by an international body like the United Nations or a regional security organization.[8] When an election has been held under UN auspices and certified as fair—as happened in Haiti—the United Nations and its members have a special responsibility, even a duty, to see that the democratic government they helped create is not destroyed.

Under most circumstances, international bodies are better used as vehicles to promote democratic processes at times when the relevant domestic parties are ready. Peacekeeping operations to help provide the conditions for free elections, monitor those elections, and advise on the building of democratic institutions are usually far more promising and less costly for all concerned than is military intervention.

With the end of the Cold War, the United Nations experienced highly publicized troubles in Somalia and the former Yugoslavia as it tried to cope with a range of challenges not previously part of its mandate. Nonetheless, its successes, though receiving less attention, outnumber the failures. It emerged as a major facilitator of peaceful transitions and democratic elections in such places as Cambodia, El Salvador, Eritrea, and Namibia.[9] Its Electoral Assistance Unit has provided election monitoring, technical assistance, or other aid to electoral processes in more than sixty states.

128   Economic interdependence is also supported by international organizations, across the globe by the World Trade Organization and regionally by the European Union. Increasingly, economic development is seen as dependent on open markets for goods and capital. Without the network of regional and global institutions to promote liberalized and expanding trade, much of the world could readily slip back into protectionism and trade wars.

The demands of growth and equality are not always well reconciled. The IMF and the World Bank have often been rightly criticized for applying to their loan policies economic and fiscal criteria that neglect equity, political liberties, and the rights of minorities such as indigenous peoples. Recently, however, those institutions have given greater attention to criteria of political responsibility, transparency, and good governance (close synonyms for democracy), and have become instruments not just to create and strengthen interdependent markets but also to ease transitions to democracy and to rebuild societies shattered by civil war.

THE EMERGING ORDER

Democracy and international peace can feed on each other. An evolutionary process may even be at work. Because of the visible nature and public costs of breaking commitments, democratic leaders are better able to persuade leaders of other states that they will keep the agreements into which they do enter. Democratic states are able to signal their intentions in bargaining with greater credibility than are autocratic states. Democracies more often win their wars than do authoritarian states—80 percent of the time (remember that the coin-flip odds would be only 50-50). They are more prudent about what wars they get into, choosing wars that they are more likely to win and that will incur lower costs. With free speech and debate, they are more accurate and efficient information processors. Authoritarian governments that lose wars may be overthrown and replaced by democratic regimes, as was the Argentine junta after the Falklands/Malvinas war. States with competitive elections generally devote lower shares of their national products to military expenditures, which in relations with other democracies promotes cooperation; as democracies' politically relevant international environment becomes composed of more democratic and internally stable states, democracies tend to reduce their military allocations and conflict involvement.[10]

The modern international system is commonly traced to the Treaty of Westphalia and the principles of sovereignty and noninterference in internal affairs that it affirmed. That settlement affirmed the anarchy of the system, without a superior authority to ensure order. It also was a treaty among princes who ruled as autocrats. Our understanding of the modern anarchic state system risks conflating the effects of anarchy with those stemming from the political organization of its founding units. When most states are ruled autocratically, then playing by the rules of autocracy may be the only way for any state, democracy or not, to survive.

But the increasing if uneven spread of democracy over the past two centuries, along with the slow emergence of new international norms and institutions, now presents an opening for change in the international system more fundamental even than at the end of other big wars—World Wars I and II and the Napoleonic Wars. For the first time ever, in 1992 a virtual majority of states (91 of 183) approximated the standards for democracy that I employed earlier. Another 35 were in some form of transition to democracy. Democracy was not consolidated in all these states, but further transitions to democracy in others have occurred, and overall the number of democratic governments increased into the twenty-first century. Yet states probably can become democratic faster than they can become rich. Some autocratically governed states will surely remain in the system. In their relations with states where democracy is unstable or where democratization is not begun at all, democracies must continue to be vigilant and concerned with the need for military deterrence. But if enough states become stably democratic in coming decades, then among them we will have a chance to reconstruct the norms and rules of the international order. We already have come a long way from 1648.

In time, the current quasi-hegemony of the United States and its allies will fade, giving way to a more diffused distribution of global power. That diffusion will occur across some very different national cultures and experiences, in Asia, Latin America, the Middle East, and perhaps Africa. It could give rise to a highly fragmented, competitive, and dangerous international system or to one in which conflicts of interest can be managed without an excessive frequency and severity of violence. In order for the less fragmented and less violent system to emerge, agreements to disagree peacefully and protections for minority needs and cultural distinctiveness—centrally associated with concepts of democracy—will have to be built into the structures of nation-states and into relations between states. Those relations will need to be further buttressed by linkages of economic interdependence and mediated by international and perhaps supranational institutions. Wide implementation of this vision offers the opportunity to manage global power changes in constructive fashion. Its elements have the ability to feed on one another in a dynamic system of reinforcing virtuous circles. Just as democracy, interdependence, and international organizations support peace, each in turn is supported by peace, and they support one another.

This vision can be and has been held by government leaders. But to achieve it in practice, among diverse countries and peoples, requires constant effort by individual citizens and by private national and transnational organizations as well as by governments. The sacrifices needed to support democracy at home and elsewhere, to share the costs of global economic interdependence, and to strengthen international organizations, must constantly be renewed. These elements can be lost, as they were in the 1930s. A placard on the wall of one of my colleagues' offices warns, "Every good thing has to be rewon each day."

These practices may well be the only alternative to disaster. The extreme "realist" precept to treat all states as potential enemies is untenable. Worse, in Michael J. Smith's words, "To treat all politics as inexpiable struggle is to propound a self-fulfilling prophecy.[11] I would go further. Except as a self-fulfilling prophecy, it is empirically erroneous. It is therefore a poor guide to practical action, and it is also therefore immoral. While we always acknowledge that some states remain outside the system of peace and thus are dangerous, we must recognize that many, while remaining self-interested actors, nonetheless can be stable and reliable partners in cooperation. That's not "idealism"; that's life.

Six

FOSTER JUST AND SUSTAINABLE ECONOMIC DEVELOPMENT

David Bronkema
David Lumsdaine
Rodger A. Payne[1]

Sustainable development is crucial for making and maintaining a just peace. "Sustainable Development" conjures up a picture of continual, yet environmentally friendly, increases in material welfare that are locally generated and controlled. Yet we should be careful when we invoke such hopes: Processes of economic and social change and aspirations to improve standards of living in poor countries and regions are complex, and catchwords that embody aspirations can often prove misleading.

WHAT IS SUSTAINABLE DEVELOPMENT?

As anybody with experience at the local level can attest, the poor, while working hard to better their lot themselves, also clamor for "development" projects from the state and from international agencies.[2] Yet well-intended development schemes have often worked out badly, frequently by failing to heed local insights and needs. Useless or destructive projects often have been undertaken on expert advice against the protests of ordinary people. Wholesome "development," then, might best be defined as "processes of change in peoples' relationships to their environment that increase their well-being, standards of living, or quality of life."[3] Increasing material welfare means changes in relationships, and working with people to help improve their material situations involves a relationship that can draw those involved together into a kind of community working toward a common goal.[4]

The Idea of Development

The words "sustainable development" have been used in many ways. "Development" generally describes a process of material and social progress; this usually leads to wider involvement in the world economy and cultural adaptation to modern world customs. Some criticize development generally as an imposition of "modern" standards and values on non-Western countries. But in poorer, Southern countries, many people live in abject poverty, lacking adequate food, shelter, medical care and clean water; and evidence suggests that this poverty most affects women, children, and all with meager political and economic power. We may not ignore the urgent, unmet, basic human needs of the earth's many peoples. Desires for material development are more than the imposition of an outside, Western standard: People in such circumstances, in almost all cultures, consistently try to become more economically prosperous; others want to try to help them; and both parties refer to this as "development."[5]

Development should not be understood, however, primarily as material accumulation, or as acquisition of the equivalent in skills ("human capital"), though those goals may often be important. Rather, at base, this aim should be thought of literally as *development*, the growth and flourishing, the cultivation, of the human person. Such human development is both the ultimate purpose and the practical foundation of other development objectives. Those concerned about modernization make an important point. Our age characteristically and easily presumes that "modern," more affluent (often American or Western) ways are the best, or the only good and acceptable ones, even though explicitly it believes the very opposite; and it tends to assume implicitly, too, that increasing material wealth and pleasure is life's chief purpose. Development needs to be concerned with building up and cultivating human persons and communities as wholes. Preserving the past and local culture and stability, limiting desires, and respecting ancient ways are not just important ends to be balanced against the ends of development (though balancing may be needed) but vital sources and constituents of human virtue, growth, and satisfaction—that is, of development.

The Idea of Sustainability

The term "sustainable" was early used to indicate people being able to improve their material welfare on their own steam and subject to their control; the term is still frequently used this way.[6] As the poor, with some help, obtain the ability to make use of local resources and local, regional, national, and international institutions in ways they weren't able to before, they are able to sustain their economic development in this first sense.

The term "sustainable" has also taken a second, "green" sense, especially since the 1987 report of the World Commission on Environment and Development (also known as the Brundtland Commission). This report, *Our Common Future*, emphasizes the need for development to include protecting the environment and natural resources for future generations.[7] Preventing economic activity from irrevocably sullying the environment is, in any case, a necessary part of living in peace, in harmony with the world of nature, and is part of the biblical mandate to "tend and dress" the land we have been given. Sustainability in either sense—enabling the poor to earn a better livelihood or meeting today's needs without threatening the needs of tomorrow—entails significant changes in the economic activities as ordinarily undertaken by individuals, transnational corporations, and nation-states. In sum, those whose needs are currently met should regulate their resource use so as to prevent exhaustion or other threats to current or future resource availability; while those who do not have adequate material and economic resources must somehow gain access to them.

These two senses are often related. Ecological destruction often threatens poor people's basic needs; poor communities often have an interest in long-term, ecologically sustainable development; and in any case, both involve a humane commitment to permanence and human flourishing. Commitment to the sustained well-being of human beings everywhere, and of their local, regional, national, and global communities, is vital to justice and peace and to care of the earth. The capacity-building and ecological aspects of sustainable development hint at a third element: the place that politics, power, justice, and peace have in development.

Sustainable Development and a Just Peace

Sustainable development is integral to making peace and to maintaining justice for several reasons. First, peace is not only an absence of war, violence, and hostility; it is also a state of reconciliation, human flourishing, and natural beauty. Severe privation and want require our response. A world in which many are trapped in dire poverty while others have abundance or in which nature is destroyed unnecessarily crushes the spirit and offends justice. Active concern for those in need and for the environment is, simply in itself, a part of living in peace. Further, developing human powers and capacities, allowing people to exercise their gifts and talents, and doing useful work and improving our surroundings are a part of any just order. Thus, sustaining, community-building, useful livelihoods are, by definition, part of a just order. A just order is organized to favor making useful and beautiful, well-made, and long-lasting goods rather than meretricious, shoddy, short-lived ones.

Second, human need and the absence of a chance to earn a useful livelihood, if unaddressed, lead to despair, societal disorder, and even war. An unjust order violates the proper patterns of human life and can erupt in open violence, especially as people find their lives futile or deteriorating.[8] Similarly, economic development that is not ecologically sustainable will cause unexpectedly worsening patterns of human life that may well lead to violence in the long run. Again, a process of sustainable development will enable people of all sectors of society to participate in governing themselves more fully than many of them are now able to do. Sustaining a just order, besides its intrinsic value, is therefore a crucial foundation for peace and justice.

135

Third, the absence of sustainable development, and impediments to it, are often bitter fruits of human greed, sin, violence, and injustice. That is, lack of sustainable development may be a result as well as a source of an absence of justice and peace. An inability to earn proper livelihoods in useful work often arises from ongoing abuses of power, perhaps even from open violence. Working for justice—including securing property rights—for peoples unable to defend themselves can be a prerequisite of their gaining opportunities for productive work and sustainable development. War and violence, too, are major causes of environmental deterioration and of people's losing control over their own lives and communities. Thus, sustainable development is also a result or fruit of justice and peace.

Thus, in sum, justice and peace are closely bound together with sustainable development. Basic development goals—providing all people with access to resources and opportunities necessary to full human flourishing, and protecting the rights of weaker people who may face opposition as they try to escape situations of dependence and poverty—are also central elements of a just and peaceful order. The absence of peace and justice undermines development and sustainability, and vice versa; justice and peace tend to foster development and sustainability and vice versa; and both areas are inherently linked concepts, even apart from their many causal connections. Together, then, the words "just and sustainable development" highlight the several crucial pillars of ethically faithful social conservation and change: preserving nature and helping the needy—in relationship and community—to preserve their rights and attain a fruitful life.

THE RECORD OF DEVELOPMENT

Broad goals of sustainable development have, in principle, been widely embraced by many individuals, nongovernmental organizations (NGOs), and governments. For instance, they were embedded in the *Agenda 21* report of the United Nations Conference on Environment and Development, produced and accepted by a large gathering of countries and NGOs.[9] Sustainability understood in "green" terms can also be important because resource scarcity, ecological deterioration, and relative deprivation might contribute to violent conflict. Positively, peace embraces as well as depends on a wholesome and ecologically aware economic order that allows human flourishing and good working relationships.

136

How is sustainable development related to peace? Where do issues of justice come in? What can be learned from recent efforts to take the preservation of natural resources seriously? What can be learned from efforts at development? How can peacemakers be most effective?

In understanding the implications of sustainable economic development, it may help to distinguish two levels. "Microdevelopment" refers to efforts made by local people on their own behalf and that of their communities, and also to nongovernmental agencies and governments targeting small-scale efforts and the poor. "Macrodevelopment" refers to efforts by governments and international agencies to increase production or decrease poverty by broad national policies and projects. Such efforts often seek to increase a country's overall production of goods and services by linking to the system of global trade. But the global system is mostly fashioned by states and international businesses, which create the economic opportunities and barriers weaker actors face. Thus, these two levels are intertwined, and the interlinkages are important.

Microdevelopment

At the micro level, the most successful development assistance taking place locally in communities has been carried out by NGOs.[10] The successful and sustainable projects are those that respond directly to the material needs identified or "felt" by the people.[11] These projects can "listen" to people, incorporating indigenous knowledge about the environment instead of assuming that the outside experts can devise the solutions unaided. Particularly important for sustainability is forming organized groups in the community that can take charge and assume leadership of projects.[12] This contributes towards "ownership" of the project by the community and also builds up the capacity to increase problem-solving skills by pooling the physical and mental resources of the community in a coordinated way. Development at this level is a slow and painstaking process, requiring a long-term committed relationship with the community in order to encourage change in the multiple areas of income-generating projects, health, agriculture, and education. The Grameen Bank in Bangladesh is a well-known example of an agency employing such practices.

Even the best of agencies cannot be assured of success (however that may be defined), and the specter of "unintended consequences" rears its head often here as well. Cooptation of the projects by elites is not the only way things go awry. Often, the political consequences of the change that begins to happen—whether within the community itself or in its relationships with elites outside the community— can bring a quick halt to the process.[13]

Macrodevelopment

Explicit macrodevelopment approaches and policies are the province of the state and international assistance agencies. The history of macrodevelopment strategies since decolonization and independence of the Global South gives at best a mixed picture of governmental success as a vehicle for development.[14] Some developing nations, notably in East Asia, have grown rapidly by building a *dirigiste* economy (directed or guided by the central government); yet most others, especially the countries of Latin America and Africa, have fared poorly.

Differences in degrees of inequality may well be an important factor. In successful East Asian economies, especially Taiwan and South Korea, major land reforms occurred prior to the market opening and state protection of infant industries, and these countries have continued to have among the world's best (least uneven) patterns of income distributions.[15] This somewhat reduced the coercive and economic power of the local elites and gave the majority of the population access to productive resources, creating a thriving domestic market for goods produced by the national industries.

There are both theoretical and historical reasons to suppose that greater equality may promote human development and welfare, human rights, and democracy. For instance, one may argue historically that Thomas Jefferson's aim and accomplishment (wrongfully achieved, to be sure, at the expense of Native Americans and African slaves) of making citizens small farmers was an effective "land reform" for citizens, which led to a historically high wage share, many small property holders, economic growth, and more effective citizen democracy. Similarly, the U.S.-mandated reforms in Japan after World War II may have contributed to the success of that country as markets took off. Generally, historical evidence suggests that the formal conditions of markets and elections—the twin pillars of neoliberalism that have long constituted the "Washington consensus"—are difficult to institute and probably less important to vital and free development than widespread citizen participation in the economy, society, and politics.

138　As a matter of theory, if one assumes capital (including control of economic processes) is most efficient when mixed relatively equally with labor, then there is every reason to suppose that a relatively equal distribution of resources, as of political power, will utilize those resources most efficiently. Furthermore, insofar as a main mechanism of efficiency in markets and of good government is accountability, a wider distribution of economic and political assets works to balance power and thus to hold wielders of economic and political resources more accountable. Principles of provision for the poor, relationship, nonmaximization, land lying fallow, and preserving family and historic preservation of assets with relatively equal distribution may be found in the biblical Jubilee legislation (Lev. 25). In the Jubilee (fiftieth) Year, slaves were to be freed, land was to lie fallow so it could be renewed, and property that had been sold was to be returned to the original owner, so that the poor would not lose ownership permanently.

In Latin America, land reforms occurred in name only. Land tenure was very—perhaps increasingly—skewed, and most people had resources barely sufficient for living. Therefore, no strong internal market developed. Control over land often let power-brokers dominate state programs aimed at modernizing agriculture. They consolidated their excessive power, including illegal land acquisitions that poorer people were unable to resist or protest effectively. In Africa, state power and bureaucracies were often used to extract resources from poorer and weaker groups (as also occurred in Eastern Europe and the former Soviet Union). Rapid "privatization" can risk further consolidating these "kleptocratic" takings as the powerful take state holdings as their personal property without paying fair amounts.

The questionable history of macrodevelopment strategy also includes a variety of unpleasant consequences resulting from actions of international assistance agencies. The World Bank—arguably the most important and powerful development institution of the past few decades—has an extensive track record of financing large capital projects that have proven environmentally destructive, socially irresponsible, and economically unproductive.[16]

Finally, the open global trading system mostly rewards those wielding the greatest economic resources and power. This is true within countries as well as among countries. Over time, many Southern nations have developed crippling levels of foreign debt—a legacy of borrowing by previous governments for unproductive development projects, corruption, and precipitous drops in the prices of primary commodities, their main exports. The interest and principle payments on the debt drastically curtail the government funds available for social goods such as education, health, environment, and infrastructure. As a result, poorer countries have to depend on international finance and development agencies like the IMF and the World Bank to keep their economies afloat. Moreover, it means that the South must toe the line of the development strategies and focuses of the international finance and trade agencies, leaving these states with very little opportunity to devise and implement their own development strategies. They are required by the banks and the World Trade Organization (WTO) to open up their economies to foreign investment and capital, doing away with tariffs and other protectionist measures, curtailing their public sectors and expenditure, reducing government involvement in the economy, and promoting agricultural exports—all measures that go under the name of "structural adjustment" or "neoliberal programs." This strategy is designed to take advantage of the cheap labor of the South. Yet this "comparative advantage" is a meaningless one for long-term development in the global economy.

While the transnational companies that have set up assembly industries in the South have provided thousands of sorely needed jobs, it is not at all apparent that they will provide a solid and sustainable industrial base for the future. A reliance on cheap labor means few if any incentives to develop domestic industries that might eventually compete internationally, reinvest many of their profits, and produce sorely needed foreign exchange to take care of debt payments. It reduces the priority of developing a highly educated population, including scientists and engineers, crucial to developing domestic industries.[17]

In sum, the claims of "injustice" in the global economic system from the Global South revolve in large measure around the structure of debt that requires the South to transfer immense amounts of money each year to the North, forces it to open its economies to northern companies, and relegates it to being a source of cheap labor, limiting the development of its own economic base while allowing consumers in the North to enjoy cheap prices for their goods. The World Trade Organization is also responsible for injustice. While trade can foster development, the WTO agenda has been driven by transnational corporations and affluent countries that embrace neoliberal ideals with little concern for the needs of the peoples of the Global South.

140   There are strong indications that link the neoliberal model to an increase in poverty and polarization of income in Latin America, although there are variations among countries.[18] Each country has distinctive sets of circumstances and implements technical models in different ways. Therefore, given past experience, one should expect a variety of results. Macrodevelopment rarely works out in the way one expects.

What is most troublesome about all macrodevelopment approaches is the fact that the poor are rarely seen as productive agents, while the wealthy are treated as the privileged catalysts to economic growth. Returning to the cases of Taiwan and South Korea, the single most important common factor in their success was the land reforms that gave the poor access to resources and educational opportunities. This provided a solid base for the internal economy. Yet even in those cases, there were unexpected consequences. In both countries, rapid industrialization has led to serious problems of environmental destruction and pollution.

CONFLICT AND THE ENVIRONMENT

To highlight some of the most recent thinking on these problems, consider more carefully possible links between environmental and resource scarcities and conflict.[19] Presumably, states might be short of resources because of their pursuit of unsustainable economic practices. Even realists in international relations concede that states might use violence to assure access to vital raw materials. The 1991 Persian Gulf war, for example, was in large part a result of overarching conflicts about the control of oil. Additionally, the 1967 Middle East war was at least partially motivated by concerns over water resources, and water remains one of the most potentially conflictive problems in that area.[20] However, Thomas Homer-Dixon's wide review of the empirical data finds absolute scarcity the least significant cause of environment/resource conflicts.[21]

A more distressing potential source of conflict comes from a combination of local politics and power structures, ethnic diversity, population growth, and environmental distress. Wealthy landowners and skewed land tenure, along with a high population growth rate, have pushed peasants to the ecologically fragile and unproductive slopes of hills and mountains. This has led to insurgencies in many places, including the Philippines and Mexico, and to ethnic conflict in countries like India. For instance, poverty and social turmoil in Bangladesh, related to high population growth, flooding, and land scarcity, have led millions of people to flee to neighboring India, "trigger[ing] serious intergroup conflict" in the state of Assam.

Moreover, people impoverished by environmental calamities may become increasingly exasperated by their plight, leading to "deprivation conflicts," which result from the gap between actual and expected living conditions. This pattern may underlie recent insurgencies in devastated rural uplands in the Philippines and in Mexico. As wealthy landowners turned to cash crops requiring fewer workers, for instance, Filipino agricultural laborers and farmers were forced to less productive uplands or to urban shantytowns, resulting in a cycle of low food production, clearing of new lands (often by burning forested areas), and further land degradation.

Development itself might provoke conflict. A look at water resources in the Middle East suggests why former UN Secretary General Boutros Boutros-Ghali, serving earlier as an Egyptian minister of state, predicted that "the next war in the Middle East will be fought over water, not politics," and why Anwar Sadat said in 1979 that "the only matter that could take Egypt to war again is water." A number of central African states have announced plans to divert Nile waters in order to secure their own development. But, according to

Robert Engelman, vice president for Programs at the Worldwatch Institute, "there is . . . not enough water in the Nile basin for all these countries to develop the way they want."[22] Egypt, a downstream nation almost totally dependent on the Nile, could suffer serious water shortages as a consequence and has threatened to respond to such acts with violence. Similarly, Turkey has planned more than three dozen hydroelectric power stations and dams that would reduce the Euphrates River's downstream flow to Iraq and Syria, which has a rapidly growing population (2.4 percent annually) and few alternative supply options. Intermittent talks about water rights over the past forty years have not produced any lasting agreements (although there are a few limited bilateral agreements among the three nations). Thus, unsustainable and conflicting development plans may wreak havoc or even provoke violent conflict, perhaps exacerbated by conflict over the status of ever more independent Kurds along joint borders.

Similarly, the Jordan River is shared by Jordan, Syria, Israel, Lebanon, and the West Bank, all of which have vital needs for its water.[23] Jordan's rapidly growing population (2.4 percent per year) will likely face an absolute water shortage by 2025. Israel's steadily growing population (1.2 percent annually) has exceeded its sustainable annual water yield since the mid-1970s. Water tables are dropping in the West Bank, where one-third of Israel's water originates, and Palestinians have been allocated far less water than Israeli citizens.

Many fear that one or more of these disputes over water could lead to internal conflict or war. Yet these experiences from the Middle East are not unique: all over the world, environment and resource disputes hold the potential for igniting violent conflict.

DEVELOPMENT LESSONS AND PRINCIPLES

Based on historical experience with development and on ethical teaching, this section sets out some essential principles for attempts at peacemaking in the area of sustainable development:

- The focus of development is on the needs, dignity, and productivity of the poor.
- Efforts to assist development must be based on lasting relationships with poor communities.
- A relational approach also leads us to the national and international political side of development.

- Development must be sustainable, in being directed toward holistic, environmentally sound, balanced development.

- It must also be sustainable in giving the people and nations being helped effective control and ownership.

- Development efforts must take into account human fallibility: ignorance, lack of complete control, desire for power and wealth, and abuse.

The Poor

The focus of development on social and economic relationships emphasizes the importance of making provision for the weak, the defenseless, the needy, the poor. This challenge is to institutionalize access to immediate provisions, resources for long-term productivity, and just institutions that defend against possible oppression. We must see poorer people not as the hapless recipients of our generous concern or pity but as fully human, dignified, responsible persons, with much to contribute. Development efforts should focus on the dignity, insight, and energy of poorer people and the value of bringing these assets to common tasks of development rather than assuming any kind of superiority. At the same time, assisting the poor with immediate help and longer-term, institutionalized access to resources is the priority in development. Much experience and development thinking suggest that this is a practical, effective, long-term approach to development and growth as well as an approach that is most just.

Recognizing the worth, intrinsic value, and contributions of poorer people—quite apart from any (also important) questions of their rights and needs or of our obligations—is an important place to start in development. People know a great deal about their own lives and what is appropriate to their specific context, and their values and practices—whether rooted in universal principles or chosen customs—have much to teach us. They have a right to their choices and ways, and often these are wiser than plans imposed by others. Subsidiarity—leaving people to do as much as possible for themselves—is also in itself a part of their development of self and of skills and of their dignity.

With specific regard to economic activities, in general poor people are often highly productive when given the resources to be so. John Farrington and Anthony Bebbington note that in several countries in

Latin America the peasants produce up to 60 percent of the food consumed nationally with very limited resources. Joe Remenyi and Bill Taylor, in a study of creditworthiness of the poor in developing countries, show how the poor have astoundingly high repayment rates and use the credit productively.[24]

Some writers on development suggest that "cultural" factors make the poor generally unproductive or even focus on how bad habits—laziness, improvidence, drunkenness, ignorance—can impede development, casting some of the poor as the sole authors of their own troubles.[25] Yet the evidence tends to show the reverse: the ability and eagerness of most poor people to be very creative in finding and utilizing good opportunities. Indeed, simply to survive, most poor people must be strongly entrepreneurial, as much research has shown.[26] This is not to say, however, that the poor do not need or want to learn from others, even as others need to learn from them.[27]

Poorer people do, however, need significant transfers of material resources, in the context of thoughtful community relationship. Globally, foreign-assistance levels do not approach the stated goals for most affluent nations (0.7 percent of GNP for members of the Development Assistance Committee) and should be substantially increased, with most assistance channeled to projects involving the poor directly.

Relationships

Human beings are not isolated individuals. Facilitating and transforming relationships is at the heart of sustainable development. First, development requires attention not only to many basic material needs but also to how poor people can identify, manipulate, and create resources—including political, social, and cultural resources—in new ways. Forming long-lasting associations and organizations with particular development projects and efforts has often proved to be of utmost value toward this end. Second, development work is likely to be more effective and helpful where there is an attempt to foster community responsibility for, and ownership of, development projects. (Many times, in fact, one of the most difficult challenges faced in development efforts is to get a large number of people from the community involved.) Development is not just a matter of individuals prospering, but of a community working together. Material improvements depend upon human skills and cooperation; and just, balanced, sustained local cooperation requires attention to and support from the communities in which it takes place.

Finally, development work is unlikely to be helpful, and may do real harm, unless efforts to help poor people and communities are based on a sustained relationship with them. Before one can offer effective assistance, one must learn about people, listen, know their situation, and develop relationships of trust. This approach is well suited to the resources of the NGO community, including churches, with their local networks and affiliations, and possibilities of relationships between individuals and organizations from rich and poor areas, in which each can learn from the other. Of course, governments play an important role in creating and maintaining the political and social opportunities in which NGOs can act.

Political Environment

Sustainable development requires a political and legal environment that will protect the rights of the poor to carry out their process of development. Rule and authority are properly part of human society; however, in a badly distorted world, they are of further importance since without just rule and institutions there will be bad, abusive rule. It is difficult to specify the role of the state in setting the economic environment, because experience has shown that while at times state planning and intervention in the economy have been disastrous, at other times they have yielded impressive results. What can be said with confidence is that the state should ensure that poor people have access to sufficient resources, such as land, technical assistance, credit, health, and education to give these people an opportunity to be productive and, above all, that the rights of the poor—including their property rights—are protected against the more powerful.[28]

Creating such a political environment includes working toward an international economic structure that will enable poor nations to seek paths of development that have their own welfare as a priority. One example is the debt problem. Debt has relegated many of the poor countries to a situation analogous to the odious debt peonage suffered by some of their own poor citizens. This situation can force countries to adopt development models favored by international capital, international banks, and the wealthy nations. A country's decision to follow a particular development model—while undoubtedly a complex one—remains better subject to that country's control; this requires that international debt problems be solved in such a way that the countries feel free to adopt, modify, or reject development models presented to them.

Sustainability

Permanence and sustainability are core moral values as well as vitally practical requisites of successful development efforts. Often, in the past, hasty consumption of resources, creation of hazards, degradation of land, and the like have led to long-term losses rather than gains; care must be exercised to see that the creation is preserved and that development can be maintained long-term. To tend and dress the garden, to care for the earth and its many creatures, species, habitats, and wonders, is part of the human mandate, a duty, and a part of what makes life interesting, beautiful, and worthwhile.

To be lasting and peace-sustaining, development must also be sustainable in the sense of giving access to resources to ordinary local people able and committed to keeping the processes going. Projects that are not locally supported are likely to decay and not be maintained, even if they were not initially ill-conceived. Thus, giving people ownership of their communities and processes of development and the skills to further those processes is an essential part of sustainable development.

Local responsibility and ownership are also logically related to environmental sustainability. Where development consists of projects not rooted in local communities, those undertaking development have little incentive to make sure that social and physical environments are protected in the long term. Alternatively, people who live in a community have a great interest in preserving their surroundings, especially its resources and natural beauty.

The question of sustainability also raises a set of ethical issues: Development, realistically understood, needs to be seen as a social, spiritual, and political issue, and not just an issue of material productivity. One reason for this is that the infinite multiplication of physical consumption is not a realistic possibility: In a world of limited resources and expanded population, part of sustainability is learning to make a good life and an improved life without ever-growing resource consumption. Moreover, the possibility of effectively maintaining development efforts rests upon community and local involvement, civil society, and opportunities in the international arena, and thus upon

146

healthy political and social development and relationships. The ability of poorer people to prosper, to lead good lives, depends upon cultivating right skills and attitudes in people at all levels. Thus, issues of simple living, such as learning to do more with less, are part of the worldwide efforts needed for sustainable development. In addition, sustainable development requires a holistic understanding of the social and political processes that bear upon people's lives; for often poverty and environmental degradation are results of unjust power structures, or arrogant quick fixes.

Human Fallibility and Humility

Two related points should be noted here. First, development needs to be seen with full awareness of political and economic structures and their potential for violence and oppression. Poverty is often an outcome of subjugation. People who are poor are easy targets for abuse by economically powerful persons and institutions, especially where there are not strong traditions of government and law. In a rapidly changing economy, powerful domestic or foreign interests may seek to expropriate the property of small cultivators or to capture and abuse government power for their own purposes. This is often particularly easy since traditional property rights of poorer parties may not be well documented. Governments and public officials can also take advantage of their positions of power, at the expense of weaker parties. The weakest and most vulnerable are the least able to resist. Again, traditional societies may keep women or other poor people dependent by charging exorbitant rates of interest and discouraging or prohibiting access to capital or property. Unfettered markets may, perhaps inadvertently at times, lead to similar results. As poor people start to acquire more resources, this itself may be seen as a threat by power holders, who may respond by disrupting and repressing community building and development. Thus sustainable development often requires defense of the rights of the poor—both human rights and economic and property rights—and is thus often inseparable from legal and political development and other elements of just peacemaking.

Second, even under the best of circumstances and without any wrongdoing, the ability to forecast the future is quite limited. This is especially true of large-scale development plans. Development plans have often failed and done harm, despite overall good intentions, through planners' overconfidence in their ability to engineer large social changes and projects or even some permanent state of growth and utopia. Peacemakers must remain humble, aware of their limits and ignorance, and not suppose that they are capable of completely controlling the future of projects. Thus, macrodevelopment strategies are not simply prescribed. It is easy to be mistaken about their conception and their implementation, even for technical experts; and an emphasis on grand plans often ignores the needs of poor people.

Our ignorance accompanies our lack of control over the process of sustainable development. This point, supported by past experience, is also an acknowledgment that human beings are not omnipotent. In efforts to bring about material or social change, an attitude that claims certain and superior knowledge is both mistaken and counterproductive. In sustainable development activities, the strategies by which social change is sought must acknowledge the relative contributions of various local, national, and foreign actors. They must begin with a humble acknowledgment that knowledge and capability do not lie with any particular actor. Much lauded development experts, pundits, and aspiring prophetic voices have frequently given unwise prescriptions that ended in disaster. Wise development requires robust respect for the lack of control anyone has over the results of social engineering. A closely related principle is the full valuation of all people involved and of the relationships among them.

STRATEGIES OF SUSTAINABLE DEVELOPMENT

The poor have, for the most part, received only the crumbs from development projects, which are often aimed at large infrastructure or economic reforms. Affluent people are often able to capture many development resources intended for the poor. Yet poorer people are not helpless; they are resilient, resourceful, and worthy of great respect. They are great, productive "engines of development" when given access to resources. Thus, advocacy of sustainable development should emphasize both the moral need to place the poor first and also the great losses society incurs when a lack of access to resources keeps poor people from their productive potential. Peacemakers must make the poor a focus of their efforts, entering into community in an attempt to help them.

What are tangible ways in which this can be done? First, agencies that carry out development by working directly with the poor should be supported. These should be agencies that establish long-term relationships with the poor, acknowledging that development is an extended process, while at the same time being aware of the dangers of creating dependency. In addition, the development work they carry out should be a holistic work, focusing on the community's many areas of need, and not just a "specialized" approach of engaging in one particular type of enterprise, such as well-drilling, which ends the relationship upon the project's conclusion. A commitment to a community requires spending a lot of time getting to know it and working with it in all aspects. (This is not to say that agencies that engage in mostly specialized projects are bad. Rather, it is to point out that those agencies that have a holistic approach are almost forced to establish a stronger bond with the community.) Peacemakers should support agencies that have an obvious respect for the poor and have established structural channels for the opinions of the poor to be incorporated into the planning, management, and execution of the projects. In addition, these should be agencies that place the responsibility for planning, direction, and implementation of development approaches in the hands of nationals. Among other things, this contributes toward building the capacity of the developing nations to manage their own development.

149

Second, peacemakers need to support creating community ties with the poor, establishing relationships that allow them to learn more about peoples living in the developing world and ways of supporting them, even as the latter learn more about the peacemakers. Many agencies are already engaged in small efforts at "development education," sharing information with their donors about the people with whom they work.[29] Perhaps even more important is promoting trips and visits by donors to specific communities in the Global South. Visits by as many people as possible to the developing world and to communities of the poor are crucial for creating opportunities to learn from one another and for keeping alive the concern for others. Agencies should be doing more to promote these visits, incorporating work opportunities for the visitors in the projects themselves. One way to institutionalize this is to create official links among churches, NGOs, and/or local communities in the North and South.[30]

Third, peacemakers should support networks of agencies that work toward protecting the legal rights of the poor or that work for trade rules that facilitate just and sustainable development. This creates a political environment that allows poor people to participate more fully in development. International networks of agencies plugged into NGOs working alongside the poor have been active for many years in bringing pressure on governments to enforce respect for the property rights of the poor and for their right to organize into groups to change their situation. They, along with some of the Northern governments, have also been working to press for creating independent judicial systems, to eliminate the favoritism shown to those who have more resources and can either bend or break the rules with impunity. It is also important to create or support organizations in the North that can monitor the situation in the various developing countries through contact with partners working directly with the poor. Such organizations can lobby the Northern governments to lend their weight to policies that will protect the poor and let the poor have access to resources that will secure their autonomy and rights.

Fourth, helping the world's neediest people will likely require sub-stantially increased transfer of material and natural resources. The poor's needs are not currently being met, as evinced by morbidity and mortality statistics, and their desperation contributes to the exhaus-tion of natural resources and the degradation of the global environ-ment. Wealthy states should increase their foreign-assistance pro-grams and work to transform bilateral and multilateral development institutions into agencies that:

- Are relatively autonomous and apolitical.
- Target the poor directly.
- Have multiyear budget appropriations to reduce the pressure to move money and treat development as a rapid process.
- Adopt a program methodology that incorporates the poor and NGOs at each stage into the decision-making processes on proj-ects in which they are involved.[31]

Fifth, sustainable development requires ecologically sensitive practices by individuals, organizations, businesses, governments, and international aid institutions. It should encourage the economic, so-cial, political, and cultural conditions necessary to carry these out. Rather than clear-cutting or burning tropical forests, people and com-panies should harvest primarily renewable products from the trees, in-cluding natural wax, resins, dyes, rattan, and even medicines. For citi-zens of the North, these practices can be extended to consumers. Individuals and private organizations can largely determine the demand for goods produced by sustainable or unsustainable means. Consumers might choose to purchase only paper products made with recycled materials. They could prefer rattan baskets to plastic containers, natural to chemical dyes, and solar water heaters to more conventional ones. Surveys have found that individuals are willing to pay a bit more for "green" products.

Instead of taking as many fish from a coastal area as possible and thereby threatening the future of the stock, individuals (with the support of states or international organizations) should manage the total catch to assure long-term supply. In both forest logging areas and coastal fishing zones, securing and maintaining indigenous ownership rights are important prerequisites to embracing sustainable practices.

Governments, of course, can do much to encourage sustainable development practices. First, rather than finance and build large capital-intensive projects like hydroelectric dams or coal-fired plants that flood valuable forest areas or pollute the air, leaders should develop a greater number of small, nonpolluting energy-generating facilities for communities in the developing world. Impoverished and rich states alike should stop rewarding unsustainable activity.

"Full-cost pricing" would be one mechanism. Rather than leasing water, land, timber, or mineral rights for arbitrarily low rates, assessments should reflect the ecological harm done by lessees like energy firms, farmers, ranchers, loggers, or miners. At minimum, states should charge market rates.

Governments are also consumers of many products (energy, paper, water, etc.). Regulations could mandate purchases from companies or states that utilize renewable resources, sustainable practices, or recyclable materials. Trade rules prohibiting such practices must be resisted.

Finally, governments and their international institutions should set regulations when necessary to limit harm to the environment. The Convention on International Trade of Endangered Species in Fauna and Flora (CITES) and the Montreal Protocol ozone accord are examples of interstate regulatory practices that work toward desired ends.

Interstate agreements are also proving indispensable in the Middle East water contexts discussed in a preceding section. For example, Sudan and Egypt signed the Nile Waters Agreement in 1959, which resolved many potential disputes between these two neighboring states. Basically, the parties agreed to allocate fixed quantities of water, thereby creating a framework for sustainable development.

Unfortunately, no other states in the region, including Ethiopia, are party to the agreement. Consequently, the treaty does not provide for a fixed allocation of Nile waters to these other states. However, there is hope for sustainable socioeconomic development if the nine riparian states partaking in the Nile Basin Initiative succeed in their joint efforts to develop the river in a cooperative and equitable manner.

Additionally, the 1994 peace treaty between Israel and Jordan addressed some of their mutual water concerns. Under the agreement, Israel each year transports seventy-five million cubic meters of water to Jordan. Moreover, Jordan, Israel, and the Palestinian Authority have agreed to work together to save the Dead Sea. The planned project, which would eventually divert water from the Red Sea, may also generate power that could be used to desalinate water for all three parties. A World Bank–funded study of the project was slated to begin in September 2007.[32] Cooperative measures like these could serve as the model for sustainable development in the region. Almost certainly, water rights will need to be addressed in any comprehensive political settlement involving Israel and the Palestinian Authority.

152

CONCLUSIONS

Advocating just and sustainable development means recommending a change in relationships that will bring about new opportunities for the poor. A peacemaker works alongside the poor, establishing direct relationships with them, advocating an increased access to resources that will allow them to flourish, and working with them to protect their property and human rights from control by the powers that would keep them in their present trap.[33] The weight of the literature and development experience shows that not only are the majority of the poor extremely creative and entrepreneurial in eking out a living from the few resources to which they have access, but also that giving them access to resources, information, and opportunities yields impressive results.

PART THREE

love and community

Seven

WORK WITH EMERGING COOPERATIVE FORCES IN THE INTERNATIONAL SYSTEM

Paul W. Schroeder

This chapter aims to correct certain widely held ideas about the international system and its connection with wars and international conflict. It has less to say than other essays in this book about concrete actions to take and particular strategies and tactics to follow in peacemaking. Yet like the other chapters, it seeks to promote a perspective so that just peacemaking can extend to the widest areas.

Not that every prevalent impression is incorrect. For example, the roots of international conflict do indeed lie deep in the very nature of international politics and therefore cannot be wished away or abolished by adopting certain rules or persuading states and peoples to be nicer to one another. In contrast, the common notion is wrong that the international system itself is the problem. I will argue that since the seventeenth century the international system (that is, the system of rules and practices governing relations between states) has represented a series of attempts at solving or at least managing an inherently insoluble problem, that of unavoidable clashes between independent states over claims, rights, and goals. While these systems have seldom met the problem of recurrent wars durably and satisfactorily and have sometimes broken down completely or made the problem worse, overall they certainly have produced more peace and less war than would have occurred without them.

The most important thing to understand about the international system is that its basic rules, institutions, and procedures do not, as some believe, stay the same forever; rather, they develop, grow, and change like other social institutions. This growth and change are unprecedentedly rapid and widespread at the present time. Fundamental changes in society and dramatic developments in international politics have combined to make the old, perennial, and apparently insoluble problem of preserving general international peace at least manageable, if not soluble.

This insight should translate into action: On one hand, peacemakers can recognize and understand the major institutions, forces, and trends working internationally toward peace as resources to encourage, support, and use. On the other hand, if would-be just peacemakers do the opposite—treat the system and its institutions not as a resource to be used and reformed but an evil to be fought or overthrown—then however well-intentioned their activities may be, they are likely to do more harm than good. The message could be put in the words, "Be wise as serpents and harmless as doves" (Matt. 10:16b). For purposes of just peacemaking in the international arena, one needs to be wise as a serpent—that is, aware of the nature of the current international system, cognizant of its possibilities for good and harm, ready to sustain it where it is vital and valuable for peace, ready to try to reform and develop it where it is inadequate or corrupt and to oppose it where it is actively evil or dangerous. Only by being wise as a serpent in this way can one be harmless as a dove—that is, engage the system for good ends without harming it, others, or ourselves.

I cannot make this case in a scholarly fashion here as I would like, but will only offer a series of propositions as guidelines for thinking about international politics in terms of just peacemaking.

1. The current international system (meaning the overall pattern of relations between international actors, mainly independent states) should not be thought of either simply as a competitive struggle for advantage based on relations of power, or as a set of relations that can and should be governed by mutual obligation, fixed norms, contract, and law. The best way to think about the system as it has evolved over centuries is to see it as an anarchic society.[1] That is, it is anarchic not in the sense of being totally chaotic or without rules but in the sense of having no recognized lawgiver or law-enforcing authority. At the same time, it is a society in the sense of having many members who are in permanent, inescapable contact with one another, who normally recognize and deal with one another as legitimate members of the

group, who engage in mutually necessary and potentially beneficial transactions, and who need rules by which to regulate and carry on these transactions.

2. This concept of the international system as an anarchic society defines what a just peace means in international relations: the best practical system of rules, norms, practices, and institutions for reducing the anarchic (conflictual, violent, destructive) elements and promoting the societal (legal, cooperative, and normative) aspects of this anarchic society, while recognizing that for profound reasons it will remain an anarchic society for the foreseeable future (in my view, for any conceivable or desirable one). Just peacemaking does not require one to be a realist in some senses of that much-abused term (e.g., to believe that international politics reduces to power politics, that there must always be great wars, that war is rooted in human nature, or the like). It does require realism in the sense of acknowledging the nature and limits of the system.

3. The root cause of destructive competition and conflict in international affairs is not simply that the various actors are competing over scarce goods (scarce in the sense of being limited, not infinite, so that one can always desire more at someone else's expense). Undoubtedly, competition over such scarce goods as territory, natural resources, wealth, trade routes, strategic positions, and the like has been a prominent cause of war and still is. More fundamental still, however, is an inherent tension within the goals to which individual governments aspire—the fact that the very aims they pursue in the international system are in a sense self-contradictory. All governments and organized societies basically need three things to survive and prosper: order (rule of law, sanctity of contract, predictability of obligations and performances, and so forth), welfare (enough material and psychic well-being among the inhabitants to sustain domestic peace), and legitimacy (a broad acceptance of governmental authority as legitimate, so that domestic law and order can be sustained with a minimum of overt force). Governments pursue these goals of domestic order, welfare, and legitimacy also, inevitably and necessarily, in international politics.[2] That is, they defend and advance their interests with regard to their borders, territory, citizens' rights, trade, governmental authority, and intangibles like their political systems, religious and cultural values, and ethnic and national honor. This frequently breeds international conflict not only because it involves scarce re-

sources and competing claims and rights, but above all because in simultaneously pursuing these three goods in the international arena, governments and peoples are demanding two contradictory things at once: order and freedom. All governments (and governments are still the dominant actors in international affairs) want to enjoy order (sanctity of contract, performance of obligations, respect for their rights and status, and the like). But they want order without sacrificing freedom—that is, independence and sovereignty, being their own source of law and authority for themselves. The deepest root of conflict in international affairs is therefore the tension and contradiction between two equally vital goals, order and freedom, within this anarchic society.

4. The contradiction has a further dimension: the free-rider problem. Most international relations theory and practice rests on rational choice theory—basically, that governments make rational choices on the basis of cost-versus-benefits utility analysis (e.g., they decide whether to make war or how to respond to a neighbor's challenge on the basis of a calculation as to the likely costs and benefits of various responses). Scholars of course debate whether governments really do act in this manner and recognize also that, even if they do, such supposedly "rational" calculation provides plenty of room and occasion for miscalculations, misperceptions, and faulty strategies, leading to conflicts and destructive consequences. Beyond these, however, there is a deeper problem with "rational choice" as the model for state action in international affairs. It involves a concealed contradiction between the "good" of the individual state or unit and the "good" of the system as a whole. Like every other society, international society, to survive and function, requires certain public goods—that is, goods that all members need and enjoy but whose costs cannot be easily imposed on individual consumers or apportioned among them. Everyone benefits in international society from general peace, freedom for trade, freedom of the seas, free exchange of information, and the like. Yet these goods all have costs attached, sometimes high ones. Who is to pay? More important still, a rational method of payment in terms of the whole system (that every member pay its fair share for these collective goods by individual restraint and performances) clashes with the most rational choice for each individual member (to make others obey the rules and pay the costs while one's own state breaks the rules and gets the benefits free). Here lies the classic clash

between rational individual state morality (*raison d'etat*) and rational international morality.

To this point, the analysis seems wholly pessimistic. It apparently suggests what many idealists, reformers, and peacemakers historically have believed—that controlling or eliminating the root causes of international conflict and war requires radically changing or eliminating the whole system, perhaps through world government or international law enforced by some supranational authority. I will not attempt to explain here why this supposed way out seems to me futile and desperate, a Utopian or rather Dystopian dream, promising far worse conflict, tyranny, and war than the present system. Instead, in what follows I want to argue that the problems and contradictions within the anarchic society of international relations, though real and ineradicable, are not fundamentally insoluble or unmanageable—at least not any longer. Rather, the current system contains trends, developments, and institutions that potentially can enable governments and societies to pursue their basic goals (order, welfare, and legitimacy) in the international arena without causing general systemic conflict, thereby managing and partially transcending the contradiction between order and freedom. Moreover, I will try to persuade readers that in conceiving the task of just peacemaking as one of encouraging and promoting these positive trends and institutions, we make it both a practical way of dealing with the realities of international politics and, at the same time, a fully justifiable one morally and ethically. This is a tall order; I can try to fill it only with some more briefly stated propositions.

5. While the anarchic society with its inherent contradictions accounts at the deepest level for international conflict and war, it also accounts for international cooperation and peace. The simultaneous, self-contradictory pursuit of order and of freedom never fully succeeds and sometimes spectacularly breaks down in great wars; but it also never totally or finally fails and often succeeds to a remarkable degree. More peace has always prevailed and still prevails in international relations than war—more peace than one should expect, given the multitude of causes and conditions making for war, and far more peace than one could explain without the existence and operation of the international system.

6. International politics furthermore is not static but rapidly changing. Four separate but interrelated trends in international history, marked since the early nineteenth century and increasingly pow-

158

erful and accelerating into the twenty-first century, have sharply altered the nature of the international system. These are:

- The decline of the utility of war, that is, a steep rise in the costs and dangers of major war as a tool of statecraft, and a corresponding decline in the applicability and potential benefits of even a successful use of large-scale military force as a way of solving major problems, securing either order or freedom.

- The rise of the trading state, that is, the priority now placed by most modern states on success in trade and the economy, as opposed to success in war, as the key to domestic order, welfare, and legitimacy.[3] Where it used to be said that war made the state and the state made war, it is now becoming more true to say that trade makes the successful state and the successful state makes trade or promotes it.

- A dramatic increase in the volume, density, and speed of international exchanges, communications, and transactions of all kinds and the increasing integration of these exchanges into organized, complex, international, supranational, and transnational networks, corporations, and other institutions. This has now developed to such a degree that the domestic economics, politics, and culture of individual states cannot be isolated from them or do without them. Along with this has gone an equally startling increase in the number, scope, durability, and effectiveness of international organizations of all kinds, both governmental and nongovernmental, to which both modern governments and nongovernmental groups must pay attention and must use for their particular purposes.

- A gradual, uneven, but unmistakable ascendancy of one form of government, liberal representative democracy, as the dominant legitimate form of governance of modern states and of one kind of economic system, market-oriented capitalism (whether of the welfare-state or a more laissez-faire variety), as the dominant form of modern economic development.

7. These four trends combine not to insure general international peace (nothing can do that) but greatly to enhance the possibilities of just peacemaking within the existing system. Some of the ways they do so are fairly obvious and frequently discussed—for example, the great rise in costs and risks of large-scale war or military coercion and

decline of its perceived benefits, together with the greater importance of non-zero-sum commercial competition in comparison to zero-sum military and power-political competition. Mature democracies seem to show less willingness either to fight one another or to resort to force generally. The dramatic rise in international transactions and organizations means far greater interdependence among states and at least potentially greater incentives for cooperation and disincentives for overt conflict. All these arguments, it must be conceded, are disputed by some observers; yet at least these trends represent potential openings for peacemakers to exploit.

8. More important and less obvious, these trends indicate how the central contradictions in international politics (that is, the contradiction between international order and freedom and the tension within rational decision making between "egoistic" *raison d'etat* morality and "altruistic" international morality) can be, if not eliminated, nonetheless sufficiently transcended or bridged so that, for most practical purposes, they no longer will be decisive. The theoretical answer to both these core problems has long been apparent: the principle of voluntary association. Every great peace plan from the Middle Ages onward, every scheme for so-called collective security from Cardinal Richelieu's to George Bush's, has called in different ways for a voluntary association or league of like-minded "peaceful" states formed to secure for all its members the common benefits of peace and to share among them the costs and burdens of defending the association against aggressors or lawbreakers. It is easy to see, purely in principle and theory, how such voluntary durable leagues for peace could solve the problem of reconciling order and freedom. Since the norms, principles, rules, and sanctions in such associations would all be decided and enforced jointly and the benefits and burdens of the association shared in common, no one's freedom or rights would be sacrificed. Even the problem of imbalances of power and weight within the association and related dangers of hegemony or domination theoretically could be managed. What weaker members would lose in decision-making power and influence they would gain in concrete protection, security, and guaranteed juridical independence, security, and voice. And since the common, shared goods would also be defined by the whole association and only available within it, the tension within rational decision making between the good of the individual state and that of the whole association would tend to disappear.

It is even easier, however, to see why such schemes and such actual associations in history (the Holy Roman Empire, various leagues of German and Italian states, the Concert of Europe, the League of Nations, the United Nations, among others) have had only partial and temporary success, and often broken down disastrously. Historically, one can list at least six reasons:

- Not enough carrot in the associations in the form of concrete payoffs to prevent defections or discourage free riders.

- Not enough stick in the form of force- and cost-effective sanctions against the same.

- No adequate mechanisms to distribute the costs, burdens, and benefits of the association equitably or to settle quarrels over them.

- No assurance that in critical circumstances the costs and risks of maintaining the association will not exceed its benefits (e.g., that the association can only be saved by a great war that will destroy some of its members).

- Insufficient unity in the form of common purposes, beliefs, and goals of members within the association, so that individual aims outweigh the common ones and internal rivalries outweigh common ties.

- Insufficient adaptability of the association and its goals to changing needs, circumstances, and aims of its members, so that on balance it hinders their pursuits rather than advancing them.

But while it is easy enough to explain why voluntary associations for peace have not worked regularly or well in the past (though they were almost always better than nothing), the point to emphasize here is that these basic obstacles no longer have the same force today. The four trends mentioned earlier have altered the conditions and practices of international relations so much that it is possible now, as it was not possible earlier, to form and sustain voluntary associations for peace and other related useful purposes that avoid or overcome the fatal weaknesses of former ones. That is, they prove to be so beneficial, cost-effective, durable, united, and adaptable that members are dissuaded from defection and outsiders discouraged from aggression, new members are attracted, and new aims and purposes developed to replace obsolete ones and to meet new challenges. This is not just theory; it is happening. The continued existence and success of organi-

161

zations like NATO, the European Union, the United Nations, and many others go a long way to make it demonstrable fact. To argue that voluntary associations for peace cannot work better today than in the past seems to me a bit like arguing that manned heavier-than-air flight is not possible for the same reasons it was impossible before 1903.

Yet, of course, none of this will happen or has happened automatically. If the system can and does work for good, as I claim, where it does and to the extent that it does it is because people—leaders and followers—make it do so. All these useful societal trends and potentially valuable peacemaking and peacekeeping organizations and developments can readily be corrupted for wrong purposes, defeated or overwhelmed by new challenges, or so stultified and confined that they become useless for meeting the emerging problems of peace today and in the future. This makes just peacemaking into a task for action—a process in which ordinary citizens individually and in groups work to sustain, criticize, goad, influence, reform, and lead the many kinds of voluntary associations—governmental and private—that can contribute to transcending the contradictions and managing and overcoming the conflicts of an anarchic international society. In other words, it means exploiting, encouraging, and strengthening the concrete world trends that enable cooperation to fly: the decline in the utility of war; the priority of trade and the economy over war; the strength of international exchanges, communications, transactions, and networks; and the gradual ascendancy in the world of liberal representative democracy and a mixture of welfare-state and laissez-faire market economy. Citizens, intermediate associations, and governments should act so as to strengthen these trends and the voluntary associations that they make possible.

To make this a bit more practical and down-to earth: In seeking to avert a crisis that could lead to war, as well as in noncrisis actions, governments should seek the counsel and the mediating help of parties that represent these international networks. And in both crisis and long-range actions, they should seek to act in a way that strengthens these networks and associations when they can assist practical problem solving. As the realist Reinhold Niebuhr observed, institutions of international cooperation are not created out of nothing by fiat or wish, but built bit by bit as nations act day by day in ways that strengthen their usefulness.

This method of building peace through durable voluntary international association both between governments and nongovernmental ac-

162

tors is applicable far more widely and effectively today than previously. However, it is, as noted earlier, not new, but it has much historical precedent and evidence in its favor. As I have argued elsewhere, one cannot adequately explain the course of international politics in earlier centuries by a version of realist theory that places all the emphasis on state security, power, and the balance of power within the system. Instead, scholars have to pay attention to transnational forces in the international system, prevailing rules and norms, and the different functions and roles filled by different kinds of states within the system in order to understand the actual historical behavior of states in international relations. For example, the long period of peace under the Concert of Europe (1815–1853) resulted not from a balance of power but from the influence of transnational ideas and forces; agreements carefully worked out among governments on a practical definition and structure of peace; a system of benign hegemonies or spheres of influence mutually agreed upon or shared; a consensus on norms and rules, rights, and the rule of law; and finally, a sense that Europe constituted a community of nations with shared responsibility to preserve the system.[4]

As Aaron Friedberg argues in a recent article, something similar but more profound is developing today. The likelihood of war in Western Europe has been reduced by "the existence of recognized rules of international conduct" and "the evolving character of the economic, institutional, and cultural inter-connections among" European states, where "barriers to the free movement of people, goods, capital, and technology have now been drastically lowered." European states have become "enmeshed in a dense web of institutions, . . . 'a thick alphabet soup of international agencies.' International institutions help to promote peace by assisting in the resolution of disputes and by easing all forms of mutually beneficial interstate cooperation. . . . Joint participation in international institutions can breed mutual understanding and an important measure of trust." In addition, growing cultural linkages increase mutual understanding and transnational loyalties; "slowly and with some difficulty, that web has begun to extend from Western to Eastern Europe." His argument posits the value of transnational linkages also where they are much less fully developed, including Africa and Latin America, but he concentrates on Asia since economic and military power are growing there with dramatic speed, remarking, "The ties among Asian states are, by comparison, much less fully developed, . . . and the possible obstacles to their growth more readily apparent." It is crucial for world peace, he concludes, that the United States and other nations contribute to strengthening the ties or linkages among nations in order to overcome instabilities that may erupt during the critical next few years as the post–Cold War world takes shape.[5]

Critics, of course, disagree. Many contend that dramatic events since the end of the Cold War—in Somalia, Chechnya, Rwanda and Burundi, the Persian Gulf, the former Yugoslavia, especially Bosnia, and elsewhere—prove clearly that conciliation, persuasion, and the influence of transnational linkages and pressures do not work in cases of real conflict. Power remains the main denominator of international politics, force the main instrument of deterrence and compellence; and an unwillingness to use force where necessary, or the failure to use it wisely and persistently, remains an invitation to failure and defeat. The argument goes beyond the bounds of this essay, and a reply could be better given by a political scientist or contemporary historian than by me, whose expertise lies in the history of international politics from the mid-seventeenth to the mid-twentieth century. Yet one might observe that the argument here is not that nonviolent strategies and tactics (which include coercive devices of various kinds, diplomatic, economic, political, and cultural) always work. To claim this would be absurd. It is only that such strategies and tactics can work far more widely and durably than they used to, or than many think; that where they do not work, often nothing else will work either; and that plenty of evidence from recent peacekeeping and peacebuilding illustrates their value. Not all leaders, governments, and peoples can be convinced through the kind of persuasion and pressure discussed earlier that they must adopt certain rules of conduct if they hope to have a decent future, but some can. This sort of pressure and persuasion by former president Carter during the Clinton presidency, and not just the intervention of American troops, led to surprising American success in ousting the military leaders in Haiti and restoring President Aristide for several years, until his eventual overthrow during the George W. Bush administration. Radovan Karadzic and Ratko Mladic in Bosnia were no doubt immune to such influences; but Franjo Tudjman in Croatia and Slobodan Milosovic in Serbia—both of them authoritarian, nationalistic politicians—were not immune, and their peoples even less so. The people turned against Milosevic in democratic elections. Whatever success the peace process has had to this point in Bosnia and can hope for in the future rests at least as much on these kinds of pressures as on NATO military intervention.

This essay, as noted, can say little about the concrete, particular ways of doing this kind of peacemaking. It will close only with another reminder of the priority of practical consequences and results, and of appraising them in terms of the whole system.

Two quotations seem to me appropriate. In a recent book, William L. Kissick writes, "As a medical student I learned an important lesson: when a patient has a host of pathologies or multi-organ-system disease, selective therapeutic strategies are critical. Any attempt to treat everything at once risks a confluence of physiological and pharmacological side effects that could overwhelm the patient; one has to address specifics and to anticipate consequences. . . . Comprehensive reform, while attractive in theory, is a high-risk venture."[6]

What Dr. Kissick says about critical patient care and the whole health-care system applies also to peacemaking and the whole, complex international system. Precisely because there are so many sources of conflict and war, so many ways for peace to break down or fail to emerge, it is essential to concentrate on doing practical good, such as saving and strengthening the system and solving or managing immediate problems, sometimes even simply limiting the damage and binding up the wounds, rather than seeking a comprehensive solution. We need a kind of Hippocratic oath in peacemaking: First, do no harm.

The second quotation comes from James Goodby, both an excellent scholar and an outstanding diplomatic negotiator for the American government in various capacities, whom I came to know at the United States Institute of Peace in 1993 to 1994. In one seminar, he remarked (I quote him from memory but accurately, I think) that he had often encountered three kinds of persons in negotiations: the "realists," for whom the essence of the question was the clash of interests, the relations of power, and the struggle to win, gain the advantage; the "idealists," for whom the vital question was a matter of principle, the vindication of a claim or the attainment of a just outcome; and finally, the problem solvers, for whom the central concern was to try to understand the problem and figure out what, in practical terms, could be done about it. As Goodby remarked, his sympathies were on the side of the problem solvers. I responded then, and remain convinced now, that history (and real morality) are also, in the long run, on the side of the problem solvers.

Eight

STRENGTHEN THE UNITED NATIONS AND INTERNATIONAL EFFORTS FOR COOPERATION AND HUMAN RIGHTS

Michael Joseph Smith

For those engaged in constructing a just peace paradigm, the traditional model of self-contained nation-states—sovereign, secure, distinct—will no longer do. Realists and just war casuists alike think of the world as made up of states (countries or nations with their governments). But the world has changed too much for this so-called Westphalian model to guide our ethical inquiry. The end of the Cold War, the rise of a genuinely global economy, the increased salience of human-rights norms, the growing demands for democratic participation, and, on the other hand, the grim operations of terrorist networks, have created new challenges and opportunities for non–nation-state actors—most prominently the United Nations (UN)—to develop policies and practices that might moderate conflicts and enhance respect for human rights. An approach to just peacemaking must encourage these international developments for the pacific settlement of a whole range of conflicts. In the most basic terms, this means support for the United Nations, associated regional international organizations, and nongovernmental organizations (NGOs) so that, collectively, we can develop the capacity to identify, prevent, and, if necessary, intervene in conflicts within and between states that threaten basic human rights. We must also work for genuine peace and reconciliation when the acute conflict has been stopped. But in this post–September 11, 2001, world we must also learn to navigate between the Scylla of inaction—as in Rwanda or Darfur—and the Charybdis of pseudo-humanitarian intervention—as in Iraq.

THE POST–COLD WAR ENVIRONMENT

What kind of international system do we now live in? Perhaps symptomatic of a major period of change and confusion is the absence of anything approaching consensus on what to call this new international system: unipolar? balance-of-power? globalist? new world order? We agree only on the term "post–Cold War" and that any historical analogy is deeply flawed at best. Let us examine the new environment from two perspectives: first, a "structural" perspective that emphasizes power and institutions; and, second, a "juridical" perspective that emphasizes changes in prevalent norms.[1]

For historians and political scientists, the traditional place to begin an analysis of the international system is with power: Who has it, and who uses it for what purposes? According to the long-dominant theory of international affairs, realism, the international system is a milieu of states, who, by their very nature, are locked in an unending and always potentially murderous competition. States seek to increase their power, and they try to prevent the rise of rivals or "hegemons" through unilateral moves as well as through balances of power. And for their survival and success, they depend above all on military might and its economic underpinnings. War is always possible, and the restraints of international law and organization can always be swept aside in the name of the "national interest."

On this view, throughout the Cold War, power was concentrated in two "poles," the United States and the Soviet Union—hence the prevalent characterization of the international system as "bipolar." The collapse of the Soviet Union and the end of the Cold War led to a "diffusion of power." But where has power gone? Here, we must make an important distinction between two arenas of simultaneous interaction—the arena of traditional military security and the arena of economic interdependence.[2]

The traditional realm of security remains relevant and potentially quite destructive: States have not dismantled their armies and weapons. But new threats to security come at least as much from internal conflict and terrorism as from external aggression. In the modern arena of economic interdependence, state actors remain relevant and important, but the character of their goals is quite different and their capacity to control events is increasingly limited. For one thing, they live in a world economy whose continuing growth is in their common interest. Competition is not "zero-sum"; my gains may well require that you make some yourself. Moreover, the stakes of competition clearly differ: physical security and the control of territory in the first arena; market shares, the creation and expansion of wealth and new markets in the other. Nor are the necessary ingredients and possible uses of power the same.

In the arena of military-security and strategic-diplomatic interaction, we have moved from bipolarity to a complex and unprecedented situation. Here, the main actors are still the states—though, even in this realm, states find themselves challenged from above and below. During the Cold War period, the security arena proved most recalcitrant to UN operations when the superpowers were themselves directly involved. Until 1989, the most powerful interstate institutions were the rival alliances. Now, one of these, the Warsaw Pact, is defunct, and the other, NATO, finds it difficult to define new purposes even as it expands its membership and adopts unfamiliar combat and peacekeeping roles in places like Kosovo or Afghanistan. The United States remains the most important player in terms of global military power, and the United States and Russia still hold the capacity to destroy the planet several times over. But Russia's economic weakness and political turbulence have somewhat reduced its ability to be a worldwide challenger. The number of other active players—China, India, Pakistan, Iran—has increased and is likely to increase still further: The proliferation of military technologies—nuclear and conventional—makes this possible.

In the new, post–Cold War world, the security worries of states are more likely to be internal, regional, and transnational; a global duopoly of power dominated by nuclear deterrence may seem simple by comparison. Local tyrants may try to become regional bullies; authoritarian regimes may seek to "solve" their ethnic and power-sharing problems by using the means of brutal military repression. And terrorist organizations move and operate across and within state borders, often without direct, traceable ties to a specific nation-state. One the one hand, the "non"- or "extra"-state component of this challenge would seem to require cooperation among states so they might develop transnational capacities, intelligence cooperation, and workable norms to damp down and even to prevent conflicts. But as an embarrassing wealth of conflicts and terrorist incidents has shown when states in the context of regional or UN diplomacy can agree that "something must be done," there has been discouragingly little exercise of the necessary collective will to deploy and equip regional or UN-sponsored forces that can even begin to deal effectively with the range of deep-seated conflicts we must confront. And yet these very failures (in Darfur, Congo, Somalia) point up the urgent necessity to develop such capacities.

In the realm of international economic interdependence—a huge subject that defies brief summary—two broad trends bear emphasis. First is the emergence of what Susan Strange has called a new "international business civilization"—a term that suggests a kind of supranational capitalism of banks, large corporations, and enterprises. This international business civilization operates beyond national borders in search of opportunities for investment and profit, and it limits the "operational sovereignty" of nation-states, who no longer can control many of the decisions that most assuredly affect them.[3] More and more of the important decisions about the direction of the global economy are made by private firms or markets, and states are left to react to these decisions.

Second, the rise of this international business civilization has meant effectively a change in the structure of the international system. In this realm, as opposed to the security realm, states jostle with other actors that in many cases have greater power and influence than they do. Nongovernmental actors and institutions make possible transnational coalitions of, say, environmentalists or mining interests. These coalitions in turn seek to influence the policy of their own nation-states. On this model, states are less like hard-boiled eggs than they are like the partial ingredients of a vast and complex global omelet.[4] Thus from a structural vantage point, the post–Cold War international system combines national sovereignty and global interdependence in a quite unprecedented way.

Beyond international structure, an understanding of the contemporary international system requires us to examine the juridical or normative environment. Here again I emphasize two broad trends. The first (rather inchoate) trend is demand from below for what might be called autonomy—in the sense of greater economic security and a greater degree of political participation and accountability. Various analysts have called this trend a demand for democratization, but this strikes me as too specifically political. Perhaps the best way to encapsulate what I am calling autonomy in the sense of security and independence is to invoke Henry Shue's notion of basic rights. People throughout the world are demanding the rights "without which the enjoyment of any other right is impossible."[5] These are rights of security and subsistence, and the demand for these rights can be witnessed in places as diverse as China, the Philippines, or Haiti. Both nation-states and international institutions such as the International Monetary Fund have had to take note of these demands and to modify policies and practices because of them.

For states, the demand for basic rights has meant a move away from the traditional realist goals of statecraft—territorial conquest and coercive political control. The long-term trends identified by Immanuel Kant in 1795—the increased destructiveness of war and preparations for it, the attractions of "greed" or commerce, combined with the spread of popular participation and "republican" forms of government—seem now to be joining to raise obstacles to the success of the traditional methods of war and occupation.[6] The United States may have defeated the Iraqi army quite easily, but political success has proven much more elusive. As the debate on the Iraq War has shown, the normative legitimacy of war, imperialism, and conquest has markedly declined. Thus, states now increasingly define even their security goals in terms of creating wealth and welfare in the context of an interdependent global economy. Even the most jingoistic American does not propose to close our trade gap with China by declaring war—though of course the Bush administration did succeed in driving the country to war with Iraq on the basis of what turned out to be a false claim that Iraq possessed weapons of mass destruction. This shows that security—defined traditionally as protection from outside attack—remains quite salient; but "security" is now widely understood to encompass more than safety from outside physical attack.

We have also witnessed long-term decline in the legitimacy of colonialism. Here, the effects of World War II were reinforced by the ideological convergence of the United States and the Soviet Union against imperial rule of the nineteenth-century style. Early in its history, the UN General Assembly effectively stripped colonial powers from exercising "domestic jurisdiction" over their colonies. The United Nations also declared that apartheid in South Africa and the unilateral declaration of independence by Rhodesia were threats to peace. In this way, the UN brought about a gradual expansion of legitimate international concern in matters that states had traditionally treated as domestic affairs.

The Holocaust and the atrocities of World War II awakened a vital concern for human rights and resulted in the Universal Declaration on Human Rights and the treaty covenants on human rights, and gave rise to the notion—ultimately quite subversive to traditional conceptions of state sovereignty—that egregious human-rights violations can be considered as a legitimate matter for international action.

International consciousness about the limits of sovereignty and the deficiency of a legal order dedicated primarily to its preservation has accelerated since the end of the Cold War. There is increasing awareness of the dangers that a variety of domestic policies may create for other states, in areas as diverse as the production of weapons of mass destruction, drugs, or the training of terrorists. Consensus on this last point explains why the American/NATO invasion of Afghanistan to remove the Taliban regime gained considerable support in the UN and international community, but the invasion of Iraq, in stark contrast, did not. Taliban support of al-Qaeda was well-documented, and after the attacks of 9/11 the United States was seen responding in self-defense against the regime that helped to sponsor them. But the invasion of Iraq occurred without this direct provocation, and ended what many considered at the time to be a largely successful containment of Saddam Hussein's ambitions through no-fly zones and international weapons inspections.

In addition to a broader conception of security, there has also been triple evolution of the idea of human rights. First, in particularly serious cases, the protection of basic human rights can now, at least in theory and occasionally in action, override the traditional norm of nonintervention (as in the case of sanctions against Iraq and the famine in Somalia). Second, the protection of minorities—neglected after the failure of the post-Versailles attempts after World War I—has again become a major concern. Given the impossibility, in most cases, of producing "ethnically pure" nation-states, protecting minorities is a major focus of international attention. Finally, there is what has been called "the emerging right to democratic governance."[7]

What has this "triple evolution" of human rights meant? More and more, individuals are seen as having not merely a right to a state providing a modicum of law and order, but also a right to a nation-state that can successfully provide and guarantee a genuine national community, and finally, a right to democratic government. In practice, of course, there are striking tensions, and even contradictions, among these rights; but together they challenge a traditional conception of state sovereignty that regards forms of government as opaque to outside and international scrutiny. The universal norms of human rights try to make the behavior of states toward their citizens transparent to all the world and subject to criticism and direct action.[8]

If this first set of normative developments—toward the achievement of basic human rights—seems cosmopolitan in its effects, a second trend appears to contradict and work against it. I refer here to demands for national and cultural self-determination, to demands for ethnic particularity in the face of an apparently homogenizing global economy. The human costs of these demands can be devastating—as events in Chechnya, Rwanda, or Darfur demonstrate. In the wake of the collapse of the Soviet empire, several national minorities have demanded states of their own. We also witnessed many examples of weak, postcolonial regimes that have failed to establish substantive legitimacy and have never solved issues of ethnic autonomy and meaningful political participation. Profound religious, ethnic, and ideological differences characterize a range of states in Africa and Asia, and when these differences are combined with widespread poverty and predatory rule by self-interested elites, horrendous conflicts can result.

These conflicts present daunting challenges to all who would manage conflict and seek peace. After this sketch of the contemporary international system, let us turn now to the developing and potential international practices that aim at establishing at least the preconditions of a just peace.

COLLECTIVE INTERNATIONAL ACTION FOR HUMAN RIGHTS

Perhaps the first step in considering any international action for humanitarian purposes is to recognize the vital role of the United Nations, both as an actor itself and as an agency to coordinate the efforts of international humanitarian relief agencies. Thankfully, demands from American citizens and changes in political leadership have resulted in the United States paying most of its back dues to the UN and the reflexive "UN-bashing" has largely ceased. Repeated polls have demonstrated that the American people believe the United

Nations to be the most appropriate agency for peacekeeping and hold the UN in much higher regard than the U.S. Congress.[9]

Citizens should urge their governments to create and support collective mechanisms for the management of conflict and the construction of peace both within and between states. Collective action for purposes of peacekeeping, humanitarian aid, conflict management, and even "peace building" are increasingly more necessary in the twenty-first century than perhaps at any time since World War II. U.S. citizens should press their government to act in small and large crises in ways that strengthen the effectiveness of the United Nations, of regional organizations, and of multilateral peacemaking, peacekeeping, and peace building. Many multilateral practices are building effectiveness to resolve conflicts and to monitor, nurture, and even enforce truces. They are initiating cooperation where violent conflict has occurred or is threatened. And they are organizing to meet human needs for food, hygiene, medicine, education, and economic interaction.

The key actor among all these NGOs remains the United Nations. Why emphasize the UN? Perhaps most obvious is that it remains the only international institution capable of sustained peacekeeping operations, and it provides the only genuinely international forum for considering, authorizing, and legitimizing multilateral action. Moreover, despite some obvious failures, it has responded to the human needs presented by conflicts throughout the world. Since 1948, the United Nations has conducted sixty-one peacekeeping operations. The number and intensity of these operations has dramatically increased since the end of the Cold War. At the end of 2007, there were 101,982 people serving in eighteen UN-led peacekeeping operations all over the world; 82, 411 were uniformed personnel coming from 114 different countries. The budget for peacekeeping operations has grown from $230 million in 1988 to $5.28 billion for fiscal year 2007.[10]

At the same time, it is widely recognized that the capacities of the United Nations are in no way equal to the magnitude of the needs. The failure of the UN to deploy a sufficient peacekeeping operation in Darfur stands as the most recent and glaring example of this failure. Without going into great detail, there is a whole range of proposals to improve the ability of the UN to identify, seek to prevent, and, if necessary, to move on to intervene in areas where humanitarian disasters are unfolding. The most promising of these proposals came in the form of the 2001 report of an International Commission on

Sovereignty and Intervention appointed by former Secretary-General Kofi Annan. This report, the result of extensive international consultation and authored by former statesmen as well as scholars from a diverse range of backgrounds, recast the whole notion of "humanitarian intervention" as a collective "Responsibility to Protect." The premise of the report was strikingly simple: rather than pitting "autonomous state sovereignty" against "outside intervention," drawing on ideas expressed both in the scholarly literature (indeed like those in the first version of this essay[11]) as well as a series of policy speeches by Kofi Annan himself,[12] the report states the following as its basic premise:

> State sovereignty implies responsibility, and the primary responsibility for the protection of its people lies with the state itself. Where a population is suffering serious harm, as a result of internal war, insurgency, repression, or state failure, and the state in question is unwilling or unable to halt or avert it, the principle of non-intervention yields to the international responsibility to protect.[13]

This redefinition of "sovereignty as responsibility" has the salutary effect of avoiding the apparent clash between cosmopolitan human rights and parochial state sovereignty. And the report rightly identifies three specific elements of our response to harm:

1. The responsibility to prevent: to address both the root causes and direct causes of internal conflict and other [hu]man-made crises putting populations at risk.

2. The responsibility to react: to respond to situations of compelling human need with appropriate measures, which may include coercive measures like sanctions and international prosecution, and in extreme cases military intervention.

3. The responsibility to rebuild: to provide, particularly after a military intervention, full assistance with recovery, reconstruction, and reconciliation, addressing the causes of the harm the intervention was designed to halt or avert.[14]

As Thomas Weiss, the staff director of the project and author of a companion research volume, has written, "the Commission sought to drive a stake through the heart of the term 'humanitarian intervention.'"[15] Among scholars and leaders in the third world, the term had taken on an aura, at best, of Western condescension toward newly sovereign states, and at worst, a euphemism for neocolonial interventionism. And, indeed, the post hoc efforts by Bush administration apologists to characterize the Iraq invasion as a "humanitarian intervention" demonstrates that this view had more than a grain of truth. Moreover, the new terminology directs our thinking not to the "rights" of the would-be interveners, but to the situation of those fellow human beings in crisis and of our responsibilities toward them. In the context of this volume, we may be tempted to think not of the "right" of the Good Samaritan to help (or forego helping) the man robbed and lying wounded on the wayside, but of our responsibility to help him in his time of need.

Of course, simply renaming the proposed action will not, in itself, resolve inevitable tensions between the values of protecting traditional state sovereignty and those that reflect a duty to act even when this would mean "violating" sovereignty. To a state at the receiving end of coercive action, justifying that action as a "responsibility to protect" is unlikely to make that action more palatable to it or its allies. Whatever the terminology, we must recognize (as the commission implicitly does) that state sovereignty is a contingent value: its observance depends upon the actions, or inaction, of the state that seeks to invoke it. Members of the international community are not obliged to "respect the sovereignty" of a state that egregiously violates human rights. Or as the Commission put it, we have a collective responsibility to act:

> when there is serious and irreparable harm occurring to human beings, or imminently likely to occur, of the following kind:
>
> A. large-scale loss of life, actual or apprehended, with genocidal intent or not, which is the product either of deliberate state action, or state neglect or inability to act, or a failed state situation; or
>
> B. large-scale "ethnic cleansing," actual or apprehended, whether carried out by killing, forced expulsion, acts of terror, or rape.[16]

How do we determine when this occurs and when our responsibility to act kicks in? The process of judgment should be multinational. For all the flaws of the United Nations, it does provide a forum for international debate and for the emergence of consensus. An insistence on collective, multilateral intervention—or, as in Haiti, collectively approved unilateral action—can correct for self-interested interventions thinly cloaked in humanitarianism. At the same time, it may be just or necessary for a state to declare its intention to act on its own; if the cause is truly just, this declaration may make collective action more possible. The intervention may still be just even if its motives are mixed. For example, India's intervention in the former East Pakistan and Tanzania's in the Uganda of Idi Amin are often cited as unilateral interventions that nevertheless ended humanitarian disasters.[17] Once again the ICISS has outlined a number of criteria that closely track the standards of the just war tradition. And they make an important suggestion on process within the Security Council that, if followed, would go far toward addressing the problem of the "veto" held by the permanent five members.[18]

CONCLUSION

An approach to just peacemaking must include a willingness to recast the sovereignty of states as an international "responsibility to protect" in cases where human rights are egregiously violated. Given the values ideally promoted by nation-states—self-determination, cultural and historical autonomy, domestic law and order, and rudimentary international order—we should not be cavalier about violating traditional sovereignty, but neither should we respect sovereignty at the cost of wholesale injustice and of ignoring grievous violations of human rights. Certainly there is an obligation to develop what might be called ready instruments of rescue, so that disasters like Rwanda or Darfur need not occur for want of a capacity to intervene. Waging peace, no less than waging war, requires us to combine capability with intention. Although the obstacles are formidable, a revitalized United Nations, following the principles of an international responsibility to protect, and equipped with a standing volunteer force ready to act, seems a minimum goal for those who would seek to wage peace in a changing world of states.

Nine

REDUCE OFFENSIVE WEAPONS
AND WEAPONS TRADE

Barbara Green
Glen Stassen[1]

Reducing offensive weapons and the weapons trade produces a more secure international community and frees money to build a more just international community, with reduced poverty. Furthermore, reducing offensive weapons and the weapons trade reduces the number of wars and the destructiveness of wars. We focus on two parts of the practice: first, reducing nuclear weapons, combating their proliferation, and, when possible, reversing it; second, reducing the weapons trade, including a ban on the production, sales, and transfers of antipersonnel land mines. Both parts of the practice significantly reduce the dangers of war; both need active support by U.S. citizens and informed citizens' groups.

REDUCING OFFENSIVE WEAPONS REDUCES INCENTIVES FOR WAR

International-relations scholars regularly note that war is no longer worth the price. With modern weaponry, the enormous destructiveness of the retaliating force means it makes no sense, by any rational calculus, to initiate a war, and then suffer the retaliation. The offensive weapons are unable to destroy the defensive response, and the likely retaliatory response is simply too enormous to risk. It was unthinkable for the United States or the Soviet Union to initiate war with each other; to do so would have been to commit national suicide. Hence, both were careful not to enter into battle where the other was engaged. During the Cold War, the Soviet Union stayed out of Korea and Vietnam, and the United States stayed out of Czechoslovakia and Afghanistan. Robert Jervis has argued cogently that in a nuclear war, the destructive response would be so thoroughly devastating that, even when it is not guaranteed but only a significant probability, deterrence still occurs.[2] When losing the gamble would mean nuclear destruction of one's whole nation, one does not enter into the gamble. This logic applies also to conventional, nonnuclear weapons because these weapons, too, are enormously more destructive than they were a century ago.

This is one major reason for the just peacemaking effectiveness of reducing offensive weapons: reduced offensive capability means one side does not have the capability to destroy the other side's ability to retaliate. If we start a war, we'll get hurt. This reduces the temptation to initiate war. War becomes less likely.

Serbia's wars in Bosnia, Croatia, and Kosovo are the counterexamples that prove the rule: Because the Serbs had controlled the Yugoslav army and kept the weapons when Yugoslavia spit up, they had the offensive capability to initiate a war without much fear of a powerful Muslim counterattack—they thought. Because of their offensive weapons, they thought war would be worth the price. They did not count on NATO intervention.[3]

Another example is the Gulf War. Iraq had built up a large offensive capability, with U.S. assistance. Next to Iraq's offensive capability, Kuwait had little retaliatory capability. Saddam Hussein calculated he could occupy Kuwait with little damage to Iraq from Kuwait's military. He was right. What he had not been told was that international forces would retaliate and cause his troops great damage. And subsequently, the international forces, led by the United States, used international sanctions to reduce Iraq's offensive capability—chemical and biological weapons, Scud missiles, and potential nuclear weapons. They did not want Iraq tempted again by a large offensive capability to attack an oil-rich neighbor or Israel. Iraq was in fact reduced to no threat to its neighbors, as the UN inspection team accurately reported.

The other major counterexample of overwhelming offensive capacity is the United States. U.S. military expenditure is greater than the sum total of all other nations combined. Hence the United States is tempted to initiate wars of intervention, believing other nations lack the power to retaliate, as in the George W. Bush administration being tempted to initiate the war in Iraq. Basic American constitutional wisdom is that concentrated power without checks and balances corrupts; it leads to injustice. The United States, with its enormous concentrated power, needs checks and balances to restrain presidents from yielding to the temptation to initiate wars of intervention (though calling them preemptive). It needs respect for international law and the wisdom of other nations.

This is one of the contributions of just peacemaking theory. Whenever a president seeks to persuade the nation that we are under threat, and it is our nation versus that other nation, and we should defer to presidential authority, that president has always been able to get initial majority support for a war.[4] This has been true in opinion polls in the last one hundred years. (Later, when people begin to realize how destructive the war has been, and that it fails tests of morality, it tends to lose support.) Only by focusing the nation's attention on a constructive alternative to war, as just peacemaking does, can opponents of the war win. Before the Iraq war, five opinion polls asked if the UN inspections should be allowed to finish their work before the war would begin. In all five, the people said yes, by a two-to-one margin. Two polls asked if first UN support should be obtained before making the war, and this question won by almost two to one.[5] Attention needs to be focused on specific alternatives like this if opposition to a war is to win; and just peacemaking generates attention to specific alternatives. We need to put clear alternatives to making war before the people, before the churches, before the Congress, and before the foreign policy elite and the president, so we can all think of better alternatives than yielding to the temptation to make unjust wars. We need an ethic of just peacemaking practices that offer alternatives to the temptation to make wars of intervention while calling them preemptive.

Aside from these counterexamples, the remaining wars have been almost exclusively internal civil wars, guerrilla wars, or terrorism—not international wars. The just peacemaking practices are in fact decreasing international wars.

The logic that war is not worth the price when the offense cannot destroy the defense argues for a change toward defensive force structures. Nations can build a force structure designed to defend against attack more than to initiate an attack. With less offensive than defensive capability, initiating a war is less attractive. For example,

Gorbachev took a dramatic independent initiative (see chapter 2). He removed half the Soviet Union's tanks from Central Europe and all its river-crossing equipment, thus reducing the Warsaw Pact's ability to make a sudden offensive attack; but the USSR retained its defensive capability. This reduced the likelihood of war, and the West realized it. Previously, NATO had worried about a possible blitzkrieg attack by Soviet tanks and so was not willing to get rid of medium-range and shorter-range nuclear missiles in Europe. But after observing the new Soviet force structure, oriented more toward defense, the West agreed to the mutual disarmament of all medium- and shorter-range nuclear missiles (the zero solution). This was the first major disarmament step toward ending the Cold War peacefully.

The practice of reducing offensive weapons has two additional advantages. If, despite the practices that widen the zone of peace, war nevertheless occurs, then there is less killing if there are fewer offensive weapons to do the killing. Let us state this carefully: The difference is not between enormous destruction and minimal destruction; modern weapons are too destructive for that. The difference is between unimaginably horrible killing and somewhat less killing. But the magnitudes are so great that merely "somewhat less" may mean a hundred thousand lives, or in the case of nuclear weapons, hundreds of millions of lives. The picture is hardly rosy, but the difference is significant for the lives of millions of potential victims.

The other advantage of reducing offensive weapons is reducing the monetary cost of weapons build-ups. This produces the ability to spend the money for real human needs that are going unfulfilled. This monetary advantage is in fact causing almost every nation in the world to reduce the percentage of its GNP that it spends for military weapons because that makes sense to realistic decision makers, Nevertheless, there are forces of resistance against reducing offensive weapons and the weapons trade—powerful forces that block sensible reductions. Offensive weapons are still in enormous oversupply in the world. Costs are still enormously destructive to many nations' economies and to human needs. Now is the time for all people who want peace to come to the aid of their countries' *real* security: cut the cost.

THE CASE OF NUCLEAR WEAPONS

A dramatic case is the reduction of nuclear weapons by the Soviet Union, the United States, and NATO as the Cold War was ending.

The break came with "the zero solution": NATO and Gorbachev agreed to destroy all medium- and shorter-range nuclear weapons. This occurred in response to extensive organization, pressure, and initiatives from European and U.S. citizen-action and peace movements. Then U.S. presidents Reagan and Bush agreed to reduce the combined nuclear warheads of the United States and the former Soviet Union from 47,000 to 15,500. Agreements were reached to ban the production of chemical and biological weapons and to destroy their stockpiles. The Comprehensive Test Ban Treaty has impeded the development of new types of nuclear weapons worldwide, even though the U.S. Senate has not yet ratified it as of this writing. Again, the CTBT was negotiated in response to extensive citizen pressure. These reductions in offensive weapons increase our security significantly.

Organized Citizen Pressure Has Been Crucial

People tend to remember these outcomes that make us all safer as the result, finally, of government decisions. But never in the last one hundred years have governments successfully negotiated arms reductions when citizen movements were not pushing strongly and effectively. Governments get stuck bureaucratically, with blocking forces from those pushing for more weapons, usually motivated by a combination of ideology and economic interest. The practices of citizen pressure for reductions, independent initiatives, and cooperative conflict resolution have shown that they can make the world safer. They have also shown the practical possibility of further reductions, which will remove offensive threats that can still cause war and unimaginable destruction by accident, by escalation, and by proliferation of weapons to other countries.[6] Just peacemaking practice is to join in groups supporting internationally mutual reductions, so the whole world is safer. Such groups have often made a significant difference for decreasing the threat and decreasing the cost of building the threat.

For one example, see the accounts mentioned in chapter 2 of the zero solution that got rid of all medium-range nuclear weapons and that was a key to ending the Cold War peacefully. For another example, the George W. Bush administration pushed for building a new nuclear bomb, the bunker buster, designed not to deter but to initiate the use of nuclear weapons even though an adversary had not thus far detonated a nuclear weapon. The peace movement, contacting their representatives in Congress, and wiser heads in Congress from both parties, prevailed, and the bunker buster was busted. It was not built, and that wrongful waste of borrowed money was prevented.

The administration then advocated "the reliable replacement warhead," a proposal to spend billions of dollars for rebuilding all nuclear weapons with new warheads. (All the varieties of nuclear bombs in the arsenal have already been tested, and are already thoroughly reliable. The true name should be "the *usable* replacement warhead," because the intention was to rebuild them in ways intended to make them more usable.) This would signal the world that the U.S. intention was not to move away from the use of nuclear weapons, but to build nuclear weapons that would be more usable. The peace movement again worked with Congress, which then gave this program zero funding in 2008. The administration then proposed to put many billions of dollars into a completely new bomb-manufacturing complex called "Complex Transformation," immediately dubbed "Bomplex Transformation." Again, citizens stated their opposition. (See www.peace-action.org or www.PeaceActionWest.org.) The worst temptation that we must not put before any president or any field commander is the temptation to initiate a nuclear war.

Security Advantages for Reductions

A National Academy of Sciences study signed by a broad array of scientists and national-security specialists who have been engaged in advising governments of both parties on national security policies recommended a first-step reduction to three thousand long-range warheads and then to one thousand for the United States and Russia.[7] The security advantages of the United States and Russia reducing to one thousand warheads each are many.

- Nuclear war is not likely to be initiated intentionally, since starting a nuclear war makes no sense when retaliation would be so devastating. The far greater danger all along has been a panicked response to a false warning of a disarming first-strike attack in a time of tension. Decreasing the number of warheads on each side greatly decreases the ability to launch a disarming first strike and thus decreases this temptation.

- The fewer nuclear weapons we and other nations have, the fewer there are to be fired in an unauthorized launch that would start a nuclear war.

- Reducing the numbers of nuclear warheads removes surplus weapons for which there are no urgent military targets. That provides incentives for obeying the rule against intentionally bombing noncombatants. "An adversary would thus not be able to use available weapons against civilian targets without leaving important military targets uncovered."[8]

- The fewer nuclear weapons there are, the fewer there are for terrorists or other nations to steal or purchase. This threat is especially real in Russia, where many nuclear weapons still remain. A global crime network is growing in strength that could make profits from selling enriched uranium or plutonium, or bomb components, or technical knowledge. And economically threatened scientists, military personnel, members of the control network, and politicians may be readily tempted by offers of money for their weapons, their plutonium or uranium, and their scientific skills. Faced with the threat of terrorism, we have enormous incentives for reducing the numbers of weapons and the amount of fissionable bomb fuel available for theft.

- If the United States and Russia agree to reduce to one thousand nuclear weapons each, they will have a stronger case for persuading other nuclear powers to reduce and restrict their arsenals. The problem is especially acute in the Middle East, where Israel has an undeclared arsenal of over two hundred weapons, and where, combined with the intense rivalries and hostilities of the region, this fuels pressures for Iran, Egypt, and Syria to go nuclear.[9]

- The fewer nuclear weapons we and other nations have, the millions or billions fewer people will be killed if they are used, and the less radiation will be spread throughout the world to make life miserable for those who survive.

The more we reduce the level of nuclear weapons worldwide, the safer we are. In December 1996 General Lee Butler, former commander-in-chief of the U.S. Strategic Command, and sixty-one other retired generals and admirals called for the step-by-step abolition of nuclear weapons, arguing that they have no use except to endanger our lives. The generals also know that the United States has such a preponderance of conventional weapons that it would be safer and actually comparatively stronger if nuclear weapons are eradicated. The peace movement has adopted the same goal, with Peace Action being the largest group working on abolition. As we approach zero, solutions to the problem of verification are likely to become clearer, and each step of multilateral reductions toward zero will make our lives safer. We need to embark on the journey toward complete abolition of nuclear weapons.

An influential editorial in *The Wall Street Journal* (January 4, 2007) by seventeen conservative U.S. former national security policy-makers, including George P. Shultz, William J. Perry, Henry A. Kissinger, and Sam Nunn, declared that the existence of large numbers of nuclear weapons in the world not only threatens to destroy untold numbers of humankind; it decreases U.S. security. With a wealth of national security experience, they argue for steps toward international elimination of reliance on nuclear weapons. They have not only made a statement; they will be organizing a movement in this direction. They are saying that today's problem is not deterring the Soviet Union, but preventing proliferation of nuclear weapons into potentially dangerous hands. Therefore, continuing Cold-War reliance on nuclear weapons is a grave danger to U.S. security as well as world security. With nuclear weapons in the hands of eight nations at present, and possibly spreading elsewhere, with enriched uranium and plutonium in several locations, there are greater chances of some getting into the hands of a terrorist organization, or of some being used by one or another nation. The United States, as well as other nations, would be far more secure in a nuclear-free world. The power of the U.S. military to deter a conventional attack is more effective than nuclear weapons are against a nuclear attack.

These conservative national security experts advocate specific steps: reducing the size of nuclear forces internationally, ratifying the Comprehensive Test Ban Treaty, halting production internationally of fissile materials for weapons, and redoubling efforts for resolving regional conflicts. The more worldwide reductions in nuclear weapons are achieved, the safer we all are. But unilateral disarmament would not solve the problem. It must be achieved by international agreements and international cooperation.

REDUCE AVAILABLE PLUTONIUM AND URANIUM FOR BOMBS

We already have a huge surplus of bomb fuel, increased daily by the plutonium (Pu) and highly enriched uranium (HEU) removed from decommissioned nuclear weapons. We do not know how to store what surplus we have. Nor does it wear out any time soon; its half-life is 2,400 years. There is no need for more until at least 4,800 years from now. Our strong concern about the spread of nuclear fissionable bomb fuel for nuclear weapons to North Korea, Iran, etc., or to terrorists, supports the need to achieve a worldwide fissionable fuels production ban; more fuel is an invitation to proliferation.

President Clinton canceled the breeder reactor, the advanced liquid metal reactor (ALMR), which would have bred more plutonium. Furthermore, "for environmental and safety reasons the U.S. has ceased producing Pu for military purposes and is not reprocessing civilian reactor fuel for recovery of Pu."[10] It has also ceased producing highly enriched uranium. In September 1993 at the United Nations, President Clinton announced a new nonproliferation policy, which included a proposal for a multilateral ban on the production of new fissile material for nuclear weapons and international monitoring of all production of fissile material. "In addition, the U.S. pledged to remove the fissile material it considers excess to its nuclear-weapon needs from military stocks and place it under international safeguards" if Russia would do the same.[11] "A multilateral, nondiscriminatory, and effectively verifiable nuclear fissile material production ban would strengthen substantially the nonproliferation regime by restraining the unsafeguarded nuclear programs of certain non-NPT states for the first time. It would also halt the production of separated plutonium and highly enriched uranium for nuclear explosives in the five declared nuclear-weapon states."[12] We can press Congress and the president to agree to talks on a fissionable fuels production ban. Other nations agreed to the Fissile Materials Cutoff Treaty, but the George W. Bush administration blocked it.

A crucial covenant that has been unexpectedly effective in halting the spread of nuclear weapons is the Nonproliferation Treaty (NPT). Since it was signed in 1968, only two nations—Pakistan and India—have developed nuclear weapons. Kazakhstan, Ukraine, and all former Soviet countries have agreed not to go nuclear and have given up their nuclear weapons to Russia. Sixteen other nations began to develop nuclear weapons, but were persuaded by assurances from other nations to reverse course and not develop them—including Libya, North Korea, South Africa, Brazil, and Argentina.[13] After six years of refusing to talk with North Korea about its nuclear program, which resulted in North Korea developing enough plutonium for about ten nuclear bombs and test-exploding one in 2006, the Bush administration finally agreed to talk, and Assistant Secretary of State Christopher Hill solved the problem in two days. Thus was demonstrated the effectiveness of the just peacemaking practice of cooperative conflict resolution over relying on threats while refusing to talk. Pressure built for the administration to agree similarly to talk with Iran, without preconditions, about their nuclear enrichment program.

Article VI of the NPT commits the nations that have nuclear weapons "to pursue negotiations in good faith on effective measures relating to cessation of the nuclear arms race at an early date and to nuclear disarmament, and on a treaty on general and complete disarmament under strict and effective international control." The United States may either comply with this promise and thus strengthen the Nonproliferation Treaty, or it may refuse and instead build more usable nuclear weapons, thus weakening the NPT while placing the temptation to initiate their use in the hands of a president or a field commander.

186

WEAPONS TRADE

The practice of reducing the weapons trade is already being carried out by many of the purchasing nations themselves. As nations turn toward democracy and respect for human rights, their governments have less need for an oversized military to keep them in power by threat of force. As their neighbors turn toward democracy, they feel less threatened and have less need for weapons. As they struggle with their deep indebtedness, they have less ability to buy weapons. Furthermore, the International Monetary Fund began requiring big reductions in expenditures for weapons if nations are to receive loans or aid. For these or other reasons,

> the real news from the 1996 Congressional Research Study released in August by Richard Grimmett is that selling arms to the third world is a dead-end market economically; at $15 billion for 1995, the developing world's arms imports dropped to just one-quarter of their peak in 1988. . . . We should recognize that the shrinking demand for high-tech armaments represents an unprecedented opportunity for controlling the arms trade.[14]

In a later report, Grimmett concluded that the developing world's arms reports continued to decrease, so that 2006 was the lowest year since the peak in 1988, once the amount is adjusted for inflation and measured in constant dollars: "In 2006, the value of all arms deliveries to developing nations was $19.9 billion, the lowest total in these deliveries values for the entire 1999–2006 period (in constant 2006 dollars)."[15] Had the U.S. government not sent large amounts to Pakistan, which they used not for weapons useful against enclaves of terrorists but for large weapons useful against India, the drop would have been greater. In 2006, Pakistan ranked first in the value of arms transfer agreements among all developing nations weapons purchasers, concluding $5.1 billion in such agreements. India ranked second with $3.5 billion in such agreements. Saudi Arabia ranked third with $3.2 billion.[16]

Poor nations whose governments spend large amounts on military weapons are being deprived of much needed money for the necessities of life and are likely to have their human rights breached by a government that relies on military weapons to dominate its people. When the George W. Bush administration declared the War on Terror, it increased its support for the military in nations like Indonesia, where the military has been a threat to human rights—as it was in East Timor. Foreign aid should be contingent on a recipient nation holding its military spending below a set percentage of its income. The precedent is straightforward: President Carter's encouragement of human rights became far more effective once U.S. foreign aid was made contingent on assessment of the human-rights record of recipient nations. This helped nudge Latin American nations to become democracies with human rights rather than national security states with dictators, as many had been prior to Carter's and the churches' push for human rights. Arms sales undermine human rights and distribute weapons that often boomerang, being used against the seller's troops, as happened to the United States in Somalia, Afghanistan, and Iraq.

The Center for Defense Information reported that "the six largest traders control over 90 percent of the arms transfers to the developing world," which is the most unstable region and which can least afford to be spending its countries' limited incomes on arms races.

Many arms sales are based on U.S. subsidies to purchasing nations (which cost U.S. taxpayers heavily) and on offsets, which are agreements to transfer U.S. manufacturing jobs to other nations in exchange for their agreeing to purchase U.S. weapons.

Because of limited regulations regarding the weapons trade, many of these weapons are not tracked. According to Oxfam and Amnesty International, thousands of people have been forced to flee, were injured or killed, and have been raped or displaced as a result of the highly deregulated international weapons trade. The United Nations has set up an arms control group to devise ways to control the illicit weapons trade. Conspicuously, during weapons trade talks on stemming illicit weapons trades, the United States opposed trade limitations and regulations. As seen in John Bolton's (U.S. ambassador to the UN in the Bush administration) arguments to the United Nations Illicit Trade of Small Arms and Light Weapons conference, the United States wanted to help stem the flow of illicit small arms but opposed any regulations or strictures on who can buy legitimate arms, how many arms are produced, or what to do with the surplus arms.[17]

188

The Dutch response, from their minister of foreign affairs in 2001, Mr. Jozias van Aartsen, straightforwardly asserted the need to limit the civilian weapons trade, eliminate surplus weapons, and place stronger regulations on the arms industry, particularly in the area of transparency. He pointed out that Cambodia started to see faster development after that country implemented a program that eliminated surplus weapons.[18]

The weapons trade can have a major impact on the development of people and nations. Some nations have been disrupted by constant conflict, such as the fighting over the uranium mines along the Congo/Rwanda border. Resources are sold, weapons are bought, and the fighting continues; it is difficult to change this, since there is no infrastructure to invest in that could supply alternative means of income. Often large-scale aid schemes proposed by the World Bank or IMF fail because they are not geared toward creating economic growth in environments where there are no functional micro-economies to network together. In *The End of Poverty*, Jeffrey Sachs suggests there is no way to capitalize in much of Africa because there is nothing to fund.[19] Years of violent warfare and massive health problems mean that there is no infrastructure and there are few healthy workers.

Despite these challenges, there are examples of people developing creative ways to change the economic realities of central Africa. A superb example is Ngoy Mulunda, a pastor in eastern Congo, who has been getting fighters to turn in their guns for bicycles. The concept is micro-economic development at work; these fighters, many very young, now have a means of moving goods and people for monetary gain. It is a first step toward breaking the cycle of warfare revolving around the exploitation of natural resources; it allows people to get onto the macro-economic ladder that Sachs describes as a way to alleviate poverty without having to rely on the uranium mines. Without replacing the mines with other forms of income, fighting will continue for whatever other natural resources can be sold. Oxfam and Amnesty International write:

> Each of the G8 governments has a particular responsibility to control arms and to respect and ensure respect for human rights and international humanitarian law. . . . Excessive or inappropriate arms purchases are also a drain on social and economic resources. In some developing countries the result is that badly needed resources are diverted away from the fight against poverty. Many of the G8 countries are large donors to aid programmes in Africa and Asia. However, continuing arms transfers to developing countries undermine their pledges to relieve debt, combat AIDS, alleviate poverty, tackle corruption, and promote good governance. The transfer of arms and related military assistance also impedes development when the items are transferred to unaccountable and poorly trained military forces that are used to suppress human rights, democracy, and socio-economic development. Such arms transfers can facilitate brutal resource exploitation, and environmental degradation. They can contribute to an increase in violence against civilians. The presence of guns in society has a particular impact on women's lives. Large numbers of women and girls are at risk of armed violence, whether they are directly involved in the fighting or dealing with the emotional, social and economic consequences of the loss of male relatives who have been killed or injured by gun violence. Given the effects of weapons misuse, it is shocking how few governments give serious thought to the impact on development and human rights of their arms exports. And for the few that do, it has yet to become a genuine priority.[20]

This is not a new concept. As early as 1982, the United Nations sponsored the Thorsson Report on arms and development. It noted that previous reports had been too cautious about noting the severity of the problems that result from arms interfering with development. The report concluded that its "investigation suggests very strongly that the world can either continue to pursue the arms race with characteristic vigour or move consciously and with deliberate speed toward a more stable and balanced social and economic development. It cannot do both."[21]

Banning Landmines

Another part of the practice of reducing the weapons trade is a ban on the production, sale, and transfer of antipersonnel landmines. In 1992, Senator Leahy and Representative Evans introduced the Landmines Moratorium Act, imposing a moratorium on the sale and export of antipersonnel land mines. People rallied in its support, and the moratorium passed and was renewed, *temporarily*. In response to extensive public pressure and endorsement from many top U.S. military leaders, General Shalikashvili, chairman of the Joint Chiefs of Staff, ordered a review of U.S. policy and indicated that he was "inclined to eliminate all antipersonnel landmines."[22] The Clinton administration almost agreed to a ban on landmines, but then refused (perhaps in the process of defending its military flank against anticipated election politics). Other nations have ratified the international treaty banning landmines, but the United States has refused, as of this writing.

The United States should lead other nations to a worldwide ban instead of resisting it. Insisting on an exception for itself legitimizes refusals by other nations. Landmines are made to hide in fields, paths, and travel routes and to kill, amputate, or maim for life whoever passes—child, adult, soldier, civilian. They are cheap, easy to acquire, and devastating—but expensive to remove. They have been used most in developing countries. Banning them is a key step in reducing the weapons trade. The U.S. military is ready to do it; what is required is for political leaders to sense that the people want it and that, thus, it would be politically advantageous. Senator Leahy announced a new bill on landmines in 1997 that mandated a permanent ban on U.S. landmine use starting in 2000, with an annually renew-

190

able exemption for Korea. That bill, though, never became law. Church groups and peace and justice groups continued to exert strong pressure to ban landmines. A Canadian proposal then successfully led to an international treaty banning landmines. Most other nations eventually entered the treaty, but the Bush administration refused. The United States needs to sign the treaty, not only to ban its own landmines but also to support the ban for other nations. This should be business for the Obama administration.

OBSTACLES

We have already mentioned some causal factors for the weapons trade in purchasing nations: authoritarian governments, influence of the military in national security states, fear of hostile neighbor nations. These factors can be reduced by practices described in other chapters: support for action to push for human rights and democratization; support for cooperative forces in the international system, including the United Nations; encouraging the U.S. government to require dramatic reductions in military expenditures before aid is approved.

Another cause is the United States' subsidies of weapons exports to other nations. The U.S. government and commercial manufacturers fan the flames of regional conflicts by subsidizing arms sales abroad. Russia, China, and France are competing ferociously for shares in the global arms market, with Britain, Germany, Israel, Italy, and the Czech Republic claiming niches for themselves. The 1996 Congressional Research Study by Richard Grimmett, cited previously, shows that for 1995 Russia surpassed the United States in arms sales to Third World countries. The Grimmett report, though, shows all sales by other countries but only country-to-country sales for the United States, leaving out commercial sales. The United States has dominated the global market since the collapse of the Soviet Union.

Additionally, the corrupting force of large contributions of money to political candidates from weapons manufacturers distorts decision-making processes regarding the weapons trade and regarding nuclear weapons. The profits are huge, so weapons manufacturers can spend lavishly to influence government spending policies. The Federal Election Commission reported these data that we cited in the first edition of *Just Peacemaking*:[23]

Selected Military Contractor Political Action Committee Contributions to 1994 Congressional Campaigns

General Electric	$328,300
Lockheed	$315,891
Martin Marietta	$285,160
General Dynamics	$258,263
Textron	$243,460
Boeing Corporation	$173,745
Northrop	$164,068
Rockwell	$160,020
McDonnell Douglas	$153,200
Loral Systems	$144,400

More recent data compare the total value of the military contracts awarded to the top nine companies for work in Iraq and Afghanistan with the amount they gave to political campaign funding from 1990 to 2003:[24]

Military Contracts in Iraq and Afghanistan Compared with Political Donations

Contractor	Military Contract Total	Campaign Contributions
Kellogg, Brown & Root (Halliburton)	$ 11,431,000,000	$ 2,379,792
Parsons Corp.	$ 5,286,136,252	$ 1,403,508
Fluor Corp.	$ 3,754,964,295	$ 3,624,173
Washington Group International	$ 3,133,078,193	$ 1,185,232
Shaw Group/Shaw E & I	$ 3,050,749,910	no data
Bechtel Group Inc.	$ 2,829,833,859	$ 3,310,102
Perini Corporation	$ 2,525,000,000	$ 119,000
Contrack International Inc.	$ 2,325,000,000	$ 2,000
Tetra Tech Inc.	$ 1,541,947,671	$ 223,770
Total	$ 35,877,710,180	$ 12,247,577

If these political donations are considered a business investment, a total of $12 million in political donations, 1990–2003, yields $35 billion in contracts, 2003–2006—not including additional military contracts outside Iraq and Afghanistan. In other words, one dollar in political investment yields $3,000 in military contracts in after-war rebuilding.

Surely these donations are designed to skew policies toward more military expenditures for their companies, while decreasing taxes for the wealthy CEOs and owners. The U.S. government's indebtedness exploded from $4 trillion total for all previous administrations since George Washington through Bill Clinton, to $10 trillion after the George W. Bush administration. So the value of these contracts is being charged to the public *with interest*. This is clearly bad for the economy as a whole, and it engenders resentment by other nations whose businesses were not considered for rebuilding contracts in Iraq. Persuading the policymakers to spend $600 billion a year for the military budget, not including the added cost of the Iraq and Afghanistan wars, amasses trillions of dollars of indebtedness. It causes the transfer of money from more-labor-intensive economic sectors to highly capital-intensive military industries, which produce far fewer jobs than money invested in roads, bridges, schools, and health care. Furthermore, it takes money away from jobs programs, neighborhood programs, drug clinics, educational improvements, health care, and help for the working poor, thus damaging the future for many young people. Sadly, corporate profits and the growth of personal fortunes for a select few have had inordinate influence in competition with the value of good governance and with regard for human life.

The war in Iraq is a prime example of the crushing costs associated with war and private interests. Columbia economist Joseph Stiglitz and Harvard lecturer Linda Bilmes have calculated that the war in Iraq will cost $3 trillion in today's money. This assumes a U.S. pull-back from Iraq after the election in 2008, but a small presence there for the next decade:

> By the end of 2008, the federal government will have spent more than $800 billion on combat operations in Iraq and Afghanistan. . . . On top of that comes a mountain of future costs: caring for war veterans . . . , replacing the military hardware that is being used and worn out in Iraq and paying interest on the enormous sums of money we've borrowed to finance the war. . . . Because of irresponsible fiscal policy (cutting taxes for the rich while a war is in progress and borrowing the money to pay for the conflict), the burden of paying for this costly adventure has been shifted to younger Americans.[25]

193

Compare this with early estimates from White House budget director Mitch Daniels, who called estimates of $100–200 billion "high."[26]

The logical way to correct this distortion of the decision process is
to limit the influence of money on political campaigns. Common
Cause and many others are pushing for limits on political contributions from all sources, and limits on campaign spending, including soft
as well as hard money. Until the power of money to corrupt the decision process is curtailed, it will be hard to make the process peaceable.

Additional Financial Incentives for Arming the World

The United States government invests large sums of money to stimu-
late distribution of weapons worldwide:

- Federal subsidies for arms exports represent the second-largest
  subsidy program for business in the entire federal budget, after
  agricultural price supports.

- The U.S. government is the world's largest arms broker, spending
  over $450 million and employing nearly 6,500 full-time personnel
  to promote and service foreign arms sales by U.S. companies. The
  Pentagon alone has a full-time arms-sales staff of 6,395.

- Federal government expenditures on promoting weapons at international air and trade shows average over $26.5 million per year.
  The Pentagon actually receives a 3 percent commission for every
  foreign arms sale it negotiates.

- U.S. arms exports in 1995 totaled an estimated $12 billion. Of that
  sum, $7.6 billion was paid by taxpayer subsidies—more than one-
  half of all exports.

Regional Arms Races

Under the excess-arms programs, the U.S. Army, Navy, and Air Force
are transferring relatively sophisticated systems to other countries.
Following the Gulf War, the Army gave Israel surplus Apache attack
helicopters, Black-hawk transport helicopters, multiple-launch rocket
systems, and Patriot tactical antimissiles. In 1995, four M-1 Abrams
tank turrets were provided to Egypt as excess defense articles. (Egypt
is building 535 M-1A1 tanks under license from General Dynamics.)

Even older equipment, like M-60 tanks and F-4 aircraft purchased
in the 1960s or 1970s, can remain quite formidable through regular
upgrades and modifications. While these weapons seem dated to the

U.S. armed services, they often become the centerpiece of foreign militaries. A discarded U.S. Navy ship, for instance, will serve as the flagship of Bahrain's navy. Similarly, Greece, Turkey, Egypt, and Morocco have each received hundreds of used M-60 tanks for free, creating large modern tank armies that they otherwise could not afford.

In other cases, American surplus arms seem to be fanning regional rivalries, as excess weapons are sent to both sides of several ongoing arms races. Significant quantities of surplus arms are going to Argentina and Chile, embroiled in a nascent arms race and ongoing border disputes. In the Middle East, American surplus arms are flowing to both Israel and Egypt, engaged in a cold peace. Most notable is the vast amount of arms that the United States has given to hostile NATO partners Turkey and Greece.

In 1994, Admiral Edward Shaefer, director of naval intelligence, called Turkish-Greek animosity "among the most worrisome situations developing in Europe, and the one most dangerous to NATO as an institution." In February 1996, this long-simmering tension boiled over. President Clinton had to intervene to head off a military confrontation. Shaefer said that the "Greco-Turkish dynamic has been exacerbated by a continuing Aegean naval buildup prompted by Western naval surplus disposals. Greece has acquired virtually a completely modernized surface force from the United States, Germany, and the Netherlands. . . . In order to redress the naval balance in the Aegean, Turkey has found it necessary to accept U.S. Navy offers for eight Knox-class frigates." The United States has transferred more than sixteen warships to this antagonistic pair and large quantities of tanks, aircraft, and artillery as well.[27]

During the 1980s, the Iran/Iraq war was one of the prime examples of the arms trade fueling warfare. The United States had built up Iran's large offensive capability, selling the Shah more weapons in ten years than it sold to all of NATO combined in the same ten-year period. After the fall of the Shah, the United States decided that Iran's military strength (which we had financed and supplied) needed to be checked; we began selling heavy weapons to Saddam Hussein's regime for use in Iraq's war with Iran.[28] While we were supplying the Iraqis, we were also secretly supplying the Iranian military in an arms-for-hostages deal.[29]

During this time period, Hussein was systematically killing Kurds in northern Iraq. The United States was still selling him weapons during this atrocity. In 1991, we wound up fighting to drive Saddam out of Kuwait, facing the weapons we had sold him during the 1980s. The costs of supplying both sides can be measured in political embarrassment when our Iran-Contra deal was exposed, and in Iranian and Iraqi lives.

The 1990s presented a new horror in the form of the genocide in Rwanda. This conflict was an example of postcolonial tension breaking into violent civil war and wholesale slaughter.[30] Providing the weapons in this conflict were France, Belgium, the United Kingdom, and others. They sold arms to both the government forces and the rebel factions that were fighting for control of the country, all the while knowing that the government forces were going after Hutu civilians. This arms race contributed to the deaths of almost eight hundred thousand people, lives that underwrote the profits of Western European arms dealers.[31]

In 2006, Israeli army and Hezbollah fighters in southern Lebanon had a two-month conflict. Hezbollah forces kidnapped an Israeli soldier and Israel retaliated with heavy shelling and bombing in both the Golan Heights region and in Beirut, killing civilians and destroying civil infrastructure. During the bombing campaign, Hezbollah forces were firing rockets into northern Israel, thus putting the lives of civilians at great risk.[32]

Both sides of this conflict have been antagonistic toward each other for years, and yet the United States still supplies huge amounts of armaments to Israel. Russia, via Iran and Syria, still supplies large numbers of conventional arms to Hezbollah and other nonstate political terrorist groups.[33] Here is yet another example of two major G-8 countries, both significant arms suppliers, fueling conflict for profit in spite of the political need to be consciously stemming the number of arms flowing into this volatile region.

If we wish to see peace in the most volatile regions of the world, we need to create an international community where peace has a chance to grow and prosper. The provision of arms and the influx of war-making capacity work in diametric opposition to the efforts of peacemakers. In terms of small arms proliferation, the threats to peace and security can be seen in the internal wars, insurgencies, and killings that have been fueled over the years by the small arms trade. In cases where government repression or other abuses are prevalent, transfers of small arms, light weapons, ammunition, bombs, and missiles are of primary concern, as these are the implements that actually kill people. From the early days of proxy warfare to the more recent conflicts spawned during the "War on Terror," we can see situations where the global arms trade has been the primary stumbling block on the road to sustainable peace.

By working together to remove weapons from the equation, we reduce the risks of offensive war, create an environment where talks and cooperative conflict resolution are more likely to occur (since armed conflict is no longer as big a temptation), and change the dynamics of the regional conflicts that are fueled by the acquisition of conventional arms.

Off-budget Procurements and Downstream Costs

As Admiral Shaefer noted, the United States is not the only country getting rid of surplus arms and contributing to regional arms races. West Germany inherited and then sold off the weapons of East Germany. Russia demobilized troops in large numbers, creating an enormous arms surplus that it sought to sell, and the Netherlands has marketed abroad its older ships, aircraft, and army vehicles. Eastern European countries sought to export tanks and other combat equipment limited by the Conventional Forces in Europe Treaty, much as the United States did. Poland and Czechoslovakia marketed their surplus weapons in Syria and Iran, causing great alarm in Washington. Particularly dangerous in this respect is an Air Force initiative to sell old weapons to fund the procurement of new weapons. In early 1994, the U.S. Air Force disclosed plans to finance the purchase of up to ninety new F-16C/D aircraft through sales of some 360 older model F-16A/B fighter jets. Air Force Vice-Chief of Staff Michael Carns, an architect of the plan, said the scheme would give him "brand new war-fighting planes at no cost to the taxpayer."

To overcome arms control opposition, the Air Force put a Madison Avenue spin on the sales plan, repackaging it as "coalition force enhancement"—a way to strengthen friendly militaries. Over a dozen countries were briefed on the availability of the cheap F-16s (at $9–14 million per plane), including Argentina, Chile, the Czech Republic, Egypt, South Korea, Malaysia, Morocco, New Zealand, the Philippines, Poland, Singapore, Thailand, and Tunisia.

The potential downstream costs of this practice are considerable, especially if other exporters also seek to fund their weapons procurement through arms sales. In fact, the U.S. government has protested vociferously in the past when other governments pursued such a policy. In 1991, China's practice of buying new weapons with the proceeds from weapons exports generated outrage in the Western press. U.S. government officials heavily denounced a Russian plan in the early 1990s to finance arms industry conversion through arms sales. In both cases, U.S. officials criticized the creation of a dangerous and short-sighted bureaucratic interest in selling weapons abroad.

With all the arms available and the instability that comes with them, the United States ends up spending a great deal of money on peacekeeping operations. In 2008 there were seventeen peacekeeping operations going on worldwide, the bulk of which were in Africa, and much of the cost was borne by the United States. Reducing the arms trade and availability of weapons to developing countries would decrease the need for expensive peacekeeping and refugee operations down the road. Arms imports to places like Sudan and the Golan Heights have fueled the violence that UN missions have tried to quell.

198   The Joint Chiefs of Staff stated in their 1992 Joint Military Net assessment that instability arises "in areas where nations are acquiring increasingly sophisticated and expensive military equipment and large armed forces. This tendency undermines regional stability and the balance of power and defers economic growth."

When we look at the sales numbers and note that 70 percent of the weapons sold are bound for the developing world, it becomes apparent that these countries are not producing the weapons used to fight their civil and guerilla wars. It is a strange and sad paradox then, that the nations that are ostensibly funding and supplying the UN peacekeeping missions are the biggest suppliers of the weapons that fuel the conflicts that create the need for the peacekeeping operations.

A NEW MODEST BEGINNING AT A TEACHABLE MOMENT

In the first edition of this chapter, we talked about linking arms trades to human rights promotion. This still needs to be our call. Several of the countries receiving large quantities of U.S. arms through surplus programs are engaged in conflict or have poor human rights records. The declared War on Terror partially shifted U.S. support from enhancing human rights to relying on military or authoritarian establishments, which have not been effective in spreading human rights or decreasing recruitment to terrorist organizations. Pakistan is one example in the news at the time of this writing—where Pervez Musharraf seized power in a military coup d'ètat, twice suspended the constitution of Pakistan, was rewarded by large amounts of heavy weapons not designed for local antiterrorist war but for battle against India, used them to get political support from the military, violated human rights, and thereby increased recruits to terrorism. He was finally overthrown in an election.

Global restraint in arms production and exports would make a true contribution to global and regional peacemaking and peacekeeping. Pursuing peace with one hand while doling out weapons with the other is cynical and counterproductive. We have described practices that are reducing offensive weapons and have demonstrated that, despite powerful obstacles, these practices are bringing significant reductions. They need the support of people who care about the peace of the world and who see a major opportunity as well as great danger at this turning point in world history. Warren Christopher, secretary of state in the Clinton administration, told Congress that the "millions spent now on multilateral preventative democracy, emergency refugee support, and peacekeeping may save hundreds of millions in defense and international relief later."[34]

As we slow the trade and sale of weapons to other countries, our own efforts to decrease our military size and increase our diplomatic and development programs would go a long way toward promoting peace and nonmilitary solutions to conflicts. We must make a concerted effort to promote an environment of trust; as we decrease the number of weapons available, we promote an international community where the ability to trust one another becomes a more attainable goal. We need to move away from the supply of weapons for profit and the gross overproduction of armaments that are sold at huge discount to violent regimes and nonstate actors.

We face many obstacles in today's political environment. As people of faith in church communities but in a social context dominated by the ideology of profit maximization, we have failed to make the most of the modest beginning proposed in the first edition of this chapter. Disaster and warfare are seen as profit-maximizing ventures and the global sale of arms to the poorest and most vulnerable regions of the world are seen as business opportunities with little regulation.

Our call now, more importantly then ever, is to demand that our fiscal resources go to development and diplomacy, not arms subsidies.

Our call is to support the lawmakers and activist groups that push for a foreign policy that does not cynically arm nations and factions that instead desperately need our help to achieve peace. We face a new "modest beginning," framed in a new global context. The risks now are as great as they have ever been, but the opportunity to change the global paradigm is upon us; in the words of Raymond Williams, "To be truly radical is to make hope possible rather than despair convincing." We have reached a new turning point in world history, a teachable moment, and the time to make hope a reality is now.

Ten

ENCOURAGE GRASSROOTS PEACEMAKING GROUPS AND VOLUNTARY ASSOCIATIONS

Duane K. Friesen

As the United Church of Christ document "A Just Peace Church" states: "Just peace requires peacemakers."[1] A just peacemaking theory presupposes not only individual peacemakers but a community of peacemakers. It requires groups of citizens who take peacemaking initiatives themselves and who encourage governments to do so. Individuals should form or join such groups; governments should support freedom of assembly, freedom of information, and the right to petition the government. And in situations where governments resist democratic institutions and democratic change, nonviolent movements and organizations have been formed and have been effective in helping create peace with justice.[2]

The ten practices of just peacemaking theory are already implicitly shared by a network of interlocking groups of people at a grassroots level. The relatively new phenomenon in history of a network of peacemaking groups can be seen in the following developments, among others:

1. A growing knowledge, awareness, and experience (recently evident in the collapse of the Soviet empire) of nonviolent movements for social change in the traditions of Gandhi and King.

2. An interlocking network of NGOs and INGOs (nongovernmental organizations and international nongovernmental organizations,

such as church organizations, Amnesty International, Peace Action, United Nations/USA, etc.) that bring pressure to bear on governments all over the globe on everything from human rights to arms control and reduction.

3. An increasing networking and cooperation worldwide of people across confessional and religious boundaries and barriers.

4. The coming together of these people into clusters of local organizations, just peace and justice groups in churches, and interfaith committees—not just isolated individuals.

5. A strengthening of international governmental organizations that may be able to work more effectively on common human problems, and perhaps the emergence of a United Nations World Disaster Relief Force (UNWDRF).

6. Increasing awareness and study of the vast repertoire of processes and skills by which most people make peace most of the time, and with that knowledge the possibility of extending those processes to an ever wider sphere of human interaction.

202

Having said this, however, we must acknowledge that this worldwide network represents a small minority (especially those who work at the peacemaking vocation intentionally) in a world that is in a rather desperate situation. We know of a number of major unresolved armed conflicts, people living in desperate situations of poverty and hunger, serious abuses of human rights, as well as a globe threatened by major environmental problems. These desperate needs of the world require that we extend and expand this global peacemaking network. One way that network can be expanded is for ethicists to seek to identify those norms that can provide a framework for increased cooperation and mission in the world by people of diverse cultural, national, and religious orientations.

Identifying ethical norms, however, will not be sufficient if we do not nurture moral communities that can form people of character. The analysis of North American society reflected in *Habits of the Heart* has shown how American society increasingly nurtures an individualism that erodes commitment to the common good.[3] Communities that nurture a commitment to a social vision are increasingly being eroded by an ethic of "self-interest" that acts on the premise that individual well-being is the ultimate value. Larry Rasmussen argues that we are living on "moral fragments" that are being destroyed more quickly than they are being replenished. He says increasingly our society is dominated by the instrumental value of "rational self-interest." In this view: "All society and its decisions can be fashioned and executed in the manner economic actors do—with the calculation of self- and group interest in relationships that are fundamentally instrumental in character. Stripped down, . . . rational self-interest is the one language everyone can understand and ought to apply to decisions and actions in every domain."[4]

We cannot take for granted the institutions of civil society (families, churches, synagogues, neighborhoods) that form people of character. Such communities can form people morally willing to commit their energies to just peacemaking because they believe it is right in and of itself. The conditions of our world require that we be willing to embrace the strangers, those with no voice, if we are really serious about just peacemaking. A calculating self-interest will not sustain us. A deep commitment to the intrinsic values of compassion and justice are essential for the costly and enduring commitment to just peacemaking required by the conditions in our world.

However, simply having a set of values is not enough to make someone an active peacemaker. In his book *Acts of Compassion: Caring for Others and Helping Ourselves*, sociologist Robert Wuthnow cites statistics to show that the likelihood for compassionate behavior requires a combination of belief in these values and regular participation in an organized religious community.

> Religious inclinations make very little difference unless one becomes involved in some kind of organized religious community. Once you are involved in such a community, then a higher level of piety may be associated with putting yourself out to help the needy. But if you are not involved in some kind of religious organization, then a higher level of piety seems unlikely to generate charitable efforts toward the poor or disadvantaged.[5]

For suggestions on how to organize a church peacemaker group, see www.ecapc.org.

As we stated in the introduction, religious communities keep alive the memory of their paradigmatic stories (such as the Exodus or the good Samaritan [Luke 18:18–30]). Such community memory is essential to the moral formation of people of character. Wuthnow notes that most Americans have a vague knowledge of the good Samaritan story as being about someone who helped a needy person. But participation in a religious community nurtures the more profound meaning of the story: the "possibility of kindness existing among strangers."[6] Wuthnow believes that keeping alive such stories is important to the continued practice of a kind of compassion that reaches across barriers to generate reconciliation. Jesus' parable jars us to consider that it is the social outcast, the excluded one, who shows compassion. The story forces us to consider ways in which divisions between rich and poor, black and white, male and female, citizen and alien can be overcome.

The sacrificial, costly work of peacemaking, illustrated in the story of the good Samaritan, is vividly represented by women who organize in the struggle for peace and justice in repressive and violent societies in Central America. In her book *Voices of the Voiceless: Women, Justice, and Human Rights in Guatemala*, Michelle Tooley documents the prominent role of women in human rights organizations in Guatemala in the last two decades. The violence of the 1980s especially served as a catalyst for women to become involved in collective action for social change. Rigoberta Menchu, winner of the 1992 Nobel Peace Prize, has been one of the primary leaders of her people in the struggle for justice amidst violence and repression.

One of the human-rights groups to survive longer than any other in Guatemala, despite the systematic repression by the police, army, and paramilitary death squads, has been Grupo de Apoyo Mutuo (GAM). Women formed the group to find their disappeared family and friends. Although GAM includes men, 90 percent of its constituency is female; 80 percent is indigenous. GAM seeks to be unified in all their activities, which have included a number of nonviolent interventions, including:

> public speeches, letters of opposition, public statements, declarations of indictment, and group petitions. They have written or supplied information for newspaper articles and have used banners and posters. They have sponsored vigils, marches, parades, funeral processions, and protest meetings. GAM has implemented sit-ins, nonviolent harassment, nonviolent occupation, and has created an alternative institution to investigate human rights abuses.

Tooley quotes an observer who says that GAM was called "the moral conscience of Guatemala and the thorn in the flesh of the military and the right-wing government ruling Guatemala."[7]

CONAVIGUA, the National Coordinator of Guatemalan Widows, formed in 1988, concludes its introductory statement of its purpose with the following words:

> In our villages only our great sacrifices have kept us alive together with our sons and daughters. Without men at home and without any help from the government, we have to take care of everything—work in the corn field, clean our house, go down to the coast for seasonal work. These and other things we have done in order that we and our children might live. So for this we have organized, to meet our needs, to defend ourselves from the abuses that we suffer, and so that we can forever live in peace.[8]

From its beginning, CONAVIGUA was the object of death threats and harassment from the military and right-wing groups closely associated with the military. Tooley concludes:

> Rigoberta Menchu and the women of GAM and CONAVIGUA tell a story—a story of exclusion from economic participation, domination by powers and authorities, exploitation by the dominant culture, and violence from repressive regimes. But as they tell their story, they resist reacting with bitterness, cynicism, and hopelessness. Instead, they act as agents of transformation, turning the conspiracy of silence and the intimacy of pain into social protest. Mothers and wives and daughters, they enter the political arena as novices, novices who defiantly and openly question the state. No longer are they silently weeping women who privately bear their pain. Through collective action they are transformed into political actors helping to gain recognition for the 60 percent indigenous, for the 87 percent majority living in poverty, for widows and orphans, and all the people who lack access to the political system.[9]

Religious organizations in less repressive and free societies are in a position to stand in solidarity with the people of Central America. Among the examples that can be cited are the following: Witness for Peace, a North American ecumenical grassroots organization that challenged U.S. policy toward Nicaragua through the 1980s; the

Roman Catholic Church, influenced by liberation theology, which served as a vehicle for lay leadership training and development through Catholic Action groups and Christian base communities; the Human Rights Resource Office for Latin America for the World Council of Churches; the American Baptist Churches, which challenged the injustice of U.S. refugee policy toward Central America by bringing a lawsuit against the Immigration and Naturalization Service[10]; and the role in the late 1980s of Moravian church leaders in Nicaragua and John Paul Lederach of the Mennonite Central Committee in North America to mediate the conflict between the Atlantic Coast Indians and the Sandinista government in Nicaragua.[11] According to Daniel Buttry, "the link in partnerships between the Nicaraguan Baptist Convention and the American Baptist Church had a definite impact upon the quest for peace."[12] The Nicaraguan bishops sent a series of pastoral letters to the churches in the United States. North American missionaries returned to the United States to provide a critique of 1980s U.S. policy toward Nicaragua, which lent support to the resistance against U.S. policy. American Baptists were also inspired to participate in Witness for Peace and the Pledge of Resistance.

Just peacemaking theory must empower ordinary people. The norms of a just peacemaking theory should not assume that the only or primary agents of action are heads of state or the leaders of revolutionary groups vying for power. Making peace is increasingly a function of a combination of many actors within the international system: people's movements, peacemaker groups in congregations and faith communities, nongovernmental organizations, leaders of nation-states, and international organizations.

Robert Putnam, international-relations scholar and political scientist, has shown the important interaction between achievements in international negotiations and the pressures of domestic politics.

> The politics of many international negotiations can usefully be conceived as a two-level game. At the national level, domestic groups pursue their interests by pressuring the government to adopt favorable policies, and politicians seek power by constructing coalitions among those groups. At the international level, national governments seek to maximize their own ability to satisfy domestic pressures, while minimizing the adverse consequences of foreign developments. Neither of the two

games can be ignored by central decision-makers, so long as their countries remain interdependent, yet sovereign.[13]

Putnam's thesis supports our argument that grassroots movements and voluntary organizations can have an important influence on the outcome of public policy regarding issues of peacemaking and justice. In his book *Peace Works: The Citizen's Role in Ending the Cold War,* David Cortright argues that citizen peace activists from 1980 to 1987 played a significant role in ending the Cold War and that grassroots social movements have the power to shape history. Although the factors that influence policy were varied and complex (for example, economic costs in both the United States and the Soviet Union, bureaucratic politics in the Soviet Union, the influence of U.S. allies), "if citizens groups had not campaigned constantly to prevent nuclear war, the military standoff between East and West might have become much more dangerous."[14] The Reagan administration's goal was to create a political climate that favored a "peace through strength" philosophy. But because of the creation of the nuclear-weapons freeze movement, the Physicians for Social Responsibility, the organization of religious leaders against the concept of nuclear superiority,[15] and media events like showing "The Day After" to a television audience of one hundred million people, the administration was forced to abandon the rhetoric and concept of nuclear superiority. Similarly, public resistance forced the administration to abandon large-scale civilian defense plans. Though the administration sought to delay arms negotiations until after a huge military build-up, pressure from the peace movements in the United States and Europe forced the administration to the bargaining table earlier and led to the moderation of U.S. positions. Massive peace mobilizations were unable to halt the deployment of intermediate-range nuclear forces in Europe, but the missiles were later abandoned in the INF Treaty.[16] There was partial success by the MX missile campaign to block mobile basing and reduce the number of missiles. The opposition to the Strategic Defense Initiative (Star Wars) by peace groups and scientists led Congress to cut funds and impose restraints, and though vast sums of money were still spent on development, no systems were deployed. Public opposition to the Reagan administration's Contra War against Nicaragua was partially successful in blocking Contra aid and preventing direct U.S. intervention (though illegal funding of the war continued until it was finally stopped by citizen pressure, congressional vote, and eventual disclosure).

The larger structures of militarism, however, continued unabated. Unfortunately the peace movement was unable to halt the overall strategy of military confrontation (which contributed to the Persian Gulf War) and the massive increase in U.S. military spending, which, combined with tax breaks for the wealthy, resulted in a huge increase in the gross federal debt (from $1 trillion in 1981, after 205 years of U.S. history, to $4.02 trillion in 1992, after only eleven more years).

The nuclear-weapons freeze campaign phenomenon is evidence that a set of shared norms that transcend national boundaries is shaping large numbers of people. The development of a just peacemaking theory, in fact, is largely possible because there exists, on an increasingly growing worldwide scale, a people's movement that shares an implicit set of norms. In part, these shared values derive from common assumptions about the importance of the implementation (not mere verbal assent) of human rights, reflected in the Universal Declaration of Human Rights (1948), and the various expansions and elaborations of those rights in the last several decades. Second, persons from both pacifist and just war traditions are increasingly emphasizing that they need to implement the shared value of peacemaking implicit in their theories. Pacifists are stressing what the label "pacifism" means: *pax*, or peacemaking, not passivity or withdrawal from conflict. Just war theorists recognize that peace should be the aim or intention of action and that war must be a last resort. Both traditions, consequently, converge (even though disagreement still exists about whether the use of violent force is ever justified) in order to identify and practice the norms of just peacemaking.

A pacifist vision continues to shape my orientation and my sensitivities, but I am less and less interested in defining the pacifist position over against other positions. We must find ways to identify common norms because of fundamental pragmatic (and ethical) reasons. Our task is to develop a "global civic culture," to use Elise Boulding's phrase, if we are to have any chance of meeting the serious challenges of our globe.[17] Trends in the international system (decline in the utility of war, economic trade and integration, transnational networks of communication and cultural exchange, the ascendancy of liberal democracy) that make just peacemaking more likely require individuals and groups to undertake kinds of action Paul Schroeder enumerated in chapter 7, "to sustain, criticize, goad, influence, reform, and wherever possible lead the many kinds of voluntary associations, governmental and private, which can contribute to transcending the contradictions and managing and overcoming the conflicts of an anarchic international society."[18]

The Internet has become a powerful tool for linking citizens within communities and across state and national boundaries. Electronic communication has become an efficient way to organize grassroots citizens groups. Because we can transcend the limits of distance and time, persons who are widely scattered geographically can be mobilized in large numbers to respond in a timely way to key public policy issues. Instant contact around the world empowers people from a diversity of nations, races, and cultures to act in concert on global issues that otherwise would take months and years to organize. Internet communication provides a powerful source of information and empowerment that even the most repressive governments find it hard to control. E-mail communication links scholars around the world to work together on scientific, moral, and public policy questions.

However, nothing can replace personal contact between people— | 209
in organizations, within communities, and with public officials. When electronic communication becomes a substitute for personal communication, it further depersonalizes the world. Electronic communication can easily abuse facts, become rude, and destroy personal reputations. Bloggers can form their own isolated communities of discourse that become immune to criticism and other sources of information. It is not clear how leaders of large movements like Move-On and True Majority are held accountable for communication they do on behalf of the group. Mass-generated responses cannot replace thoughtful and carefully formulated communication by individuals on complex moral issues. Access to Internet communication still privileges the more educated and affluent. Electronic communication can empower citizen groups, but it can also corrupt and be abused.

Why is a "citizens' movement" of peacemakers and peacemaking groups so important? What do they do?[19]

1. A transnational network of people who are organized to learn from one another and act in concert can partially transcend the narrow self-interest and myopia that often characterize groups in conflict. A longer view of the root causes of a conflict can help overcome the failure to see the adversary's point of view.[20]

2. A citizens' movement, committed more to peacemaking processes than to defense of governmental or bureaucratic interest or to quick fixes (often with armed force) in a single conflict, can help maintain the long view, the kind of perseverance that is needed so that a just peace can emerge over generations. The ashram was central to the success of Gandhi's nonviolent struggle in India. Bishop Desmond Tutu and the South African Council of Churches were in the forefront in advocating nonviolence in the struggle in South Africa. As movements come and go and the popularity of a cause begins to wane, people's organizations and their leaders often provide key support and staying power. Rosa Parks had long been an active member of an ongoing organization, the NAACP, when she took her seat in the front of the bus in Montgomery, Alabama.

3. Citizens' groups often serve as advocates for the voiceless, especially those who are poor and powerless. Religious institutions, for example, can establish a space (a sanctuary), even in the most repressive societies, that is not easily controlled by the dominating political system. They can thus become a center for teaching and organizing. In 1981, a youth pastor and some young people started weekly Monday prayer services for peace at the St. Nicholai Church in Leipzig, East Germany, one of the small seeds planted early that contributed to the crumbling of the Berlin Wall. In 1988, these prayer services became the locus of increasingly larger groups of East German citizens who gathered to discuss social issues. By October 1989, three hundred thousand persons gathered in Leipzig to demonstrate despite police harassment and arrests.[21] In communist Czechoslovakia, the theater provided a space for social transformation. Vaclav Havel's courageous action is a profound demonstration of what it means "to live within the truth" rather than "living a lie."[22]

4. A transnational people's network has less investment in defending what has been. Persons in the movement can free our imaginations to think of alternatives to established patterns of behavior and the narrow range of options we often consider in resolving conflict. International nongovernmental institutions can model alternative ways of living that put the lie to so-called inevitable hatreds by bringing together persons of diverse religious, national, racial,

ethnic, ideological, and economic background. Out of these inter-actions, people's imaginations are freed to consider ways of making peace where hatred and violence are assumed to be inevitable. An example is the effort in Bosnia and Croatia of David Steele and colleagues to work at local levels across lines of culture, religion, language, and class.[23]

5. People within citizens' movements can play a servant role, working behind the scenes in mediating conflict without needing to be in the limelight or to take credit. People without strong attachment to governments, or people who do not bring to a conflict a strong self-interest, can gain the trust of parties and serve in a mediating role. American Methodist leaders and a Baptist church peacemaker group behind the scenes sought to help resolve the Iranian hostage crisis. This conflict might have led to a much more positive outcome if their advice had been heeded.[24]

6. Citizens' movements often help to initiate, foster, or support transforming initiatives,[25] where existing parties need support and courage to take risks to break out of the cycles that perpetuate violence and injustice. Charles Osgood's method of "independent initiatives" was widely adopted by church statements and peace movements in Europe and the United States. Eventually, they persuaded governments to adopt it, with striking success. Stassen tells the fascinating story of the role of citizens' groups in encouraging the adoption of the "zero solution" in the late 1980s on intermediate-range missiles in Europe.[26]

7. A citizens' network (particularly as that is institutionalized in voluntary associations) sustains concern and interest when the media and world opinion are unaware, forget, or flit about from one thing to the next. One year it was Somalia; then it was Iraq. Where will our attention be next year? Sustainable development, one of the norms of just peacemaking theory, requires long-term advocacy and commitment by a host of citizens' groups.[27]

8. A citizens' network of NGOs and INGOs can often be a source of information and knowledge that persons in positions of governmental authority lack. One of the most important services performed by the Washington, D.C., office of the Mennonite Central Committee is to circulate returned workers from around the globe to the U.S. Congress. I have seen the power and significance of

such testimony on a number of issues, as well as their impact in informing their home communities.[28]

9. Citizens' groups also sometimes resist governments when they behave unjustly, are short-sighted or arrogant, thinking they know more than they do or thinking they can control futures that are in fact not under their control. The revival of Islam nurtured in the mosques throughout Iran was critical in the overthrow of the Shah in 1978–79. Islamic women played a vital role in the mass protests. While resistance to tyranny is sometimes called for, at other times religious groups and individual leaders can help to nurture a spirit of repentance and forgiveness in the political culture. Alan Geyer cites a number of cases where repentance and forgiveness, nurtured by church groups and church confessions, prepared the climate in which governmental leaders could then make repentance and forgiveness a public event, advancing international peacemaking and reconciliation.[29]

10. Churches and other religious groups can serve a special role in nurturing a spirituality that sustains courage when just peacemaking is unpopular, hope when despair or cynicism is tempting, and a sense of grace and the possibility of forgiveness when just peacemaking fails. In Vietnam, Thailand, and Burma, Buddhist monks have given leadership in protest of human-rights violations and movements for nonviolent social change. Aung San Suu Kyi, daughter of Burma's national hero, winner of the Nobel Peace Prize, and advocate of nonviolence and democracy, connects her struggle explicitly to the teachings and institutions of Buddhism.

Out of intense loyalty grounded in the authority of religious tradition, ordinary people act and shape social reality regardless of whether they are always conscious of how they impact the world. Religious organizations are especially important in nurturing a spirituality that is essential to peacemaking: courage and the willingness to suffer; overcoming hatred of the enemy and the ability to endure abuse without retaliation; hope and patience during a long period of struggle; trust in the possibility of the miracle of transformation when the evidence for change appears bleak; joy even in the midst of suffering and pain; realism that guards people from disillusionment by making them aware of the depth of human evil and the persistence of systems of domination and injustice; and humility about one's own lack of knowledge and need for wisdom.

Prayer and meditation are spiritual disciplines that open people to a transcendent reality beyond themselves. Dag Hammarskjold cautioned us that "your cravings as a human animal do not become a prayer just because it is God whom you ask to attend to them."[30] Nonidolatrous prayer does lead to repentance for militant nationalism and forgiveness for offenses, to increased compassion for envisioning the sufferings of victims of war and injustice, revised priorities about how we spend our own lives, and increased courage for making a peacemaking witness in our own communities. Malcolm X was converted from racism while praying with persons of different races on his pilgrimage to Mecca. The frequent repetition of "forgive us our sins, as we forgive those who sin against us" in the Lord's Prayer was a key factor in the remarkable public witness of the quietist Amish when they forgave the killer in the 2006 West Nickel Mines school shooting.[31] There are reasons why persons who practice silent, listening prayer, like Quakers with unprogrammed meetings, like Thomas Merton and Glenn Hinson, have historically been strong leaders for peacemaking.

Prayer helps us to be more aware of our limits to predict and control the future. Still we can embrace our common humanity through simple deeds of kindness and charity. In the context of hatred and violence, such deeds may disarm an opponent and provide the possibility for a transforming initiative for justice and peace. Any genuine religious act is potentially an act of peacemaking because it touches people with a transcendent spirit and power, which opens us to our common humanity and exposes the lie of human systems of injustice and violence.[32] In the words of Vaclav Havel:

In today's multicultural world, the truly reliable path to coexistence, to peaceful coexistence and creative cooperation, must start from what is at the root of all cultures and what lies infinitely deeper in human hearts and minds than political opinion, convictions, antipathies, or sympathies: it must be rooted in self-transcendence. Transcendence as a hand reached out to those close to us, to foreigners, to the human community, to all living creatures, to nature, to the universe; transcendence as a deeply and joyously experienced need to be in harmony even with what we ourselves are not, what we do not understand, what seems distant from us in time and space, but with which we are nevertheless mysteriously linked because, together with us, all this constitutes a single world. Transcendence as the only real alternative to extinction.

The Declaration of Independence, adopted two hundred and eighteen years ago in this building, states that the Creator gave man the right to liberty. It seems man can realize that liberty only if he does not forget the One who endowed him with it.[33]

A just and peaceful society protects in law, nourishes and encourages, and informs accurately rather than untruthfully, associations of citizens organized independently of governmental organizations that are linked together across the boundaries of nation, class, culture, and race. Governments that claim to seek peace are obligated to such protection, encouragement, and truthfulness. Even when this freedom of association is not protected by law and is threatened by hostile conditions, still the mystery of the human spirit is that independent associations of people emerge who seek the shalom of the city where they dwell, as did the Jews in ancient Babylon and as did people in our time in the churches of East Germany and the theaters of Czechoslovakia.

NOTES

Introduction

1. Michael Walzer, *Just and Unjust Wars* (New York: Basic Books, 1977), 197. Walzer was my much admired teacher; he taught us this understanding long before the current focus on terrorism. —Glen Stassen

2. The weakness of Jean Bethke Elshtain, *Just War against Terror* (New York: Basic Books, 2003). Not one sentence in the book advocates any action it contends is effective in preventing causes of terrorism. It's all about justifying war.

3. John Keegan, *A History of Warfare* (New York: Knopf, 1993).

4. Fareed Zakaria, "Suicide Bombers Can Be Stopped," msnbcnews, December 2003 (http://www.msnbc.com/news/953555.asp). Accessed December 2003.

5. Svante E. Cornell, "The Kurdish Question in Turkish Politics," *Orbis* 45/1 (Winter 2001): 42.

6. Michael Radu, "The Rise and Fall of the PKK," *Orbis* 45 no 1 (Winter 2001): 58.

7. Cornell, "Kurdish Question," 37.

8. Ibid., 40.

9. Ibid., 45.

10. Radu, "Rise and Fall," 47.

11. Peter Woodman, "Stay Away from Istanbul, Britons Told," The Press Association Limited, Nov. 20, 2003.

12. National Counterterrorism Center, "2007 Report on Terrorism," April 30, 2008, 21; see www.cfr.org/publication/16320/.

13. Alexander Lennon, ed., *The Battle for Hearts and Minds: Using Soft Power to Undermine Terrorist Networks* (Cambridge, Mass: MIT Press, 2003), 69, 286, et passim; Arnold Howitt and Robyn Pangi, ed., *Countering Terrorism: Dimensions of Preparedness* (Cambridge, Mass: MIT Press, 2003), chapter 5 et passim.

14. (Princeton, N.J.: Princeton University Press, 1970).

15. Audrey Kurth Cronin in Cronin and Jmaes M. Ludes, ed., *Attacking Terrorism: Elements of a Grand Strategy* (Washington, D.C.: Georgetown University Press, 2004), 25.

16. Krueger and Malecková, "Education, Poverty, Political Violence and Terrorism: Is there a Causal Connection?" manuscript, May 2002.

17. Reports in 2002 by Peter Hansen, commissioner-general of UN Relief; Jean Ziegler, Swiss sociologist and UN envoy for the UN Human Rights Commission Agency; and U.S. AID.

18. Michael Radu, "Terrorism after the Cold War: Trends and Challenges," *Orbis* (Spring 2002), 286.

19. Susan Thistlethwaite, "New Wars, Old Wineskins," in *Strike Terror No More: Theology, Ethics, and the New War*, ed. Jon L. Berquist (St. Louis: Chalice Press, 2002), 264–79.

20. Zachary Abuzah, "Al Qaeda's Southeast Asian Network," *Contemporary Southeast Asia* 24/3 (December 2002): 428.

21. Ibid., 433. For a wider-ranging historical study of terrorism in a readable format, see Walter Laqueur, *The New Terrorism: Fanaticism and the Arms of Mass Destruction* (New York: Oxford University Press, 1999), 79–156; and Paul Gilbert, New Terror, New Wars (Washington, D.C.: Georgetown University Press, 2003).

22. Fareed Zakaria, "The Arrogant Empire," *Newsweek* (March 24, 2003): 19–33.

23. See further Edward LeRoy Long Jr., *Facing Terrorism: Responding as Christians* (Louisville: Westminster John Knox Press, 2004).

24. Glen Stassen, "The Unity, Realism, and Obligatoriness of Just Peacemaking Theory," *Journal of the Society of Christian Ethics* 23/2 (Spring/Summer 2003), 181–6.

25. National Conference of Catholic Bishops, *The Challenge of Peace: God's Promise and Our Response* (Washington, D.C.: U.S. Catholic Conference, 1983), par. 23 and excerpts, copyright © 1983 United States Catholic Conference, Inc., Washington, D.C. Used by permission. All rights reserved.

26. Ibid., 22.

27. Ibid., 22.

28. Ibid., 23.

29. Peter Ackerman and Christopher Kreugler, *Strategic Nonviolent Conflict: The Dynamics of People Power in the Twentieth Century* (Westport, Conn.: Praeger Publishers, 1994).

30. Gene Sharp, *Waging Nonviolent Struggle: Twentieth Century Practice and Twenty-first Century Potential* (Boston: Porter Sargent Publishers, 2005).

31. James B. Burke, *Crafting a Global Just Peacebuilding Ethic from Just War Theory and Strategic Nonviolent Conflict*, unpublished dissertation, May 2007.

32. Larry L. Rasmussen, *Moral Fragments and Moral Community* (Minneapolis: Fortress Press, 1993), 142.

33. See, for example, John H. Yoder, *The Politics of Jesus* (Grand Rapids: Eerdmans, 1972); Walter Wink, *Engaging the Powers* (Minneapolis: Fortress Press, 1992); and Glen H. Stassen, *Just Peacemaking: Transforming Initiatives for Justice and Peace* (Louisville: Westminster John Knox Press, 1992).

34. Glen Stassen, *Living the Sermon on the Mount* (San Francisco: Jossey-Bass, 2006).

35. Stassen, *Just Peacemaking: Transforming Initiatives*, 46.

36. Willard M. Swartley, *Covenant of Peace: The Missing Piece in New Testament Theology and Ethics* (Grand Rapids: Eerdmans 2006).

37. Donald Shriver, *An Ethic for Enemies: Forgiveness in Politics* (New York: Oxford University Press, 1995).

38. Wink, *Engaging the Powers*, 114.

39. David Hollenbach, S.J., *Justice, Peace, and Human Rights: American Catholic Social Ethics in a Pluralistic World* (New York: Crossroad, 1988), 16. He quotes the U.S. Bishops from Synod of Bishops, *Justitia in mundo*, no. 6.

40. This is taking place, however, not without defeats and subterfuges. See Tooley, *Voices of the Voiceless: Women, Justice, and Human Rights in Guatemala* (Scottdale, Pa., and Waterloo, Ontario: Herald Press, 1997), chap. 2.

41. David Hollenbach, S.J., *Justice, Peace, and Human Rights: American Catholic Social Ethics in a Pluralistic World* (New York: Crossroad, 1988); Glen Stassen, "Human Rights," *Global Dictionary of Theology* (Downers Grove: InterVarsity, 2009).

42. John Langan, S.J., "Defining Human Rights: A Revision of the Liberal Tradition," in *Human Rights in the Americas: The Struggle for Consensus*, ed. Alfred Hennelly, S.J., and John Langan, S.J. (Washington, D.C.: Georgetown University Press, 1982), 70, 74, 82.

43. Ibid., 81, 85.

44. Ibid., 99.

45. Policy Planning Staff, United States Department of State, "Review of Current Trends: U.S. Foreign Policy," Foreign Relations of the United States 1.2 (1948), 524.

46. For a lucid account of American interventions, see Stephen Kinzer, *Overthrow: America's Century of Regime Change from Hawaii to Iraq* (New York: Times Books, 2006).

47. Antonia Juhasz, *The Bush Agenda: Invading the World, One Economy at a Time* (New York: Regan Books, 2006), 197, 211–12.

48. Judith Gundry, "Spirit, Mercy, and the Other," *Theology Today* 51 (January 1995): 508, 510, 516, and 518–22.

49. Duane Friesen, *Christian Peacemaking and International Conflict: A Realist Pacifist Perspective* (Scottdale, Pa.: Herald Press, 1986), 87, 89.

50. Lisa Sowle Cahill, *Love Your Enemies: Discipleship, Pacifism, and Just War Theory* (Minneapolis: Fortress Press, 1994), 244.

51. Yoder, *Politics of Jesus*, 40.

52. Robert Wuthnow, *Acts of Compassion* (Princeton, N.J.: Princeton University, 1991), 179–84.

53. Anthony Spaeth Davos, "Web of Power," *Time* (February 17, 1997), 58.

54. Ibid, 59.

55. See also John H. Yoder, "To Serve Our God and to Rule the World," in Yoder, *The Royal Priesthood: Essays Ecclesiological and Ecumenical*, ed. Michael Cartwright (Grand Rapids: Eerdmans, 1994), 128–40.

56. (Maryknoll, NY: Orbis, 1996).

57. Glen Stassen, "Just Peacemaking Theory as Hermeneutical Key: For International Cooperation in Preventing Terrorism," *Journal of the Society of Christian Ethics* (Fall 2004).

58. Michelle Tooley, *Voices of the Voiceless: Women, Justice, and Human Rights in Guatemala* (Scottdale, Pa., and Waterloo, Ontario: Herald 1997), 21–25 and chaps. 3, 6.

CHAPTER 1. Support Nonviolent Direct Action

1. Jonathan Schell, *The Unconquerable World: Power, Nonviolence, and the Will of the People* (New York: Henry Holt & Company, 2003).

2. Daniel L. Buttry, *Christian Peacemaking: From Heritage to Hope* (Valley Forge, Pa.: Judson Press, 1994), 63ff.

3. Mark W. Charlton, *Do Economic Sanctions Work?* (Wynnewood, Pa.: Evangelicals for Social Action, forthcoming).

4. Joseph Stephanides, foreword, *Smart Sanctions: Targeting Economic Statecraft*, ed. David Cortright and Gorge Lopez (Lanham, Md.: Rowman & Littlefield, 2002), vii.

5. Ibid., vii. See chapter 3 of this book for the practice of conflict resolution.

6. See David Cortright and Gorge Lopez, "Containing Iraq: Sanctions Worked," Foriegn Affairs (July/August 2004), 90–103.

7. Mohandas Gandhi, *Nonviolence in Peace and War*, 2:363, as cited in *Gandhi on Nonviolence*, ed. Thomas Merton (New York: New Directions, 1965), 27.

8. Martin Luther King Jr., "Letter from Birmingham Jail," *Why We Can't Wait* (New York: Harper & Row, 1964), 88.

9. Henry David Thoreau, "On the Duty of Civil Disobedience," in *Social and Political Philosophy*, ed. John Somerville and Ronald Santoni (New York: Doubleday, 1963), 283.

10. Margaret Miles, "The Female Body as Figure," in *Carnal Knowledge: The Female Nakedness and Religious Meaning in the Christian West* (Boston: Beacon Press, 1989), chap. 4.

11 Gandhi, *Nonviolence in Peace and War*, 1:282, as cited in *Gandhi on Nonviolence*, 27.

12. Dom Helder Camara, *The Spiral of Violence* (London: Sheed and Ward, 1975).

CHAPTER 2: Take Independent Initiatives to Reduce Threat

1. Charles E. Osgood, *An Alternative to War or Surrender* (Urbana: University of Illinois Press, 1962).

2. See Stassen, *Just Peacemaking: Transforming Initiatives*, chap. 5, and David Cortright, *Peace Works: The Citizen's Role in Ending the Cold War* (Boulder, Colo.: Westview Press, 1993), chap. 8.

3. Harold Saunders, Address to the Middle East Institute of the World Affairs Council, Washington, D.C., Jan. 17, 1991 (manuscript), 6ff.

4. Svenn Lindskold, "Trust Development, the GRIT Proposal and the Effects of Conflict and Cooperation," *Psychological Bulletin* 85 (1978): 770–93. See also Lindskold's research reports in *Journal of Conflict Resolution* (September 1983): 521–32; *Personality and Social Psychology Bulletin* 12 (June 1986): 179–86; in *Personality and Social Psychology Bulletin* 14 (June 1988): 335–45. See also E. H. Boyle and E. J. Lawler, *Social Forces* 69 (June 1991): 1183–1204.

5. Deborah Welch Larson, "Crisis Prevention and the Austrian State Treaty," *International Organization* 41 (Winter 1987): 27–60.

6. Robert Jervis, *Perception and Misperception in International Politics* (Princeton, N.J.: Princeton University Press, 1976).

7. National Council of Catholic Bishops, *The Challenge of Peace* (Washington, D.C.: United States Catholic Conference, 1983), par. 204–6.

8. Schritte zur Abrüstung, *Von der Abschreckung zur Sicherheitspartnerschaft* (Bonn: n.p., May 1985); *Ökumenische Versammlung für Gerechtigkeit und Bewarhung der Schöpfung* (Berlin: Aktion Sühnezeichen/Friedensdienste, 1990), 21, 92–93, 97–98, 196.

9. National Council of Catholic Bishops, *Challenge of Peace*, par. 204–6.

10. Susan Thistlethwaite, ed., *A Just Peace Church* (New York: United Church Press, 1986), 136f., 142f.

12. Robert Pape, "The Strategic Logic of Suicide Terrorism," *The American Political Science Review* 97/3 (August 2003) 355.

12. Ibid., 352, 353.

13. Ibid., 348.

14. Ibid., 354.

15. Ibid., 348, 352, 353, 354.

16. Ibid., 353.

17. Ibid., 356.

18. Khalil Shikaki, "Palestine Divided," *Foreign Affairs* (January/February 2002) 90ff.

19. Scott Atran, *The Strategic Threat from Suicide Terror*, AEI-Brookings Joint Center (December 2003) 9.

20. Bruce Hoffman, "The Logic of Suicide Terrorism," *Atlantic Monthly* 291/5 (June 2003) 44.

CHAPTER 3: Use Cooperative Conflict Resolution

1. Some practitioners refer to this practice as partnership conflict resolution, echoing the use of the term "partnership" by Olaf Palme and Helmut Schmidt (Dieter S. Lutz, *Lexikon: Rüstung, Frieden, Sicherheit* [Munich: C. H. Beck, 1987], 132–291). In the concept of security partnership Palme and Schmidt's recognition that each party's security depends on the degree of security felt by its adversary certainly states one important part of what we mean by conflict resolution. CCR, however, goes beyond security issues and reciprocal process. Other practitioners refer to this practice as collaborative conflict resolution, a phrase used widely in peer mediation programs in schools across the United States. The term "collaboration" is used to indicate the active nature of the engagement. It affirms that the goal is not only passive compliance or compromise. The problem with "collaboration" is the quisling connotation the term holds for many people who have suffered under fascism or communism. In contrast, CCR is never secretive or subversive.

2. According to Moltmann, unavoidable differences can be localized and relativized in a way that enables people to attend to common concerns. Jürgen Moltmann, *The Experiment Hope*, ed. and trans. with a foreword by M. Douglas Meeks (London: SCM, 1975), 175.

3. In the last two centuries, proponents of these teachings have included Native Americans like Chief Joseph (*Chief Joseph's Own Story*, [Fairfield, Wash.: Ye Galleon Press, 1984]), Quakers opposing world wars, civil rights workers in the southern United States, Gandhian disciples in India, liberation theologians (like Jan Sobrino, José Míguez Bonino, and Gustavo Gutiérrez in South and Central America), religious and lay leaders in Eastern Europe during the fall of Communism in 1989, the Catholic Church opposing Marcos in the Philippines in 1986, and more recently those following Desmond Tutu's and Nelson Mandela's paths in the anti-apartheid movement in South Africa. Contrast these approaches with the unilateral and often militarist approaches to conflict that are documented in James Carroll's history of the Pentagon, *House of War* (New York: Houghton Mifflin, 2006). For a more recent exploration of both paths, see David Cortright *Gandhi and Beyond* (Boulder, Colo.: Paradigm, 2006). For an articulation of a foreign policy framework based in CCR see Glen Stassen and Steven Brion-Meisels, "Real Security in the Future: International Cooperation, Human Rights and Freedom from Weapons of Mass Destruction," in *Peace Action: Past, Present and Future*, ed. Glen Stassen and Lawrence Wittner (Boulder, Colo.: Paradigm, 2007).

4. Armstrong (*The Great Tradition* [New York: Random House, 2006], xix) explores several streams that all share this commitment to compassion—and by extension to social justice. In *The Great Transformation: The Beginning of Our Religious Traditions* (New York: Knopf, 2006), she focused on ways in which Judaism, Hinduism, Confucianism and classical Greek ethics all shared a commitment to compassion as a core value of their religious traditions; compassion is closely connected to several of the CCR principles we discuss in this chapter. One non-Christian example can be found in Islam, which stresses the interrelationship between forgiveness and justice. Though the Koran states that justice must come first, it also emphasizes that a special reward will come to one who forgives: "Those who avoid the greater crimes and shameful deeds and when they are angry even then forgive. . . . The recompense for an injury is an injury equal thereto (in degree): but if a person forgives and makes reconciliation his reward is due from Allah. . . . But indeed if any show pa-

tience and forgive that would truly be an exercise of courageous will and resolution in the conduct of affairs" (Surah Ash-Shura, sec. 4, ll. 37, 40, 43).

5. Mohammad Abu-Nimer, "Conflict Resolution in an Islamic Context," *Journal of Peace & Change*, 21/1 (January 1996), 22.

6. Abdul Azis Said, Nathan C. Funk, and Ayse S. Kadayifci, eds., *Peace and Conflict Resolution in Islam* (Lanham: University Press of America, 2001), 10, praise John Paul Lederach for his distinction between rationalistic Western conflict resolution and culturally sensitive cooperative conflict transformation. See also David Augsburger, *Conflict Mediation Across Cultures: Pathways and Patterns* (Louisville: Westminster John Knox Press, 1992) and Douglas Johnston and Cynthia Sampson, eds., *Religion: The Missing Dimension of Statecraft* (New York: Oxford University Press, 1994), and Carolyn Schrock-Shenk and Lawrence Ressler, eds., *Practical Skills for Conflict Transformation* (Scottdale, Pa.: Herald Press, 1999).

7. Niebuhr, "Why the Christian Church Is Not Pacifist," *The Essential Reinhold Niebuhr: Selected Essays and Addresses*, ed. Robert McAfee Brown (New Haven, Conn.: Yale University Press, 1986), 24.

8. Richard Cohen, *Students Resolving Conflicts: Peer Mediation in Schools* (Glenview, Ill.: Scott Foresman, 1995), 42–43.

9. Brian Frost, *The Politics of Peace* (London: Darton, Longman and Todd, 1991), 85–100.

10. "Six Steps for Nonviolent Social Change," from the Martin Luther King Jr. Center for Nonviolent Social Change, Inc., (Atlanta, 1990), printed in *Nonviolence Anthology* (n.p.: Golubka, 1991), 20. For an exploration of King's approach to conflict resolution in the broader context of twentieth-century politics, including its relevance to the new challenges of terrorism, see David Cortright, Gandhi and Beyond.

11. Cohen, *Students Resolving Conflict*.

12. Albert J. Reiss Jr., and Jeffrey A. Roth, *Understanding and Preventing Violence* (Washington: National Academy Press, 1993), 8, 108–9.

13. For more on this approach to CCR, see Linda Brion-Meisels, Steven Brion-Meisels, and Catherine Hoffman, "Creating and Sustaining Peaceable School Communities," *Harvard Educational Review* 77/3 (Fall 2007).

14. Manu Meyer and Albie Davis, "Talking Story: Mediation, Peacemaking, and Culture," *Dispute Resolution Magazine*, (Fall 1994).

15. See Howard Zehr, *Changing Lenses: A New Focus for Crime and Justice* (Scottdale, Pa.: Herald Press, 2005), and Christopher D. Marshall, *Beyond Retributio : A New Testament Vision for Justice, Crime, and Punishment* (Grand Rapids: Eerdmans, 2001).

16. Patti DeRosa and Ulric Johnson, "The Ten C's : A Model of Diversity and Social Change. *The Brown Papers* vol. 6, no. 5, Boston: Boston Women's Theological Center, May/June 2002.

17. Steven Brion-Meisels and Casey Corcoran, *Peacemaking in Boston and Los Angeles: A Study of Peacemaking in Two Cities*, unpublished report, Boston: Peace Games, 2006.

18. One example of this is the 2006 documentary film *Encounter Point*, dir. Ronit Avni and Julia Bacha, prod. Ronit Avni, Joline Makhlouf, and Nahanni Rous, ©2006 Encounter Point. All rights reserved.

19. Ivo Markovich, Franciscan priest from Guca Gora, Bosnia, as told during a roundtable, "The Role of Religion in the Conflict in Serbia, Croatia, and Bosnia and Herzegovina," sponsored by the Mennonite Central Committee and co-led by N. Gerald Shenk and David Steele, Vienna, Austria, May 16–18, 1993.

20. For further treatment of this subject, see David Steele, *Role of the Church as an Intermediary in International Conflict: A Theological Assessment of Prinicipled Negotiation,* Ph.D. dissertation, University of Edinburgh, Scotland, 1991.

21. Steven Brion-Meisels, "Developing peace and disarmament education initiatives to disarm children and youth: Evaluation of the two-year country project reports organized by the United Nations Department for Disarmament Affairs and the Hague Appeal for Peace. In G. Levitas ed., *Peace and Disarmament Education: Changing Mindsets to Reduce Violence and Sustain the Removal of Small Arms* (New York: Hague Appeal for Peace), www.haguepeace.org.

22. Sandy Tolan, *The Lemon Tree: An Arab, a Jew, and the Heart of the Middle East* (New York: Bloomsbury, 2006).

23. This section draws particularly on research and practice in CCR that has been led by Meenakshi Chhabra. For another view of this approach to peacemaking across religious differences, see the personal account provided by Greg Mortensen and David Oliver Relin in *Three Cups of Tea* (London: Penguin Books, 2006).

24. Glen Stassen, *Just Peacemaking: Transforming Initiatives for Justice and Peace* (Westminster John Knox Press: 1992), 236–41.

25. Thomas E. Ricks, *Fiasco: The American Military Adventure in Iraq* (New York: Penguin, 2006), 70, 73, 102–5, 167, 169, 176, 209, et passim.

26. Joseph Cirincione, et al., *WMD in Iraq: Evidence and Implications* (Washington, D.C.: Carnegie Endowment for International Peace, January 2004), 8; http://www.ceip.org/files/pdf/Iraq3FullText.pdf, accessed February 9, 2004.

27. Hans Blix, *Disarming Iraq* (New York: Pantheon Books, 2004), 259.

28. Dick Cheney, "Vice President Speaks at VFW 103rd National Convention," speech, Nashville, Tennessee, August 26, 2002, http://www.whitehouse.gov/news/releases/2002/08/20020826.html, accessed 5 February 2004.

29. Barton Gellman, "Iraq's Arsenal Was Only on Paper; Since Gulf War, Nonconventional Weapons Never Got Past the Planning Stage," *Washington Post,* 7 January 2004, A01.

30. George A. Lopez and David Cortright, "Containing Iraq: Sanctions Worked," *Foreign Affairs* 83/4 (July/Aug. 2004), 1.

31. Helene Cooper and David E. Sanger, "With a Talk over Lunch, a Shift in Bush's Iran Policy Took Root," *New York Times,* June 4, 2006.

32. David Isenberg, "Talk Is Win-Win," *Defense News* (July 17, 2006): 76.

33. Ibid.

34. "Americans Distrust Iran, but Back Talks," Fox News poll June 20, 2006, www.angus-reid.com/polls/index.cfm/fuseaction/viewItem/itemID/12283.

35. Gareth Porter, "Iran Proposal to U.S. Offered Peace with Israel," Inter Press Service, May 25, 2006.

36. For a definitive study, see Robert Jervis, *Perception and Misperception in International Politics* (Princeton,N.J.:Princeton University: 1976).

37. Walter Wink informs us that, in this seminal text from Jesus' teaching, *antistenai,* the Greek word translated "resist not" (also the term used in Rom. 13) actually means "do not revenge violently." So Romans 12 reports the teaching as "do not seek revenge or repay evil for evil." Jesus repeatedly resisted evil, but not by evil means. Wink interprets turning the other cheek, giving one's cloak, and walking the second mile as actions that rob the oppressor of the power to humiliate by taking the initiative oneself and publicly unmasking the oppression. He presents Jesus' teaching as a strategic measure for empowering the oppressed by pushing the unjust laws of the day

to the point of absurdity in order to reveal them for what they are. At the same time, he portrays Jesus as preserving respect for the rule of law and lovingly challenging the Roman powers to change (Walter Wink, *Violence and Nonviolence in South Africa: Jesus' Third Way* [Philadelphia: New Society Publishers, in cooperation with the Fellowship of Reconciliation, 1987], 13–21, 58–61). See also Glen Stassen, "The Fourteen Triads of the Sermon on the Mount: Matthew 5:21–7:12, *Journal of Biblical Literature* 122/2 (Summer 2003), 267–308, and *Living the Sermon on the Mount* (Jossey-Bass, 2006), chapters 4 and 5.).

38. See David Cortright, *Ghandi and Beyond*.

39. The origins of the realist paradigm reach back to Thucydides, Machiavelli, Hobbes, and Clausewitz. Modern proponents include George Kennan (see *American Diplomacy 1900–1950* [New York: Mentor, 1952]) and Hans J. Morgenthau and Kenneth Thompson, *Politics among Nations: The Struggle for Power and Peace*, 6th ed. (New York: Knopf, 1985).

40. Robert Axelrod, *The Evolution of Cooperation* (New York: Basic Books, 1984).

41. Robert Jervis, "Realism, Game Theory, and Cooperation," *World Politics* (April 1988): 336–40.

42. Axelrod, *The Evolution of Cooperation*.

43. See James Carroll, *The House of War* (2006).

44. There are countless educational and civic engagement programs around the world that are doing precisely this work—often with little recognition and minimal funding. This chapter has been shaped in part by work done at Peace Games (a small NGO currently working in four U.S. cities as well as with colleagues in Colombia and the Middle East: www.peacegames.org), by colleagues working through the Center for Children, Families, and Public Policies at Lesley University, and by colleagues and students in the Risk and Prevention Program at the Harvard Graduate School of Education.

CHAPTER 4: Acknowledge Responsibility for Conflict and Injustice and Seek Repentance and Forgiveness

1. This analysis of forgiveness is basic to the arguments of the book *An Ethic for Enemies: Forgiveness in Politics* (New York: Oxford University Press, 1995), by Donald Shriver. See especially page 9, which defines forgiveness as a synthesis of these four elements.

2. Reinhold Niebuhr, *An Interpretation of Christian Ethics* (New York: Meridian Books, 1956), 45. Copyright ©1935 HarperCollins Publishers.

3. Ibid., 118.

4. Reinhold Niebuhr, *The Irony of American History* (New York: Charles Scribner's Sons, 1952), 42.

5. Andre Trocmé, *The Politics of Repentance* (New York: Fellowship Publications, 1953), 72, 74, 111.

6. Shriver, *An Ethic for Enemies*, 71.

7. Frost's line comes from his poem "The Star Splitter." Among political philosophers the most prominent advocate of this view—that the formation or reformation of a society requires forgiveness—is Hannah Arendt. See *The Human Condition* (New York: Doubleday), 214–15, where she credits Jesus as "the discoverer of the role of forgiveness in human affairs."

8. Dietrich Bonhoeffer, "Guilt, Justification, Renewal," *Ethics* (Minneapolis: Fortress, 2005), 134–45.

9. Shriver, *An Ethic for Enemies*, 108.

10. Ibid., 108, 110.

11. See Michelle Tooley, *Voices of the Voiceless: Women, Justice, and Human Rights in Guatemala* (Scottdale, Pa., and Waterloo, Ontario: Herald Press, 1997).

12. Shriver, *Honest Patriots: Loving a Country Enough to Remember Its Misdeeds* (New York: Oxford University Press, 2005), 105.

13. Alan Geyer and Barbara G. Green, *Lines in the Sand: Justice and the Gulf War* (Louisville: Westminster John Knox Press, 1992), 170.

14. George F. Kennan, *At a Century's Ending* (New York: W. W. Norton, 1996), 186–87. See also Richard Ned Lebow and Janice Gross Stein, *We All Lost the Cold War* (Princeton, N.J.: Princeton University, 1994).

15. For one study of American high school history books 1950–2000, cf. Shriver, *Honest Patriots*, chapters 3 and 4, paralleled by a similar study of high school history books in Germany and South Africa in chapters 1 and 2.

16. Gerald Ford, quoted in Shriver, *An Ethic for Enemies*, 165.

17. George Bush, quoted in ibid., 166.

18. George Bush, quoted in ibid., 143.

19. Gordon Craig, "History as a Humanistic Discipline," in *Historical Literacy*, ed. Paul Gagnon (New York: Macmillan, 1989), 134.

20. James Juhnke and Carol Hunter, *The Missing Peace: The Search for Nonviolent Alternatives in United States History* (Kitchener, Ontario, and Scottdale, Pa: Pandora and Herald, 2001).

21. Arthur Moore, quoted in Michael McIntyre, "Efforts to Organize an 'Act of Repentance' in Washington," February 15, 1980; memo to Bishop James K. Mathews et al.

22. "A Call to Repentance and Prayer for Iran and the United States," leaflet from Office of Bishop James K. Mathews, Washington, D.C., February 1980.

23. Mansour Farhang, quoted in Walter Taylor, "Iranian Aide Suggests U.S. Apologize for Its Past Policy on Shah," *The Washington Star,* January 30, 1980, 1.

24. Alan Geyer, "A Proposal for a Presidential Statement on U.S.–Iranian Relations," Washington, D.C., draft memo, February 22, 1980, 1. A parallel grass-roots effort was initiated by the Crescent Hill Baptist Church peacemaker group in Louisville, using connections with Jimmy Carter through his Baptist friend Jimmy Allen and simultaneously through a high-level Baptist member of the U.S Department of State. They reminded President Carter that in his campaign for the presidency, he had said that the United States had been too close with dictators and not close enough with human rights. All he needed to do was to remind Iran of that campaign theme, and that he believed it was true as well in the present crisis, and that if the new government in Iran would respect human rights, the U.S. government would give Iran its respect. In the passion of the Iranian revolution, the question in Iran was whether the United States sided with the Shah, whom National Security Director Zbigniew Brzezinski had invited to come to the United States for surgery and thus had appeared to be siding with the dictator. President Carter would answer the Iranian question, and indicate the United States had been too close with the Shah, without losing face if he would only reissue the statement he had already made in the campaign, and say it was true still. The group was told, however, that both routes of access were blocked by Brzezinski, who was running Iran policy and defensive about having brought the Shah to the United States. Two different Christian groups, independent of each other, but aware of the just peacemaking practice of acknowledg-

223

ment, repentance, and forgiveness, were thinking similarly. They were prodding the government to engage in this just peacemaking practice, which might have saved that administration.

25. William Shakespeare, *King Henry IV*, Part I, II.iii.10.

CHAPTER 5: Advance Democracy, Human Rights, and Interdependence

1. For comments on this chapter, I am indebted to Glen Stassen, and I have incorporated some passages on human rights and religious liberty from a draft paper on just peacemaking by John Langan, S.J. The chapter summarizes research reported in detail in Bruce Russett, *Grasping the Democratic Peace: Principles for a Post–Cold War World* (Princeton, N.J.: Princeton University Press, 1993), Bruce Russett and John R. Oneal, *Triangulating Peace: Democracy, Interdependence, and International Organizations* (New York: W. W. Norton, 2001), and many scholarly articles with John Oneal and other co-authors. See also Bruce Bueno de Mesquita, Alastair Smith, Randolph Siverson, and James Morrow, *The Logic of Political Survival* (Cambridge, Mass.: M.I.T. Press, 2003); Charles Lipson, *Reliable Partners: How Democracies Have Made a Separate Peace* (Princeton, N.J.: Princeton University Press, 2003); David Rousseau, *Democracy and War* (Stanford, Calif.: Stanford University Press, 2005); Rudolph Rummel, *Power Kills: Democracy as a Method of Nonviolence* (New Brunswick, N.J.: Transaction, 1996).

2. My assertions have not gone uncontested, but the predominant evidence remains strongly in their favor. For a reply to some early critiques, see Bruce Russett, "Counterfactuals about War and Its Absence," in *Counterfactual Thought Experiments in World Politics: Logical, Methodological, and Psychological Perspectives*, ed. Philip Tetlock and Aaron Belkin (Princeton, N.J.: Princeton University Press, 1996). On the continuing evidence for the peace-inducing effect of democracy and also of economic interdependence and international organizations, see Russett and Oneal, *Triangulating*, and Oneal, Russett, and Michael Berbaum, "Causes of Peace: Democracy, Interdependence, and International Organizations, 1885–1992," *International Studies Quarterly* 47, no. 3 (September 2003), 371–93.

3. Samuel Huntington, *The Third Wave: Democratization in the Late Twentieth Century* (Norman: University of Oklahoma Press, 1991). 3. Edward Mansfield and Jack Snyder, *Electing to Fight* (Cambridge, Mass.: M.I.T. Press, 2005).

4. Edward Mansfield and Jack Snyder, *Electing to Fight* (Cambridge, Mass.: M.I.T. Press, 2005).

5. Rudolph Rummel, *Power Kills: Democracy as a Method of Nonviolence* (New Brunswick, N.J.: Transaction, 1996).

6. Boutros Boutros-Ghali, *An Agenda for Peace* (New York: United Nations, 1993), par. 81; and Boutrous Boutros-Ghali, *An Agenda for Democratization* (New York: United Nations, 1996).

7. John Pevehouse and Bruce Russett, "Democratic International Organizations Promote Peace, *International Organization* 60, no. 4 (Fall 2006): 969–1000.

8. See Bruce Russett, "Bushwhacking the Democratic Peace," *International Studies Perspectives* 6, no. 4 (November 2005): 395–408.

9. See Michael Doyle and Nicholas Sambanis, *Making War and Building Peace: United Nations Peace Operations* (Princeton, N.J.: Princeton University Press, 2006).

10. James Fearon, "Domestic Political Audiences and the Escalation of International Disputes," *American Political Science Review* 88, no. 3 (September 1994): 577–92; David Lake, "Powerful Pacifists: Democratic States and War,"

American Political Science Review 86, no. 1 (March 1992): 24–37; Daniel Reiter and Allan C. Stam, *Democracies at War* (Princeton, N.J.: Princeton University Press, 2002); Bueno de Mesquita et al, *Logic*; Michelle Garfinkel, "Domestic Politics and International Conflict," *American Economic Review* 84, no. 5 (December 1984): 1294–1309; Zeev Maoz, *Domestic Sources of Global Change* (Ann Arbor: University of Michigan Press, 1997).

11. Michael J. Smith, *Realist Thought from Weber to Kissinger* (Baton Rouge: Louisiana State University Press, 1986), 48.

CHAPTER 6: Foster Just and Sustainable Economic Development

1. Rodger Payne wishes to thank Joshua Easton and Jason Renzelman for research assistance.

2. See Gustavo Esteva, "Regenerating People's Spaces," *Alternatives* 12, no. 1 (1987): 125–52, and Gustavo Esteva, "Development," in *The Development Dictionary: A Guide to Knowledge as Power*, ed. Wolfgang Sachs (London: Zed Books, 1992). There is a vast recent literature on development, looking at the ways that words embody values and an exercise of power of which people are only dimly aware. Generally, these authors are writing about the set of techniques, attitudes, and prescriptions found in large, "official" development agencies like the World Bank, UNDP, AID, and other Northern governmental aid organizations, and not as much about nongovernmental organizations (NGOs). This literature is insightful and useful but rarely includes the perspective of the poor on development. See Geof Wood, "Labels: A Shadow across Reality: An Introductory Note," *Development and Change* 16, no. 3 (July 1985): 343–45, and Geof Wood, "The Politics of Development Policy Labelling," *Development and Change* 16, no. 3 (July 1985): 347–74; James Ferguson, "The Anti-Politics Machine: "Development," *Depoliticization, and Bureaucratic Power in Lesotho* (Cambridge: Cambridge University Press, 1990); Tim Mitchell, "America's Egypt: Discourse of the Development Industry," *Middle East Report* (March–April, 1991): 1834; Stacy Leigh Pigg, "Constructing Social Categories through Place: Social Representation and Development in Nepal," *Comparative Studies in Society and History* 34 no. 3 (1992): 491–513; Arturo Escobar, *Encountering Development: The Making and Unmaking of the Third World* (Princeton, N.J.: Princeton University Press, 1995).

3. The problems of defining "the poor" are outside of the scope of this paper. We refer the reader to any number of definitions available in the literature on development.

4. This includes changes in attitudes, in values, in morals, concerning others and oneself. In addition, it also includes changes in relationships among nation-states. It can also be seen as including changes in relationships with one's God. This last one is trickier to define, requires a whole theology, and is beyond the scope of this essay. Development as consisting of changes in relationships is not a new idea. See Patrick Breslin, *Development and Dignity: Grassroots Development and the Inter-American Foundation* (Rosslyn, Va.: Inter-American Foundation, 1987), for how one agency, the IAF, defined it this way already in the 1970s. The stark human need of poor people in poor countries is an obvious rationale for development aid. Further, the suggestion that development may not be a good or ought to be subordinated to ecological or spiritual concerns is often offensive to people from those countries, because richer or "more developed" countries evidently seek further wealth for themselves. This has been an issue of contention at least since the 1928 International Missionary Conference, and it has surfaced in international events such as conferences on the environment.

5. Of course, many times the two parties attach different meanings to the word "development." Nevertheless, material (or economic) progress is always one of the most important meanings attached by both sides. Depending on the context and people involved, other meanings include political, social, cultural, spiritual, and personal changes. As indicated below, we adopt the more holistic definition. The "South" is used to refer to those countries considered "poor." Previous designations such as "underdeveloped," "developing," "less developed," and "Third World" have dropped by the wayside in an attempt to avoid pejorative connotations. Another alternative use that has found favor in the literature, especially in the missiology literature, is "Two-Thirds World." (See Vinay Samuel and Chris Sugden, eds., *Sharing Jesus in the Two Thirds World: Evangelical Christologies from the Contexts of Poverty Powerlessness and Religious Pluralism*, The Papers of the First Conference of Evangelical Mission Theologians from the Two Thirds World, Bangkok, Thailand, March 22–25, 1982 [Grand Rapids, Mich.: Eerdmans, 1983]).

6. See Norman Uphoff, "Assisted Self-Reliance: Working with, Rather than for, the Poor" in *Strengthening the Poor: What Have We Learned?* ed. John P. Lewis, *U.S.–Third World Policy Perspectives*, No. 10, Overseas Development Council (New Brunswick, N.J.: Transaction Books, 1988); Norman Uphoff, "Fitting Project to People," in *Putting People First*, ed. Michael M. Cernea, 2nd ed. (New York: Oxford University Press, 1991), 467–511; Thomas F. Carroll, *Intermediary NGOs: The Supporting Link in Development* (Hartford, Conn.: Kumarian Press, 1992); and John Farrington and Anthony Bebbington, with Kate Wellard and David J. Lewis, *Reluctant Partners? Non-governmental Organizations, the State, and Sustainable Agricultural Development*, Non-Governmental Organizations Series, Coordinated by the Overseas Development Institute (London and New York: Routledge, 1993). This "capacity-building" literature has roots in the work done by Norman Uphoff and Milton Esman, *Local Organization for Rural Development: Analysis of Asian Experience*, Special Series on Rural Local Government (Ithaca, N.Y.: Rural Development Committee, Cornell University, 1974), and Norman Uphoff et al., *Local Institutional Development: An Analytical Sourcebook with Cases* (Hartford, Conn.: Kumarian Press, 1986). The concepts on which it is based have much in common with those employed in the community development efforts of the 1960s and with those advanced by Paulo Freire's work on education, *Pedagogy of the Oppressed*, trans. Myra Bergman Ramos (New York: Seabury Press, 1970). These commonalities are seldom mentioned in the literature cited above, which focuses on detailed comparative development case-study research designed to identify the crucial variables in development-project success.

7. John W. Sewell, "Foreword" in Lewis, ed., *Strengthening the Poor*.

8. See Ted Gurr, *Why Men Rebel* (Princeton: Princeton University Press, 1970).

9. The so-called "Earth Summit" was held in Rio de Janeiro, Brazil, in June 1992.

10. Roger C. Riddell and Mark Robinson, with John de Coninck, Ann Muir, and Sarah White, *Non-Governmental Organizations and Rural Poverty Alleviation* (Oxford: Clarendon Press; London: ODI, 1995) have an excellent summary of the literature comparing NGOs to "official" agencies, and the meteoric trend toward funding NGOs.

11. This refers not just to the "physical" aspects of their environment but also to the political ones.

12. See Uphoff et al., *Local Institutional Development*.

13. "Political consequences" is an easy way to refer to changing relationships of power. As people acquire increased access to resources, they can become less dependent on others, who may resent it for a variety of reasons. As examples, the

wealthy may lose the labor, market, and deference of those who had depended on them, and men may lose leverage and control over the women as the latter engage in their own productive activities.

14. See Farrington and Bebbington, *Reluctant Partners*, for a good summary of the rise and decline of state-driven development. For additional material on the state and development and development ideas and theories in general, see H. W. Arndt, *Economic Development: The History of an Idea* (Chicago and London: University of Chicago Press, 1987), and A. F. Robertson, *People and the State: An Anthropology of Planned Development* (Cambridge: Cambridge University Press, 1984).

15. Among others, see Stephan Haggard, *Pathways from the Periphery* (Ithaca and London: Cornell University Press, 1990), and Duncan Green, *Silent Revolution: The Rise of Market Economics in Latin America* (London: Cassell, 1995). Singapore and Hong Kong are essentially city-states lacking rural peasants.

16. Bruce Rich, *Mortgaging the Earth: The World Bank, Environmental Impoverishment, and the Crisis of Development* (Boston: Beacon Press, 1994).

17. Green, *Silent Revolution*.

18. Ibid., 202.

19. Thomas F. Homer-Dixon, "On the Threshold, Environmental Changes as Causes of Acute Conflict," *International Security* 16 (Fall 1991): 76–116, and Thomas F. Homer-Dixon, "Environmental Scarcities and Violent Conflict, Evidence from Cases," *International Security* 19 (Summer 1994): 5–40.

20. The Arab League and Syria in the early and mid-1960s attempted to divert Jordan River headwaters away from Israel. Israel responded with air strikes, creating tensions that contributed to the 1967 war. For details of the Middle East conflicts over water, see Peter H. Gleick, "Water and Conflict, Fresh Water Resources and International Security," *International Security* 18 (Summer 1993): 79–112, and Peter H. Gleick, Peter Yolles, and Haleh Hatami, "Water, War and Peace in the Middle East: Conflict over Water Rights," *Environment* 36 (April 1994): 6–15, 35–42.

21. Thomas F. Homer-Dixon, *Environmental Scarcity and Global Security*, Headline Series, no. 300 (New York: Foreign Policy Association, 1993), 52, and Ashok Swain, *The Environmental Trap: The Ganges River Diversion, Bangladeshi Migration and Conflicts in India*, Report No. 41 (Uppsala, Sweden: Department of Peace and Conflict Research, Uppsala University, 1996). See also by Homer-Dixon, "On the Threshold" and "Environmental Scarcities and Violent Conflict."

22. Boutros-Ghali is quoted in Anthony Shadid, "Cairo May See Waters of Nile Diminish," *Los Angeles Times*, December 17, 1995, A38. Sadat is quoted in Gleick, "Water and Conflict"; Engelman is quoted in Shadid.

23. Information in this section comes mostly from Miriam R. Lowi, "Bridging the Divide: Transboundary Resource Disputes and the Case of West Bank Water," *International Security* 18 (Summer 1993): 113–38.

24. Joe Remenyi and Bill Taylor, "Credit-Based Income Generation for the Poor," in *Christianity and Economics in the Post–Cold War Era: The Oxford Declaration and Beyond*, ed. Herbert Schlossberg, Vinay Samuel, and Ronald J. Sider (Grand Rapids, Mich.: Eerdmans, 1994); Farrington and Bebbington, *Reluctant Partners*.

25. See, for example, Herbert Schlossberg, "Destroying Poverty without Destroying Poor People," in *Christianity and Economics*, 116, 117. The "cultural" characteristics listed by Schlossberg and those he quotes come from a stream of analysis introduced in the 1960s by Oscar Lewis in "The Culture of Poverty," *Scientific American* 214, no. 4 (1966): 19–25. At its worst, the legacy of this literature sees the

"cultural" characteristics of the poor as the main barriers to their own success and implies that the poor have different values than the middle classes. At its best, this literature shows that many of the poor share middle- and upper-class values and pays close attention to the complexity of the interaction of structural and cultural constraints that perpetuate poverty and lead to differences in the behavior of some of the poor.

26. See, for example, Gavin Smith, *Livelihood and Resistance: Peasants and Politics of Land in Peru* (Berkeley: University of California Press, 1989).

27. See Farrington and Bebbington, *Reluctant Partners*, and Remenyi and Taylor, "Credit-based Income Generation."

28. The literature on linking the state with efforts at the micro level for maximum impact is important here. See Farrington and Bebbington, *Reluctant Partners*; Lewis, ed., *Strengthening the Poor*; John Friedmann, *Empowerment: The Politics of Alternative Development*. (Cambridge, Mass.: Blackwell, 1992). However, these sources do not address how these efforts are linked up with the structure of the international economic system.

29. For references to development education, how it came about, and the difficulties agencies have with it, see material throughout Maggie Black, *A Cause for Our Times: Oxfam the First 50 Years*. (Oxford: Oxfam, 1992); Ian Smillie, *The Alms Bazaar: Altruism under Fire: Nonprofit Organizations and International Development* (Ottawa, Can.: International Development Research Centre, 1995); Anne Gordon Drabek, ed., "Development Alternatives: The Challenge for NGOs," *World Development* 15, Supplement (1987).

30. Robert Moffitt, "The Local Church and Development," in *The Church in Response to Human Need*, ed. Vinay Samuel and Christopher Sugden (Grand Rapids: Eerdmans, 1987), advocates church-community links and details some experience in this area. The "Sister City" projects are another example.

31. The Global Environment Facility, a new multilateral agency that targets assistance to make ongoing development projects sustainable, is required to consult extensively with NGOs, and is therefore a step in the right direction. See Rodger A. Payne, "The Limits and Promise of Environmental Conflict Prevention; The Case of the GEF," *Journal of Peace Research* vol. 35 (May 1998): 363–80.

32. Toby Ash, "Jordan: Water Authority Forges Links with Israel," *MEED Middle East Economic Digest* 39 (March 10, 1995): 14.

33. As argued in this chapter, this is not meant to deny that there are cultural traits that prevent some poor from making a transition to a new style of social, economic, and political relationships inside and outside of their community. However, a significant body of anthropological literature on development shows that cultural traits are not the major impediment to development and that many times what appears to be a cultural barrier is really a way in which the poor resist and rework changes that are detrimental to their welfare. See James Scott, *Weapons of the Weak: Everyday Forms of Peasant Resistance* (New Haven, Conn.: Yale University Press, 1985); Thayer Scudder, "The Institute for Development Anthropology: The Case for Anthropological Participation in the Development Process," in *Production and Autonomy: Anthropological Studies and Critiques of Development*, ed. John W. Bennett and John R. Bowen (Lanham, Md.: University Press of America, 1988); Anne Fleuret, "Some Consequences of Tenure and Agrarian Reform in Taita, Kenya," in *Land and Society in Contemporary Africa*, ed. R. E. Downs and S. P. Reyna (Hanover, N.H., and London: University Presses of New England, 1988), 136–58, among many others.

CHAPTER 7: Work with Emeerging Cooperative Forces in the International System

1. Hedley Bull, *The Anarchical Society: A Study of Order in World Politics* (London and New York: Columbia University Press, 1977).

2. I am borrowing this scheme (acronym OWL) from a colleague in political science, Edward A. Kolodziej, "Order, Welfare, and Legitimacy: A Systemic Explanation for the Soviet Collapse and the End of the Cold War," *International Politics* 34 (June 1997): 111–51.

3. Richard Rosecrance, *The Rise of the Trading State: Commerce and Conquest in the Modern World* (New York: Basic Books, 1986).

4. I develop this historical perspective more fully in the following works: "Historical Reality vs. Neo-Realist Theory," *International Security* 19, no. 2 (Summer 1994): 108–48; "The Nineteenth Century Balance of Power: Balance of Power or Political Equilibrium?" *Review of International Studies* 15 (April 1989): 135–53; "Did the Vienna Settlement Rest on a Balance of Power?" *American Historical Review* 97, no. 2 (June 1992): 683–706, 733–35; and *The Transformation of European Politics, 1763–1848* (Oxford: Clarendon Press, 1994).

5. Aaron L. Friedberg, "Ripe for Rivalry," *International Security* 18 (Winter 1993–1994): 10–13, 19ff.

6. William L. Kissick, *Medicine's Dilemmas* (New Haven, Conn.: Yale University Press, 1994), 150.

CHAPTER 8: Strengthen the United Nations and International Efforts for Cooperation and Human Rights

1. Throughout this chapter, and especially in this section, I substantially rely on a joint work in progress with Professor Stanley Hoffmann of Harvard University.

2. On this distinction, see Stanley Hoffmann, *Primacy or World Order* (New York: McGraw-Hill, 1978). Of course, the distinction in reality is far from perfect. In the realm of economic interdependence, states try to combine the logic of competition (the quest for relative gains) with that of a world economy that has rules and a dynamism of its own. Chaos or crises caused, in that realm, either by aggressive state competitiveness or by economic recessions and dislocations, can spill over into the traditional arena.

3. Susan Strange, "The Name of the Game," in *Sea Changes*, ed. Nicholas X. Rizopoulos (New York: Council on Foreign Relations, 1990), 238–73.

4. The omelet image comes from Hoffmann, *Primacy or World Order*.

5. Henry Shue, *Basic Rights* (Princeton, N.J.: Princeton University Press, 1980; 2nd ed. 1996).

6. Cf. Carl Kaysen, "Is War Obsolete? A Review Essay," *International Security* 14, no. 4 (1990): 42–64.

7. Thomas M. Franck, "The Emerging Right to Democratic Governance," *American Journal of International Law* 86, no. 1 (January 1992): 46–91.

8. Stanley Hoffmann, "The Delusions of World Order," *New York Review of Books* 39, no. 7 (April 9, 1992): 37–42.

9. See Jessica Matthews, "The UN and the Congress," *Washington Post*, March 5, 1995.

10. These figures are taken from the UN Department of Peacekeeping Operations website, http://www.un.org/Depts/dpko/dpko/bnote.htm.

11. See my discussion in the first edition of *Just Peacemaking*, ed. Glen Stassen (Cleveland: Pilgrim Press, 1998), 163–65.

12. See, for example, Kofi Annan, "Two Concepts of Sovereignty, *The Economist* 352 (September 18, 1999): 49–50.

13. *The Responsibility to Protect: Report of the International Commission on Sovereignty and Intervention*, December 2001 (Ottawa, Canada: International Development Research Centre, 2001), xi, http://www.idrc.ca/en/ev-9436-201-1-DO_TOPIC.html.

14. Ibid.

15. Thomas G. Weiss, *Humanitarian Intervention* (Cambridge, U.K.: Polity Press, 2007), 102.

16. *Responsibility to Protect*, xii.

17. Michael Walzer, *Just and Unjust Wars* (New York: Basic Books, 1977), 102–8.

18. "The Permanent Five members of the Security Council should agree not to apply their veto power, in matters where their vital state interests are not involved, to obstruct the passage of resolutions authorizing military intervention for human protection purposes for which there is otherwise majority support" (*Responsibility to Protect*, xii).

CHAPTER 9: Reduce Offensive Weapons and Weapons Trade

1. For the first two editions, we thank Fran Teplitz of Peace Action Education Fund and Lora Lumpt, senior researcher at the Federation of American Scientists, for research assistance. For this new 2008 edition, we thank Charles Martin-Shields for research assistance and suggested wording at several points.

2. Robert Jervis, *The Meaning of the Nuclear Revolution* (Ithaca, N.Y.: Cornell University, 1989).

3. Most of the cases of war we cite to illustrate our theme also illustrate additional factors described in other chapters: isolation from international forces of cooperation, including the United Nations; authoritarian rather than democratic leaders; historical guilt and resentment unforgiven and unhealed; negative economic development; lack of respect for human rights; lack of willingness to engage in cooperative conflict resolution; lack of a civil society with strong grassroots peace groups. All were true of Serbia under Milosevic.

4. Glen Stassen, "Just Peacemaking Theory as Hermeneutical Key: For International Cooperation in Preventing Terrorism," *Journal of the Society of Christian Ethics* 24/2 (Fall 2004).

5. Ibid.

6. For a shorter, narrative account of this history, see Glen Harold Stassen and Lawrence S. Wittner, eds., *Peace Action: Past Present and Future* (Boulder, Co: Paradigm, 2007). For a fuller account, see Lawrence Wittner's award-winning trilogy, *The Struggle against the Bomb*, especially *Toward Nuclear Abolition: A History of the World Nuclear Disarmament Movement, 1971 to the Present* (Stanford, Calif.: Stanford University Press, 2003).

7. National Academy of Sciences, *The Future of the U.S.–Soviet Nuclear Relationship* (Washington D.C.: National Academy Press, 1991), vii.

8. Jonathan Dean and Kurt Gottfried, *A Program for World Nuclear Security* (Cambridge, Mass.: Union of Concerned Scientists, February, 1992), 8.

9. Ibid., 12–13.

10. National Academy of Sciences, *Future of U.S.–Soviet Nuclear Relationship*, 37.

11. Lisbeth Gronlund and David Wright, *Beyond Safeguards: A Program for More Comprehensive Control of Weapon-Usable Fissile Material* (n.p.: Union of Concerned Scientists, 1994), 11.

12. Thomas Graham Jr., acting deputy director, USACDA, "The Nuclear NPT: A Twenty-five-year Success Story," Rome, Italy, July 2–3, 1994, 3.

13. Kurt Campbell, Robert Einhorn, and Mitchell Reiss, eds,, *The Nuclear Tipping Point: Why States Reconsider Their Nuclear Choices* (Washington, D.C.: Brookings Institution Press, 2004), 329–30; Mitchell Reiss, *Without the Bomb: the Politics of Nuclear Nonproliferation* (New York: Columbia University Press, 1988), 263–68. See www.matthew5project.org for a brief summary of how this was achieved, and for a Christian advocacy of learning from that history for how to engage in cooperative conflict resolution talks with potential new nuclear powers such as North Korea and Iran in order to persuade them not to go nuclear.

14. William D. Hartung, quoted in Jim Bridgman, ed., "September 1996 Weapons Trafficking Campaign Update," *Peace Action Grassroots Organizer*, September 1996.

15. Richard F. Grimmett, "Conventional Arms Transfers to Developing Nations, 1999–2006" (Congressional Research Service Report for Congress, September 26, 2007), 2. Accessed at Federation for American Scientists, www.fas.org/sgp/crs/weapons/RL34187.pdf, March 26, 2008.

16. Ibid.

17. http://disarmament.un.org/cab/smallarms/statements/usE.html, UN Conference on the Illicit Trade in Small Arms and Light Weapons in All its Aspects, July 9, 2001.

18. http://disarmament.un.org/cab/smallarms/statements/netherlandsE.html, UN Conference on the Illicit Trade in Small Arms and Light Weapons in All its Aspects, July 9, 2001.

19. Jeffrey Sachs, *The End of Poverty*, (New York: Penguin, 2006), chapters 10, 11.

20. Oxfam/Amnesty International, www.controlarms.com, "The G-8, Global Arms Exporters, Failing to prevent irresponsible arms transfers," June 2005, 4.

21. Richard Jolly, United Nations Group of Governmental Experts on the Relationship between Disarmament and Development, disarmament.un.org/DDA publications/OP9art03.pdf.

22. Peace Action Education Fund, "Factsheet: Timeline of U.S. Landmine Policy."

23. "A U.S. Conventional Arms Transfer Policy," *The Defense Monitor* 23, no. 7 (1994): 5.

24. Contract totals are for postinvasion contracts. Campaign contribution totals are from the Federal Election Commission database from 1990 through mid-year 2003.

25. Linda J. Bilmes and Joseph E. Stiglitz, "War's Price Tag," *Los Angeles Times*, March 16, 2008, M1.

26. Linda J. Bilmes and Joseph E. Stiglitz, "Iraq War Costs Could Top $2 Trillion," *Christian Science Monitor*, January 10, 2006.

27. 1994 Director of Naval Intelligence posture statement, quoted in Paul F. Pineo and Lora Lumpe, "Recycled Weapons: American Exports of Surplus Arms, 1990–1995: A Study by the Arms Sales Monitoring Project of the Federation of American Scientists," May 1996; see http://fas.org/asmp/library/publications/recycle.htm.

28. Dobbs, Michael; "U.S. Had Key Role in Iraq Build-up," *Washington Post*, December 30, 2002, A1.

29. Wolf, Julie; "The Iran/Contra Affair," *The American Experience: Reagan*, Public Broadcasting Service, http://www.pbs.org/wgbh/amex/reagan/peopleevents/pande 08.html.

30. This information was found at Never Again's website, http://neveragain.epov .org/Arms_shipments_and_the_Rwandan_Genocide. The article was a compendium of documents written by witnesses and United Nations arms embargo agreements, which can be found on the site.

31. http://neveragain.epov.org/Arms_shipments_and_the_Rwandan_Genocide.

32. Anthony Shadid, "Israel, Hezbollah Vow Wider War," *Washington Post*, July 15, 2006, A1.

33. The Council on Foreign Relations published analysis of Russia's arms trade with Iran, including a section on whether Iran sends these weapons to terrorist groups, in CFR document #11869. The U.S. Department of State also publishes information about Iran and Syria supplying weapons to Hezbollah, which can be seen on the International Information Program website, accessible at: http://usinfo .state.gov/xarchives/display.html?p=washfile-english&y=2006&m=August&x=2006 0822163831ndyblehs0.6180689.

34. Secretary of State Warren Christopher, "Foreign Assistance Priorities after the Cold War," U.S. Department of State dispatch, May 31, 1993.

CHAPTER 10: Encourage Grassroots Peacemaking Groups and Voluntary Associations

1. Susan Thistlethwaite, ed., *A Just Peace Church* (New York: United Church Press, 1986), 60.

2. See chapter 1, "Support Nonviolent Direct Action," by John Cartwright and Susan Thistlethwaite.

3. Robert Bellah et al., *Habits of the Heart: Individualism and Commitment in American Life* (Berkeley: University of California Press, 1985).

4. Larry Rasmussen, *Moral Fragments* (Minneapolis: Augsburg Fortress, 2000), 48.

5. Robert Wuthnow, *Acts of Compassion: Caring for Others and Helping Ourselves* (Princeton, N.J.: Princeton University Press, 1991), 156.

6. Ibid., 179–84.

7. Tooley, *Voices of the Voiceless*, 81. See particularly chapter 3, entitled "Voices of the Voiceless: The Response of Women in Guatemalan Human Rights Groups."

8. Ibid., 86.

9. Ibid., 96.

10. Tooley describes the American Baptist case, ibid., 177.

11. See the documentation of this case in Buttry, *Christian Peacemaking*, 132f.

12. Ibid., 182f.

13. Robert D. Putnam, "Diplomacy and Domestic Politics: The Logic of Two-Level Games," in *Double-Edged Diplomacy: International Bargaining and Domestic Politics*, ed. Peter B. Evans, Harold K. Jacobson, and Robert D. Putnam (Berkeley: University of California Press, 1993), 436. Copyright © 1993 The Regents of the University of California. Cf. Lawrence Wittmer, *Toward Nuclear Abolition* (Stanford University, 2003).

14. Cortright, *Peace Works*, 248. The summary of the impact of the peace movement on policy is taken from a chart on page 247.

15. For example, in the early 1980s, major statements were made by the U.S. Roman Catholic Bishops, the General Assembly of the United Presbyterian Church, the United Methodist Council of Bishops, as well as other denominations. Riverside Church in New York City, through the leadership of William Sloan Coffin, played a very significant role through its convocations and publications.

16. Richard C. Eichenberg corroborates Cortwright's argument. An initial hard-line U.S. position against negotiation with the Soviet Union was changed by the pressures of domestic politics. "This flexibility on the part of the American administration represented a shift from its initial preference, and it was the result of domestic pressure within the United States as well as West Germany." Richard C. Eichenberg, "Dual Track and Double Trouble: The Two-Level Politics of INF," in *Double-Edged Diplomacy*, 54.

17. Elise Boulding, *Building a Global Civic Culture: Education for an Interdependent World* (New York: Teachers College, Columbia University, 1988).

18. See chap. 7, "Work with Emerging Cooperative Forces in the International System," by Paul Schroeder.

19. Parts of the concluding section of this chapter have been published by Duane K. Friesen in the essay "Religion and Nonviolent Action," in *Protest, Power, and Change: An Encyclopedia of Nonviolent Action from ACT-UP to Women's Suffrage* (New York: Garland, 1997).

20. See chapter 4, "Acknowledge Responsibility for Conflict and Injustice and Seek Repentance and Forgiveness," by Alan Geyer, which cites the conflicts in Somalia and the Persian Gulf War as case studies of this myopic view.

21. For an account of the role of the churches in East Germany, see Jörg Swoboda, *The Revolution of the Candles: Christians in the Revolution of the German Democratic Republic* (Macon, Ga.: Mercer University Press, 1996). For an eyewitness account of the events, see Mark Jantzen, *The Wrong Side of the Wall: An American in East Berlin during the Peaceful Revolution* (Beatrice, Nebr.: Author Press, 1993). Jantzen was a student studying in East Germany under the auspices of the Mennonite Central Committee. The book is available through Henry and Gretl Jantzen, 1415 Summit St., Beatrice, NE.

22. See chapter 1, "Support Nonviolent Direct Action," by John Cartwright and Susan Thistlethwaite, who cite numerous examples of practices by citizens' groups that advocate for the voiceless.

23. See chapter 3, "Use Cooperative Conflict Resolution," by David Steele, Steven Brion-Meisels, Gary Gunderson, and Edward LeRoy Long Jr.

24. See chapter 4, "Acknowledge Responsibility for Conflict and Injustice and Seek Repentance and Forgiveness," by Alan Geyer.

25. Stassen, *Just Peacemaking: Transforming Initiatives*, chaps. 3, 4, and 5.

26. See chapter 2, "Take Independent Initiatives to Reduce Threat," by Glen Stassen.

27. See chapter 6, "Foster Just and Sustainable Economic Development," by David Bronkema, David Lumsdaine, and Rodger A. Payne.

28. See the documentation of this impact in Keith Graber Miller, *American Mennonites Engage Washington: Wise as Serpents, Innocent as Doves?* (Knoxville: University of Tennessee Press, 1996).

29. See chapter 4, "Acknowledge Responsibility for Conflict and Injustice and Seek Repentance and Forgiveness," by Alan Geyer.

30. Dag Hammarskjold, *Markings* (New York: Alfred A. Knopf, 1964), 11.

31. Donald Kraybill, Steven M. Nolt, and David L. Weaver-Zercher, *Amish Grace: How Forgiveness Transcended Tragedy* (New York: John Wiley and Sons, 2007), 90–98.

32. Several paragraphs of this paper are included in Friesen, "Religion and Nonviolent Action."

33. Vaclav Havel (former president of the Czech Republic), "Post-Modernism: The Search for Universal Laws," speech delivered on the occasion of the Liberty Medal Ceremony, Philadelphia, Pa., July 4, 1994.